AGRICULTURE ISSUES AND POLICIES

PEANUTS AND SUGAR

BACKGROUND, POLICY AND PROVISIONS OF FEDERAL PROGRAMS

AGRICULTURE ISSUES AND POLICIES

Additional books in this series can be found on Nova's website under the Series tab.

Additional eBooks in this series can be found on Nova's website under the eBooks tab.

AGRICULTURE ISSUES AND POLICIES

PEANUTS AND SUGAR

BACKGROUND, POLICY AND PROVISIONS OF FEDERAL PROGRAMS

EDITH PEREZ
EDITOR

nova publishers
New York

NOTICE TO THE READER

Library of Congress Cataloging-in-Publication Data

ISBN: 978-1-63485-487-0

Published by Nova Science Publishers, Inc. † New York

CONTENTS

PREFACE

According to the U.S. Department of Agriculture (USDA), the United States is expected to be the fourth largest producer and exporter of peanuts in the world in 2015. In addition to its prominent role in international markets, U.S. peanut production and marketing is an important activity in several states located in the southeastern and southwestern United States. The U.S. sugar program is singular among major agricultural commodity programs in that it combines a floor price guarantee with a supply management structure that encompasses both domestic production for human use and sugar imports. The sugar program provides a price guarantee to the processors of sugarcane and sugar beets, and by extension, to the producers of both crops. This book provides a review of the background, policies and provisions on federal programs for both peanuts and sugar.

In: Peanuts and Sugar
Editor: Edith Perez
ISBN: 978-1-63485-487-0

Chapter 1

U.S. PEANUT PROGRAM AND ISSUES*

Randy Schnepf

SUMMARY

According to the U.S. Department of Agriculture (USDA), the United States is expected to be the fourth largest producer and exporter of peanuts in the world in 2015. In addition to its prominent role in international markets, U.S. peanut production and marketing is an important activity in several states located in the southeastern and southwestern United States. The U.S. peanut crop has been eligible for certain federal farm support programs since the 1930s—initially under a quota system and, since 2002, under the income support programs available for other major program crops like corn, wheat, soybeans, and rice.

Today, under the 2014 farm bill (Agricultural Act of 2014, P.L. 113-79), the major income support programs are marketing loan benefits and either the price loss coverage (PLC) or agriculture risk coverage (ARC) program (as determined by a one-time producer choice). For peanuts, almost all producers (99.7%) chose PLC because they expected it to provide higher payments and greater risk protection than would be available under ARC.

Marketing loan benefits are available immediately after harvest and are coupled directly to planting and production. In contrast, PLC and

* This is an edited, reformatted and augmented version of a Congressional Research Service publication R44156, prepared for Members and Committees of Congress, dated November 18, 2015.

ARC payments are made to 85% of historical base acres and thus decoupled from producer crop choices. Also, PLC and ARC payments are not available until nearly a full year after harvest—October 1 following the end of the marketing year when full information on farm prices is available. The 2014 farm bill also created "generic" base acres—former cotton base acres from the 2008 farm bill. Generic base is added to a producer's total base for potential payments, but only if a covered crop is planted on the generic base. In other words, PLC payments on generic base acres are coupled to actual plantings (although payments remain subject to the 85% factor applied to eligible acres).

Under current peanut program provisions, peanuts have a separate program payment limit—a consequence of the quota buyout (P.L. 107-171; §1603). As a result of this feature, a farmer that grows multiple program crops including peanuts has in effect two different program payment limits: the first payment limit (of $125,000) is for an aggregation of program payments made to all program crops other than peanuts; and the second (also of $125,000) is for program payments made exclusively to peanuts. Thus, under an extreme scenario involving large payments for both peanuts and other program crops, this could potentially double a farmer's payment limits.

Farm policy economists have noted that peanuts have a statutory reference price that is set disproportionately above historical market prices, particularly when compared to other major program crops. Some contend that this potential advantage favors peanut production on generic base acres. However, the extent to which this scenario might play out is unclear, and both agronomic and market circumstances suggest that it might be somewhat limited.

Estimates of peanut program outlays for FY2016 vary. USDA (February 2015) projects FY2016 costs at $379 million, Food and Agricultural Policy Research Institute (August 2015) projects USDA program outlays for peanuts at $431 million, and the Congressional Budget Office (August 2015) projects $232 million. As a point of reference, the annual market value of U.S. peanut production has traditionally been in the range of $1.1 billion to $1.4 billion.

INTRODUCTION

According to the U.S. Department of Agriculture (USDA), the United States is expected to be the fourth largest producer and exporter of peanuts in the world in 2015.[1] In addition to its prominent role in international markets, U.S. peanut production and marketing is an important activity in several states located in the southeastern and southwestern United States. Peanuts have participated in federal farm support programs since the 1930s—initially under a quota system, and since 2002 under the income support programs available for other covered commodities like corn, wheat, soybeans, and rice. This report updates and revises an earlier August 19, 2015, version. It provides a brief overview of the U.S. peanut sector and reviews current U.S. farm policy including a discussion of how peanuts (following market adjustments spurred by a 2002 federal quota buyout) fit within current policy relative to other program crops.

Peanut Industry Basics

Production Areas

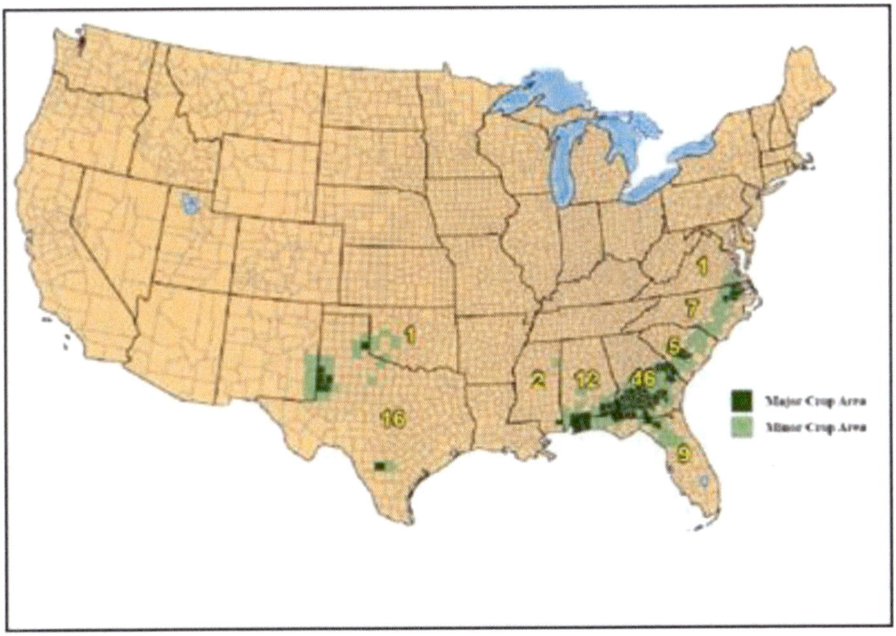

Source: U.S. Department of Agriculture, Office of the Chief Economist, World Agricultural Outlook Board, http://www.usda.gov/oce/weather/pubs/Other/MWCACP/namerica.htm.

Notes: Alaska and Hawaii do not produce peanuts.

Figure 1. U.S. Peanut-Producing Areas. (Yellow number indicates state share of U.S. production. (2006-2010))

U.S. peanut production is located primarily in the southeastern United States. The crop is planted in an arc stretching from southern Mississippi to southern Virginia, but with some additional smaller clusters of production in Texas, Oklahoma, and New Mexico (*Figure 1*). Georgia accounts for just under half of U.S. production, and Alabama has 12%. Most neighboring states account for single-digit shares.

This geographic location of production reflects the peanut plant's need for 120-160 frost-free days and soil that is sandy and loamy (relatively equal amounts of sand, silt, and clay) for optimal crop performance. The peanut industry is also geographically concentrated within each state, with peanuts accounting for a large share of farm and related agribusiness income earned in a number of peanut-producing counties. About three-fourths of U.S. peanut acreage is dryland (1.1 million acres in 2012), and the remainder is irrigated (0.5 million acres).

Peanut Varieties and Uses

Table 1. Peanut Types and Uses

Peanut type	Share of U.S. peanut crop	Primary use and characteristics	Where grown
Runner	80%	Manufacture of peanut butter; kernel size is uniform, which allows for even roasting	Georgia, Texas, Alabama, Florida, South Carolina, and Oklahoma
Virginia	15%	Snack peanuts and in-shell; kernel is large and known as "ballpark" peanut	SE Virginia, NE North Carolina, South Carolina, and western Texas
Spanish	4%	Snack peanuts, peanut butter and confections; kernel is small and round, with red skins	Texas and Oklahoma
Valencia	1%	Used for all-natural peanut butter and sold in shell for roasting and boiling; sweet flavor; each shell contains 3 to 5 kernels	New Mexico

Source: National Peanut Board and American Peanut Council.

The major types of peanuts grown in the United States are Runner, Virginia, Spanish, and Valencia (*Table 1*). The Runner is the most common variety and is used in the manufacture of peanut butter. Peanut butter is the leading use of peanuts produced in the United States (45%), according to the American Peanut Council (APC). Snack nuts and in-shells account for approximately 30% of use. Candy and confections and peanut oil for cooking account for the remainder. According to APC, peanuts are the leading snack nut consumed in the United States, with a two-thirds share of the snack nut market.

Industry Structure

Peanuts were grown on 6,561 farms in the United States in 2012, according to the 2012 *Census of Agriculture*, with an average farm size of 247 harvested peanut acres per farm (*Table 2*). Similar to output for other commodities, peanut production is primarily through larger farms that typically have lower per-unit costs of production. Peanut farms with at least 250 acres account for one-third of all peanut farms and three-quarters of national production. Most peanut farmers also plant other crops such as cotton, corn, or soybeans in multi-year rotations with peanuts in order to maintain soil health and crop yields.[2] The farm value of peanut production was $1.1 billion in 2014.

After harvest, farmers move peanuts to buying points or stations located throughout the production regions. Buying stations are operated by shellers, independent dealers, or warehouse owners. These "first handlers" purchase the peanuts and provide services such as drying, cleaning, and arranging for marketing assistance loans provided by the U.S. Department of Agriculture (USDA). Shellers sell edible peanuts to processors for manufacturing and bid on USDA-owned stocks of peanuts (forfeitures under the marketing loan program) for processing or export. Sales between shellers and processors are arranged by brokers or done directly.

Unlike markets for major crops like corn and soybeans, the U.S. peanut market is considered "thin," with only two peanut shellers reportedly buying over 80% of all peanuts from growers. No futures market exists for peanuts, and private contracts between producers and shellers reportedly account for most transactions. Given the peanut industry's structure and pricing practices (contracting), little public price and other market information is available to USDA.

Table 2. Number of Peanut Farms and Harvested Acreage, 2012

State	Number of Farms	Harvested Acres	Average Peanut Acres per Farm
Georgia	2,833	731,946	258
Alabama	772	217,940	282
Florida	698	196,320	281
North Carolina	636	105,739	166
Texas	552	148,795	270
South Carolina	493	106,746	217
Virginia	170	20,208	119
Oklahoma	166	21,926	132
Mississippi	128	48,306	377
Other	113	23,705	210
United States	6,561	1,621,631	247

Source: 2012 Census of Agriculture, http://www.agcensus.usda.gov/Publications/2012/Full_Report/ Volume_1,_Chapter_2_US_State_Level/.

Notes: Other states reporting acreage in 2012 were Arkansas (36 farms), Tennessee (22), New Mexico (21), California (15), Louisiana (11), Kentucky (5), Missouri (2), and Maryland (1).

Production and Market Trends

Two opposing but related trends have shaped peanut production during the last quarter century. Planted acreage has declined while productivity (yield measured in pounds per acre) has increased (see *Figure 2*). Acreage had been declining even prior to the policy change in 2002 from a quota system, which tended to lock acreage in place, to traditional commodity support programs (see "U.S. Farm Policy and Peanuts"). The policy change allowed market forces to play a stronger role in producer decision making. As a result, peanut production shifted to higher-yielding land with lower production costs. This acreage shift, including a greater proportion of plantings in Georgia, along with improvements in varieties and management practices, propelled a long-term uptrend in peanut yields that helped to lift peanut production in recent years (*Figure 2*). Another phenomenon associated with the 2002 peanut quota buyout has been a substantial increase in market volatility as evidenced by the sharp up-and-down cycle of plantings and production since 2002.

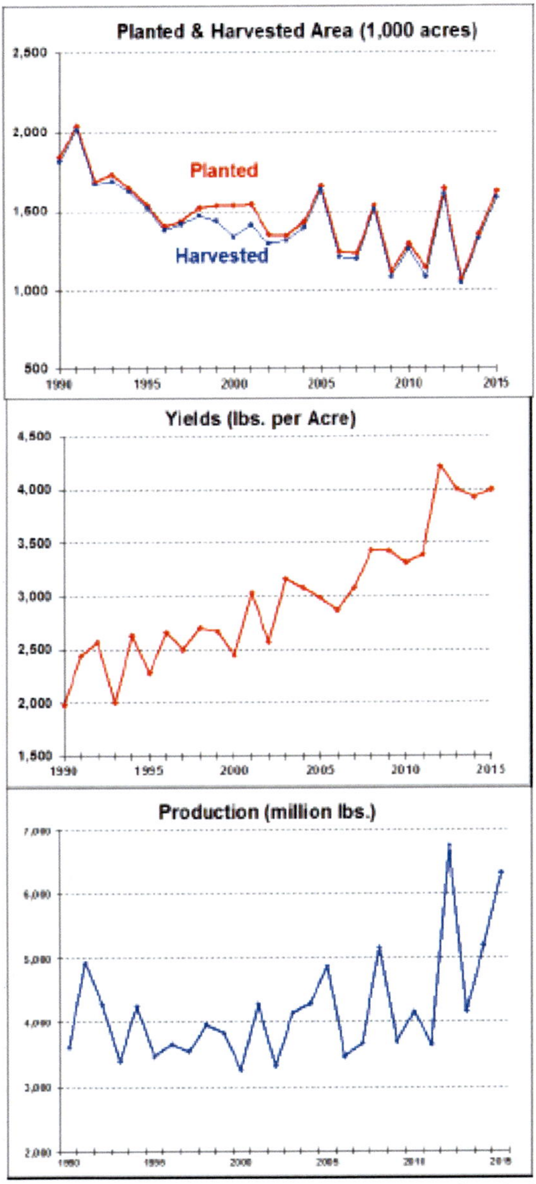

Source: National Agricultural Statistical Service, USDA, October 9, 2015.

Figure 2. U.S. Peanuts: Planted and Harvested Area, Yield, and Production.

A critical long-run factor influencing peanut output is the nature of demand for peanuts. In general, the demand for peanuts and peanut products (especially peanut butter) is fairly inelastic.[3] This implies that even small changes in supply can result in large price movements.

Domestic food use has grown slowly but steadily over time. After averaging a 14% share of total use during the 2002 to 2011 period, U.S. peanut exports jumped sharply in 2012 and have over 20% of total use since. China entered the market that year as a buyer because their regular supplier (India) had encountered yield problems due to drought. Canada, the Netherlands, and Mexico are the top export markets and account for about half of U.S. exports. Argentine peanuts compete with U.S. peanuts in the European market.

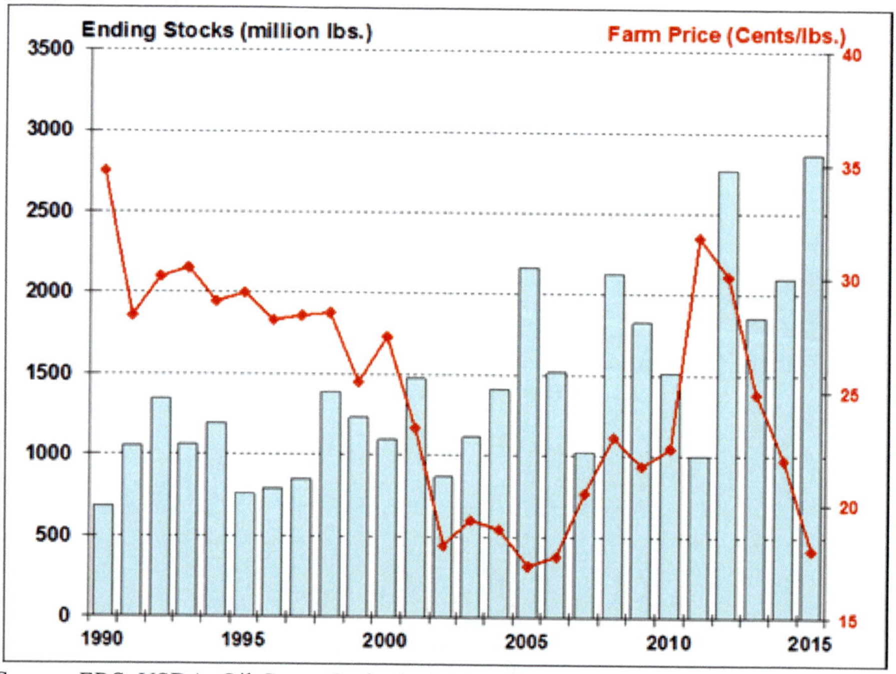

Source: ERS, USDA, Oil Crops Outlook, OCS-15k, November 13, 2015.
Notes: Farm prices are in current dollars. The peanut marketing year begins August 1.

Figure 3. Peanut Ending Stocks and Season-Average Farm Price.

High farm prices in 2011 encouraged U.S. producers to sharply increase plantings in 2012 (up 44% from 2010 plantings). A record U.S. peanut harvest in 2012—driven by both large plantings and record yields—resulted in record large domestic ending stocks despite record exports and strong domestic use

(*Figure 3*). The 2012/13 marketing year ending stocks were also record large in terms of their relative size as a share of total use (54%). Large domestic supplies have contributed to a strong downward trend in U.S. farm prices for peanuts since 2012. In 2015/16 (August-July season), the average farm price of peanuts is expected to be in a range of 16.75 to 19.25 cents per pound (with a midpoint of 18 cents per lb) and ending stocks are projected at a new record high.[4]

U.S. FARM POLICY AND PEANUTS

Current U.S. farm policy provides three income support programs for several major crops including peanuts.[5] However, farm policy for peanuts has followed a different policy trajectory from the other program crops for most of the last century. From the 1930s until 2002, peanuts operated under a system of marketing quotas that rigidly controlled domestic supplies and prices.[6] In 2002, Congress eliminated peanut quotas under a new farm bill (Farm Security and Rural Investment Act of 2002, P.L. 101-171, §1301-§1309) through a series of payments that offset the loss of quota rights—these payments are referred to as a "buyout."[7]

Since the 2002 buyout, farm policy for peanuts has followed essentially the same structure as for other "covered" program commodities.[8] In addition to eligibility for major farm support programs, peanuts initially retained their long-standing eligibility for Commodity Credit Corporation (CCC) monthly storage payments (similar to the cotton storage payment program) when put under a 9-month nonrecourse marketing loan. However, eligibility for storage payments was terminated with the 2007 peanut crop.

The current farm commodity program provisions in Title I of the 2014 farm bill (Agricultural Act of 2014; P.L. 113-79) include three types of support for covered commodities for crop years 2014-2018:

- Marketing Assistance Loan benefits, which offer interim (up to nine months) financing for loan commodities (covered crops plus several others) at statutory loan rates and, if prices fall below loan rates, additional low-price protection in the form of marketing loan gains or loan deficiency payments;
- Price Loss Coverage (PLC) payments, which are triggered when the national season average farm price for a covered commodity is below its statutorily fixed "reference price"; and

- Agriculture Risk Coverage (ARC) payments, as an alternative to PLC, which are triggered when annual crop revenue is below its guaranteed level based on a multiyear moving average of historical crop revenue.

Under the 2014 farm bill, farmers with base acres of covered commodities were given a one-time irrevocable choice between PLC and "county" ARC (based on a county guarantee) on a commodity-by-commodity basis for each farm. Alternatively, all covered crops on a farm can be enrolled in "individual" ARC, which is based on a farm-level guarantee. If no choice was made, the producer forfeited any payments for the 2014 crop year and the farm was enrolled automatically in PLC for the 2015-2018 crop years.

For peanuts, almost all producers (99.7%) selected PLC because they expected it to provide higher payments and greater risk protection than would be available under ARC. Similarly most rice producers (100% for long grain and 96% for medium grain) and large majorities of barley (75%), canola (97%), sorghum (66%), and minor oilseed producers (56% to 84%) also selected PLC. In contrast, a near-unanimous majority of corn (93%) and soybean (97%) producers, and a large majority of wheat producers (56%), selected ARC.

A Separate Program Payment Limit for Peanuts

Under current peanut program provisions, the primary advantage that peanuts have over other program crops is that peanut producers participating in government support programs have a separate program payment limit—a consequence of the peanut quota buyout (P.L. 107-171; §1603). As a result of this feature, a farmer that grows multiple program crops including peanuts has essentially two different program payment limits:

- the first payment limit of $125,000 per person is for an aggregation of program payments made to all program crops other than peanuts;
- the second payment limit of $125,000 per person is for program payments made exclusively to peanuts.

Thus, under an extreme scenario involving large payments for both peanuts and other program crops, this could potentially double a farmer's payment limits to as much as $250,000.

Marketing Assistance Loan Program

Peanuts and other designated crops are eligible for benefits under the Marketing Assistance Loan (MAL) program. MAL provides interim financing in the form of a government loan for up to nine months for participating producers following harvest of their crops.

A farmer must produce a crop to benefit from the program because the crop serves as loan collateral if the producer applies for a loan. The MAL process begins after harvest, when farmers may request a marketing loan, which is offered by USDA at a loan rate established in statute for pledged production (P.L. 107-171; §1202)—for peanuts the loan rate is $355 per ton or equivalently, 17.75 cents per pound. If a farmer puts their crop under a marketing loan, then they receive loan proceeds equal roughly to the quantity of peanuts placed under loan times the loan rate. Farmers then closely watch the relationship between market prices and the loan rate. In the case of peanuts, USDA estimates and announces a weekly national posted price to be used in determining the marketing loan repayment rate and other benefits. Prior to loan maturity, a farmer may repay the loan principal and interest if the posted price is at or above the loan rate. As a result, the loan provides interim financing, allowing the farmer to receive cash as soon as the crop is harvested and avoiding sale of the crop during harvest when prices tend to be at their seasonal low. The program essentially provides a price floor for producers because the government will take ownership of the loan collateral (i.e., the pledged crop) if prices drop below the statutory loan rate.

Special Marketing Loan Benefits

Defaults (or forfeitures) on marketing loans are not common because USDA provides the producer the opportunity to capture benefits even when the posted price is below the loan rate. In this case, farmers are allowed to repay the loan at the lower posted price, thus receiving a "marketing loan gain" (MLG) from the government because farmers do not repay the loan in full. The MLG is equal to the difference between the loan rate and the weekly national posted price.

Also, accrued interest is waived, but the producer pays storage and handling charges for the quantity of peanuts under loan. As an alternative to putting the crop "under loan" when prices are low, farmers may request a "loan deficiency payment (LDP)," with a payment rate equal to the difference between the loan rate and the posted price (same as the MLG). Farmers then receive an LDP payment without going through the loan process.

For most of the last decade, the farm (and posted) price of peanuts has been above the loan rate, so annual marketing loan benefits have been either zero or minimal (*Figure 4*).

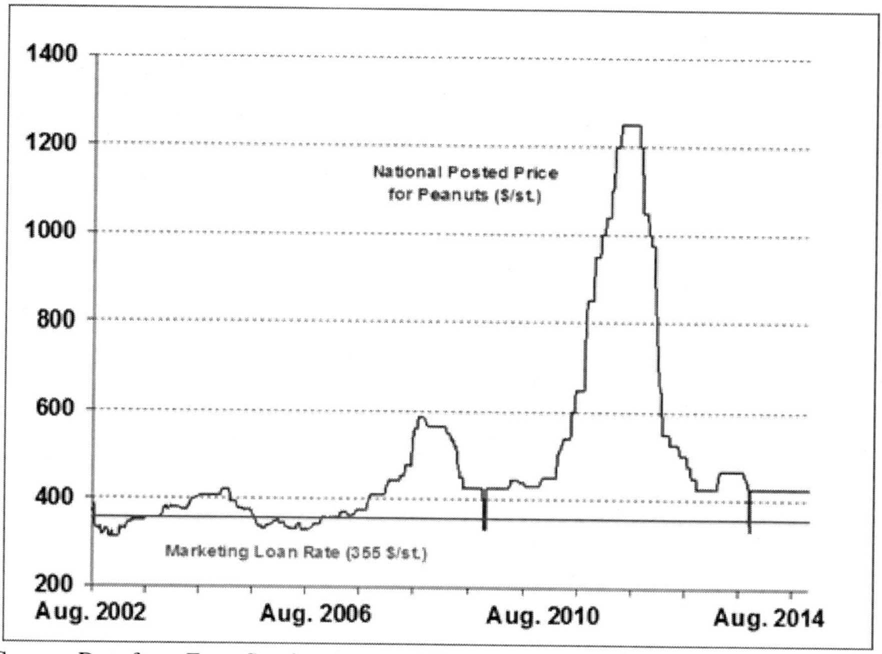

Source: Data from Farm Service Agency, USDA.

Notes: Posted price data are for Runner-type peanuts, with an average loan rate during entire period (August 2002 - June 2015) of $355 per ton. During periods of weak market prices marketing assistance loan benefits have resulted, including $49 million for crop year 2002/03 and $31 million for crop year 2005/06.

Figure 4. Peanut Prices and Marketing Loan Rate. (Producers receive benefits when the weekly national posted price is below the loan rate)

Forfeiture of the Pledged Crop

Forfeiture of the pledged crop in lieu of loan repayment is an option that is available for all marketing loan crops. Rather than repaying the loan with cash, farmers can fulfill their loan obligation by forfeiting the crop pledged as collateral. This option can be attractive for peanut producers if the posted price is below or even slightly above the loan rate because USDA, by law, then pays for costs associated with storage, handling, and interest. For large producers, another key feature of the forfeiture option is that the "gain" associated with forfeiting the crop, unlike a gain from repaying the loan with cash (or receiving an MLG or LDP), does not count toward the payment limit of $125,000 per person. Producers decide which route to pursue (repay loan with cash or forfeit) depending on the expected value of each option, their need for loaned funds, and their likelihood of exceeding the payment limit. If a farmer chooses to forfeit the crop, USDA takes ownership of the crop. Storage costs continue to accrue to USDA until it sells the crop or, in the case of peanuts, uses the CCC-owned peanuts for domestic nutrition programs.

Price Loss Coverage (PLC) Payments on Peanut Base

In addition to marketing assistance loan benefits, producers with base acres for any covered commodity (including peanuts) are eligible for a second (and higher) layer of income protection under the Price Loss Coverage (PLC) program. For peanuts, PLC payments are triggered when the annual farm price is below the statutory PLC reference price of $535 per short ton (i.e., 2,000 lbs) or equivalently, 26.75 cents per pound, as established under the 2014 farm bill (*Figure 5*).[9]

PLC and ARC payments are made after October 1 following the end of the marketing year.[10] As a result, government payments arrive more than a year after the crop is harvested. For example, the payment associated with the 2014 peanut crop (planted in spring 2014 and harvested in summer 2014) will be made after October 1, 2015.[11] (In contrast, marketing loan benefits are available immediately upon harvest for crop years 2014-2018.)

For individual farms, payments are calculated using the national PLC payment rate and individual farm information on historical program yield and acres. The PLC payment formula is the *PLC payment rate times historical farm program yield times* 85% of *historical peanut base acres.*

- The national PLC payment rate is equal to the PLC reference price minus the higher of the season-average farm price or the marketing loan rate.
- With respect to farm program yields, during program signup in early 2015, producers were given the choice of keeping the same farm-level program yield used for calculating the farm's counter-cyclical payments under the 2008 farm bill (generally based on 1998-2001 yields or earlier) or updating the farm program yield according to the

formula of 90% of the 2008-2012 average yield per planted acre for the farm.

- Peanut base represents historical peanut planting on each farm and totals 2 million acres nationwide.12 As with program yields, the 2014 farm bill provided farmers with a one-time opportunity to update individual crop base acres by reallocating acreage within their previous base to match their actual crop mix (plantings) during 2009-2012.

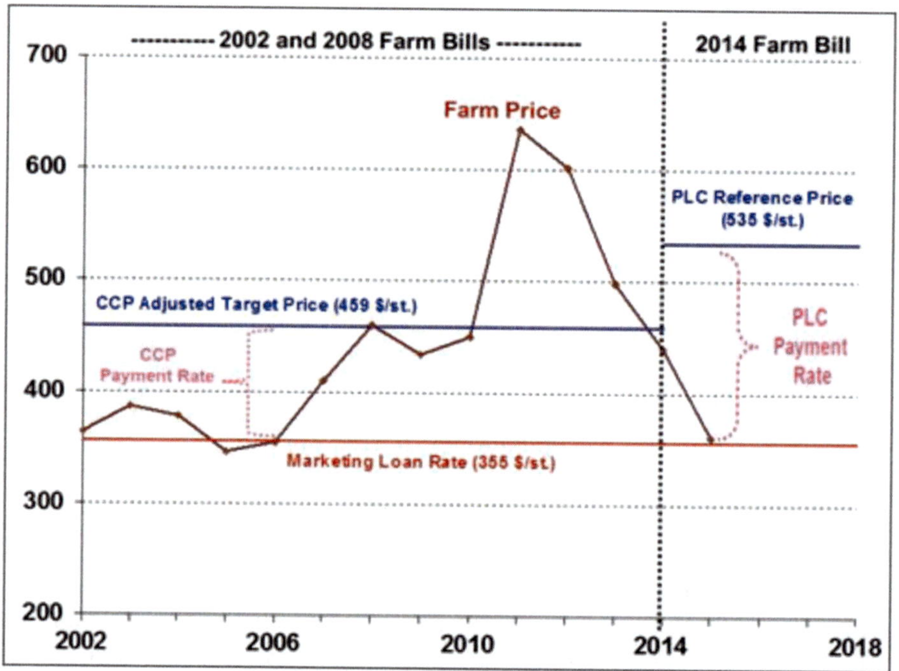

Source: Farm price data are from ERS, USDA, Oil Crops Outlook, OCS-15k, November 13; farm program parameters are from respective farm bills—2002, 2008, and 2014.

Notes: Under the 2014 farm bill, the PLC payment rate is the reference price of $535 per ton minus the annual farm price (or loan rate if higher). Under the 2002 and 2008 farm bills, the trigger for counter-cyclical price (CCP) payments was $459 per ton, which equaled the target price of $495 per ton minus the direct payment rate of $36 per ton. The loan rate is part of the formula because marketing loan benefits provide additional price protection when prices fall below the loan rate.

Figure 5. Peanut Income-Support Program Price Triggers Since 2002. (Payment rate = Reference price minus national farm price (or loan rate, if higher)

A new feature of the 2014 farm bill income support programs is that, unlike income support programs from previous farm bills, payments under PLC and ARC are made on base acres, not current plantings. This feature—decoupling payments from current plantings—is intended to better comply with World Trade Organization (WTO) commitments on domestic support and to minimize any influence on producer behavior and subsequent market distortion. The payments are considered "partially decoupled" because the payment amount remains connected to current market prices. An exception to the decoupling is payments associated with generic base acres, whereby current plantings can affect payment acreage.

PLC Payments for Peanuts Planted on "Generic" Base

PLC payments can also be made on "generic base acres." Generic base acres are the renamed cotton base acres from the 2008 farm bill. Under the 2014 farm bill, cotton is no longer a covered commodity and thus no longer eligible for PLC or ARC payments. Instead, the former cotton base, now "generic base," is added to a producer's total base for potential payments, but only if a covered crop is planted on the generic base.[13] In other words, PLC payments on generic base acres are fully coupled to actual plantings (although payments remain subject to the 85% factor applied to eligible acres).

Unlike PLC payments on peanut base acres, which are made regardless of which crop is planted, the PLC payment on generic base in any given year is proportional to a farm's plantings of peanuts and other covered crops on the entire farm. More specifically, for each crop year, generic base acres are attributed to a particular covered commodity base (for potential payment) in proportion to that crop's share of total plantings of all covered commodities on the farm in that year.[14] The coupled nature of PLC payments on generic base is an important new program feature because of the large number of generic base acres available under the 2014 farm bill—17.5 million acres.[15] Substantial coupled plantings could potentially occur to the extent that this land remains under cultivation (as discussed below in "Relative Planting Incentives Under Farm Programs"). It is likely that many of the former cotton base acres are no longer used for annual crops—similarly, the original decoupling under the 1996 farm bill resulted in base acres in many places returning to pasture or fallow, but still remaining eligible for assistance).

Expanded Federal Crop Insurance Coverage in 2014 Farm Bill

Federal crop insurance is available for about 130 crops, including peanuts. Traditionally, a yield-based federal crop insurance policy was available for peanut producers to protect against yield loss due to weather, if purchased by producers. The insurance guarantees are established just prior to planting, based on historical yields and expected market prices (not statutory prices used in farm programs). The insurance premiums are subsidized by USDA, and subsidy rates vary based on the type of policy and coverage selected.[16]

The 2014 farm bill mandated a peanut revenue insurance product for the 2015 crop year so farmers could choose between a traditional yield-based policy and one that protects against declines in revenue (yield times price). Revenue policies have been available for many other farm program crops for almost two decades, but developing one for peanuts has been problematic because its relatively small market is considered "thin" and futures market prices are not available for setting the price guarantee. After considerable study, USDA's Risk Management Agency decided to base prices for the new revenue product on several factors, including the futures prices of cotton, wheat, soybean oil, and soybean meal, as well as the Brazilian price of peanuts, peanut stocks, and the FSA loan rate for peanuts.[17]

The rapid adoption of the new revenue insurance policy by peanut producers suggests that there was a strong demand for this product. For the 2015 crop, peanut producers purchased a total of 23,434 federal crop insurance policies covering nearly 1.5 million acres. Of this total, 44% of the policies and 68% of the covered acres were enrolled in revenue insurance.[18] Under the 2015 peanut policies, $9.6 million was paid out in indemnities including $7.1 million under revenue policies.

Adjusted Gross Income Limit

As with other farm program crops, payment eligibility depends on a gross income limit and rules on being "actively engaged." To qualify for any commodity program benefits, recipients must pass an eligibility requirement based on adjusted gross income (AGI) used for federal taxes. The AGI limit is a single, total (farm and non-farm) AGI limit of $900,000 (using a three-year average). Also, to be eligible for payments, persons must be "actively engaged" in farming.

Actively engaged, in general, is defined as making a significant contribution of (i) capital, equipment, or land, and (ii) personal labor or active personal management.[19]

Relative Planting Incentives Under Farm Programs

Crop planting choices in general, and on base acres in particular, are based on relative net returns among competing crops, plus rotational considerations. Farm program payments do not figure in the determination because they are decoupled from planting decisions. In contrast, crop choices on generic base acres must consider both relative net returns as well as potential proceeds from government programs (i.e., both ARC and PLC) because of their coupling to crop plantings.

Market conditions vary widely based on relative crop prices, yield prospects (both irrigated and non-irrigated), and production costs. A preliminary assessment of potential market conditions for 2016 using a combination of data from USDA and the University of Georgia suggests peanuts could be a very competitive option for producers behind soybeans on irrigated acres and wheat on non-irrigated acres when comparing cost and returns for competing crops (*Table 3*).

It is important to note that *Table 3* excludes fixed costs and thus does not attempt to predict actual profitability across crops. In the short run, crop choices can be made by comparing returns above variable costs; however, to ensure economic viability in the long run, producers must also cover fixed costs, which are not considered in this table. This consideration is particularly valid for peanuts, where equipment lines are unique to the crop and represent significant up-front costs. Also, the variable cost estimates used in Table 3 represent the estimate for a single point in time and are subject to changing market conditions for a host of farm inputs including fuel, fertilizer, pesticides, labor, and land.

A similar preliminary outlook for 2016 PLC and ARC payments for major covered commodities—using a combination of data from USDA and the Food and Agricultural Policy Research Institute (FAPRI)—suggests that peanuts may be an attractive planting option on generic base acres relative to most other competing crops (*Table 4*). Peanut program payments under PLC (the program choice of over 99% of peanut base owners) are projected at $270 per acre. However, most corn and soybean base owners chose the ARC program. Under the ARC scenario presented in *Table 5*, corn and soybeans are projected to receive ARC payments of $139 and $117 per acre, respectively.

Table 3. Comparison of Net Returns for Peanuts and Competing Crops, 2015/16

Crop	Prices Projections		Expected Yield		Expected Revenue	Variable Cost (VC)	Net Returns Above VC
Irrigated Crops							
Cotton	$0.59	$/lb.	1,200	lbs./acre	$708	$524	$184
Soybeans	$8.90	$/bu.	60	bu./acre	$534	$294	$240
Peanuts	$0.18	$/lb.	4,700	lbs./acre	$846	$653	$193
Corn	$3.65	$/bu.	200	bu./acre	$730	$662	$68
Wheat	$5.00	$/bu.	75	bu./acre	$375	$323	$52
Sorghum	$3.60	$/bu.	100	bu./acre	$360	$349	$11
Non-irrigated Crops							
Peanuts	$0.18	$/lb.	3400	lbs./acre	$612	$550	$62
Cotton	$0.59	$/lb.	750	lbs./acre	$443	$423	$20
Wheat	$5.00	$/bu.	55	bu./acre	$275	$199	$76
Soybeans	$8.90	$/bu.	30	bu./acre	$267	$212	$55
Corn	$3.65	$/bu.	85	bu./acre	$310	$313	-$3
Sorghum	$3.60	$/bu.	65	bu./acre	$234	$223	$11

Source: Calculations are by CRS. Prices are from USDA, WASDE, November 9, 2015, and ERS, USDA, Oil Crops Outlook, OCS-15k, November 13, 2015; yield and variable costs of production data are from University of Georgia, College of Agricultural and Environmental Sciences, Extension, Cost Enterprise Budgets, January 2015, http://www.agecon.uga.edu/extension/budgets/cct/index.html.

Notes: The calculations above are illustrative only. They combine 2015 pre-planting yield and costs estimates from Georgia—the leading U.S. peanut-producing state, with USDA post-harvest price estimates. Individual farm agronomics including irrigation availability and rotational considerations related to cropping patterns, soil types, plant disease and insect infestations, etc. are also important factors in crop selection, but are not included here.

When potential PLC and ARC program payments (Table 4 and Table 5) are combined with potential market returns (Table 3), peanuts appear to have an advantage over other program crops in competing for generic base acres.

Table 4. Comparison of Potential PLC Program Payments for Peanuts and Competing Crops, 2016 Projections

Crop	Prices				National Average Program Yield		National Average Payment Rate ($ Per Acre)[a]
	PLC[b]	SAFP[c]	Per-Unit Payment Rate[d]	Unit			
Peanuts	$535.00	$392.20	$142.80	$/ton	1.897	tons/acre	$270.85
Peanuts	$0.2675	$0.1961	$0.0714	$/lb.	3,793.4	lbs./acre	$270.85
Corn	$3.70	$3.71	$0.00	$/bu.	132.0	bu.acre	$0.00
Sorghum	$3.95	$3.73	$0.22	$/bu.	67.6	bu.acre	$14.87
Soybeans	$8.40	$9.15	$0.00	$/bu.	37.4	bu.acre	$0.00
Wheat	$5.50	$5.05	$0.45	$/bu.	45.3	bu.acre	$20.39

Source: CRS calculations using national average program yields (FSA, USDA) and expected national season-average farm prices (SAFPs) for 2016/17 from FAPRI, Baseline Update for U.S. Agricultural Markets, FAPRI-MU Report #03-15, August 2015.

Notes: This table is illustrative only. Program yields used here are the national average for both irrigated and non-irrigated crops. The calculation above assumes that the farm program yield is the same as the national average program yield. In practice, each individual farm has its own specific program yield for each program crop (differentiated by irrigated versus non-irrigated) based on its historical data. PLC payments (paid on 85% of base acres) are made when the SAFP for a crop is below its 2014 farm bill reference price. At this early stage, projections for the 2016 SAFP are speculative and subject to substantial variation with changing prospects in domestic and international markets.

[a] The per-acre payment rate equals the per-unit payment rate times the program yield. It is applied to 85% of an eligible producer's base acres for the respective program crop.

[b] The statutory PLC reference price.

[c] The FAPRI August 2015 projection of national season average farm-prices received for 2016/17.

[d] The payment rate is the PLC reference price minus the SAFP (or loan rate, if higher). If the SAFP exceeds the reference price, then no payment is available. If the SAFP is below the marketing loan rate, additional benefits accrue under the MLP (but paid on actual production).

This competitive edge will vary across producing zones with yield and cost conditions, as well as changes in relative prices.

In an extreme case, if a producer with generic base acres expected a sizeable peanut PLC payment rate relative to other program crops, their entire farm could be planted to peanuts (or peanuts and no other covered crop), and their PLC payments on generic base would be calculated using exclusively the payment rate for peanuts.

Table 5. Comparison of Potential ARC Program Payments for Peanuts and Competing Crops, 2016 Projections

	Prices			Yield			Revenue ($/acre)		ARC Payment Rate ($/acre)[d]
Crop	ARC MA[a]	SAFP[b]	Unit	ARC MA[a]	US AVG[c]	Unit	ARC MA[a]	US AVG[d]	
Peanuts	513.33	392.20	$/ton	2.0	1.9	st./ac.	$1,011.82	$750.47	$261.34
Peanuts	0.257	0.196	$/lb.	3,942	3,827	lb./ac.	$1,011.82	$270.85	$261.34
Corn	4.79	3.71	$/bu.	158.2	166.8	bu./ac.	$758.24	$618.83	$139.42
Sorg-hum	4.77	3.73	$/bu.	60.6	64.0	bu./ac.	$288.78	$238.27	$50.06
Soy-beans	11.87	9.15	$/bu.	44.5	44.9	bu./ac.	$528.13	$410.84	$117.30
Wheat	6.70	5.05	$/bu.	44.5	45.9	bu./ac.	$298.41	$231.80	$66.61

Source: CRS calculations using national average farm prices and yields (NASS, USDA) and expected national season-average farm prices (SAFPs) for 2016/17 from FAPRI, Baseline Update for U.S. Agricultural Markets, FAPRIMU Report #03-15, August 2015.

Notes: This table is illustrative only. Yields used here are national averages. The calculation above assumes that county-level yields are the same as the national average yield. In practice, each county will have its own specific program yield for each program crop based on its historical data. ARC payments (paid on 85% of base acres) are made when the county-level revenue for a crop is below the calculated product of the 5-year Olympic moving averages for national prices and county yields. At this early stage, projections for 2016 prices and yields are speculative and subject to substantial variation with changing prospects in domestic and international markets. Peanuts are added to this table purely to facilitate comparisons with other crops. Less than 1% of peanut base owners chose to participate in the ARC program.

[a] ARC moving averages (ARC MA) are calculated using the Olympic average (i.e., throw out the high and low years) of the preceding five years.

[b] FAPRI August 2015 projection of national season average farm-prices received for 2016/17.

[c] The U.S. average (US AVG) is a FAPRI August 2015 projection for 2016/17.

[d] The payment rate is the ARC MA for revenue minus the actual county revenue. If the actual county revenue exceeds the ARC MA revenue, then no payment is available.

Alternatively, if expected market returns and PLC payment rates do not favor peanuts, farmers with generic base acres could plant their entire farm to crops other than peanuts. An outcome between these two extremes is expected to prevail if farmers maintain typical rotations, which are needed to maintain soil health and long-term yield potential for all crops. Nevertheless, high potential PLC payments on generic base could cause producers to "stretch" their rotations and benefit from additional peanut payments on generic base.

Farm policy economists have noted that peanuts (and rice) have a statutory reference price that is set disproportionately above historical market prices, particularly when compared to the reference prices for other major program crops.[20] Since the peanut quota buyout in 2002, monthly peanut farm prices have been below their respective reference price 87% of the time, and below the marketing loan rate 18% of the time.[21] This compares with monthly corn farm prices (56% of the time below the reference price and 5% of the time below the marketing loan rate); soybeans (39% and 4%), wheat (22% and 4%), sorghum (59% and 12%), and barley (65% and 0%). Rice has comparable "in-the-money" percentages with the announced Adjusted World Price (AWP) for rice with 90% of monthly farm prices falling below the reference price, and 32% below the marketing loan rate. Some contend that this potential advantage favors peanut production (relative to other program crops) on generic base acres. However, the extent to which this scenario might play out is unclear, and both agronomic and market circumstances suggest that it might be limited.

The outlook for average farm prices across major program crops is likely to be a key determinant of both farm program payments and crop planting choices on generic base. This is because the size of the farm program payments increases in proportion to the decline in farm price below the reference price and loan rate. The largest impacts on planting decisions could be in states where the generic base is large relative to the total base (*Figure 6*) because the planting mix determines the payment. At one extreme is a farm with 100% generic base, when acreage eligible for specific crop payments corresponds directly to the covered crops that are planted. At the other extreme, for a farm with no generic base acres, the payment acres are predetermined and will not change regardless of what the farmer plants—namely covered crops to the individual crop base acres.

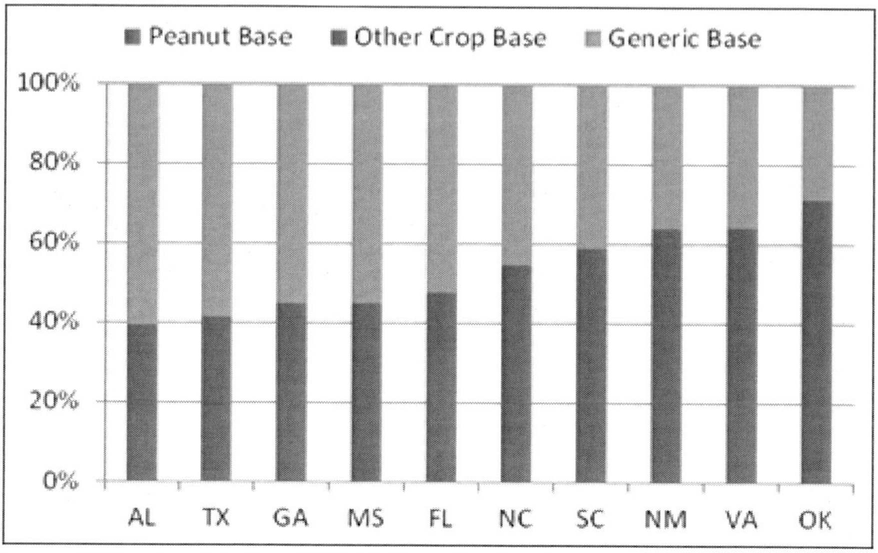

Source: CRS, using data from USDA's Farm Service Agency.
Notes: Other crop base includes primarily corn, soybeans, rice, and sorghum.

Figure 6. Shares of Total Base on Farms with Generic Base.

The share of generic base is more than 50% for several peanut-producing states, including Alabama, Texas, and Georgia (*Figure 6* and *Table 6*). These states could see additional plantings of peanuts in future years if relative returns (including government payments) favor peanuts.

Table 6 summarizes peanut base acres and total generic base under the 2014 farm bill. Planted peanut acreage for major producer states for 2012-2015 is also shown.

Table 6. Peanut Base, Generic Base, and Peanut Planted Area by State

			Peanut plantings			
State	Peanut base	Generic base	2012	2013	2014	2015
Georgia	753,328	1,456,949	735,000	430,000	600,000	790,000
Texas	401,032	7,204,323	150,000	120,000	130,000	165,000
Alabama	260,991	657,231	220,000	140,000	175,000	200,000
N. Carolina	157,643	866,638	107,000	82,000	94,000	90,000
Florida	152,206	105,308	210,000	140,000	175,000	185,000
Oklahoma	93,010	589,031	24,000	17,000	12,000	10,000
S. Carolina	78,770	347,713	110,000	81,000	112,000	113,000

			Peanut plantings			
State	Peanut base	Generic base	2012	2013	2014	2015
Virginia	75,516	103,423	20,000	16,000	19,000	19,000
New Mexico	24,267	98,088	10,000	7,000	4,500	5,000
Mississippi	14,144	1,623,887	52,000	34,000	32,000	43,000
Subtotal	2,010,907	13,052,591	1,638,000	1,067,000	1,353,500	1,620,000
Arkansas	6,177	1,148,575	NA	NA	NA	NA
Louisiana	1,288	995,813	NA	NA	NA	NA
Tennessee	1,125	743,850	NA	NA	NA	NA
Arizona	428	406,931	NA	NA	NA	NA
Missouri	211	440,015	NA	NA	NA	NA
Colorado	75	0	NA	NA	NA	NA
Nebraska	34	8	NA	NA	NA	NA
Other states	0	795,128	NA	NA	NA	NA
Total	2,020,243	17,582,911	1,638,000	1,067,000	1,353,500	1,620,000

Source: Base acres: Farm Service Agency (FSA), USDA; planted acreage: NASS, USDA, October 9, 2015.

Notes: NA = not estimated by NASS, USDA.

Selected Policy Issues

Generic Base Acres

The domestic and trade policy concern is that farm program payments made to plantings on generic base are fully coupled to production and thus potentially market distorting. As a result, program payments made to generic base would likely count toward the U.S. amber box limit of $19.1 billion. Furthermore, if such payments are substantial and can be linked to a surge in exports, they could potentially be vulnerable to challenge by another WTO member.[22]

Potential Marketing Loan Forfeitures

As mentioned earlier, large peanut producers who have pledged their peanut crops as collateral for nine-month USDA marketing loans could confront a payment limit issue leading to forfeiture of their crop to USDA. This situation could result if incurring marketing loan benefits (i.e., marketing loan gains or loan deficiency payments) would cause them to surpass the payment limit of $125,000. In such a situation, a producer could simply forfeit the collateral peanuts to USDA (via the Commodity Credit Corporation) and keep the original loan value. The CCC would then be responsible for handling and storage costs and the eventual marketing of the peanuts.

USDA, in its November 2015 crop forecast, projected U.S. peanut ending stocks for the 2015/16 crop year to be record large at 2.87 billion pounds or 52.3% of total use.[23] If such an oversupply situation continues into the future, USDA could face challenges with the marketing loan program for peanuts. If supplies are large enough to depress prices for successive years, but farm subsidies (via generic base) provide incentives to plant peanuts, a large amount of peanuts could go under loan and forfeitures could accumulate. In a severely depressed market, USDA might have difficulty finding a buyer without offering a deep discount, which would result in large net outlays for the government. USDA could wait for a price recovery, but doing so would result in additional storage charges. Sufficient storage capacity might also be an issue if stocks increase substantially.

Prospective Government Farm Program Outlays

Following the 2002 buyout of the peanut quota program, federal peanut income support payments (excluding storage payments and the buyout) have averaged $192 million per year. Additionally, peanut storage payments averaged $79 million per year from 1996 to 2007 (the last year of eligibility), and $0 since their elimination in 2007 (*Figure 7*).

With ongoing congressional concern for budget deficits and federal spending, the cost of the peanut programs might garner the attention of policymakers who want to reduce federal spending. In April 2014, two months after the 2014 farm bill was signed into law, the Congressional Budget Office (CBO) projected CCC program outlays for peanuts of $84 million for FY2016 and an annual average of $71 million for the five-year 2014 farm bill period (FY2014-FY2018). As new information on market conditions as well as producer participation and program outlays for FY2014 and FY2015 have become available, projections of potential outlays have been revised upward. In February 2015 USDA projected peanut program costs of $379 million for FY2016 .[24] In June 2015, FAPRI projected farm program outlays for peanuts of $431 million for FY2016 and an annual average of $337 million for the five-year 2014 farm bill period (FY2014-FY2018).[25] Finally, in August 2015, the CBO projected CCC program outlays for peanuts at $232 million for FY2016, and at an annual average of $198 million the five-year 2014 farm bill period.[26] As a point of reference, the annual market value of U.S. peanut production has traditionally been in the range of $1.1 billion to $1.4 billion, depending on crop size.[27]

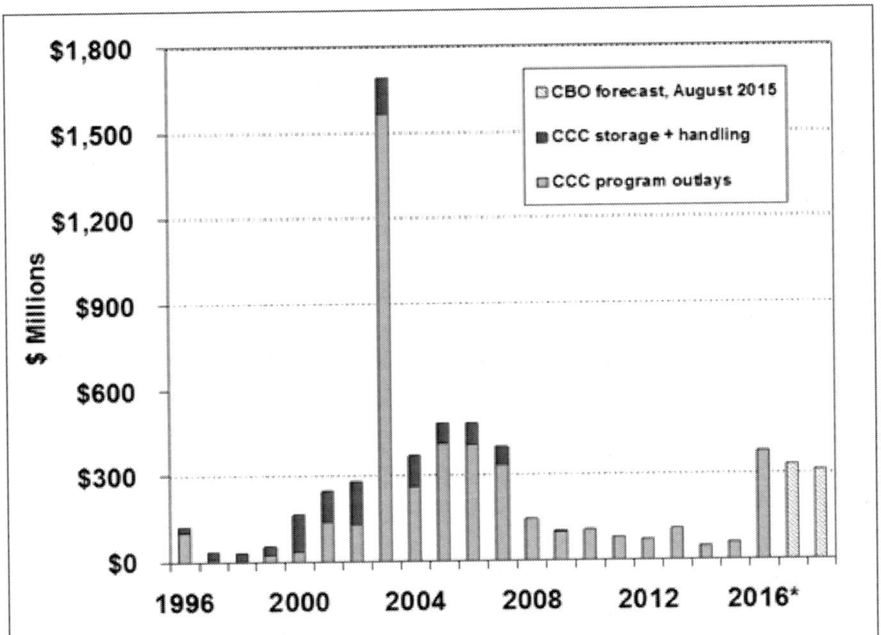

Source: Farm Service Agency (FSA), USDA, "Table 35—CCC Net Outlays by Commodity & Function, Fiscal Years 2007-2016E," CCC Budget Essentials, February 2015; and CBO, "August 2015 Baseline for Farm Programs," August 26, 2015.

Notes: FY2003 costs include the CCC buyout of peanut quotas. CBO projections do not include storage and handling costs of CCC-owned peanuts. 2016 is a USDA forecast; 2017 and 2018 are CBO projections.

Figure 7. USDA CCC Net Outlays for Peanuts. (Fiscal years 1 996 to 2016 estimated; 20 1 7-20 1 8 projected)

Government payments for the 2016 crop will depend on how low the average peanut price is relative to the reference price. USDA will make its first forecast of 2016 farm prices in May 2016. The current 2015 outlook for peanut farm prices of $360 per ton (or 18 cents per pound) implies a PLC payment rate of $175 per ton. When combined with a total peanut base of 2 million acres and an average PLC payment yield of 1.5 tons per acre, total PLC payments on 85% of peanut base acres would be $446 million for the 2015 crop or about $68,000 per farm using the number of peanut farms (6,561) in the 2012 Census of Agriculture.[28] Additional PLC payments on generic base (attributed to peanuts) could push total PLC payments substantially higher in 2016 and beyond. Under expectations for larger peanut crops and the ensuing low market prices, additional costs would be associated with the marketing loan program, including storage and handling costs.[29]

Market Development

The American Peanut Council (APC) administers the U.S. peanut industry's export market development program, receiving approximately $2 million per year in government funds under the Market Access Program (MAP).[30] MAP aids in the creation, expansion, and maintenance of foreign markets for U.S. agricultural products.[31] MAP funding has been targeted for reductions by some Members of Congress, who maintain that it is a form of "corporate welfare," or to help offset increased expenditures on other programs. Such efforts have been unsuccessful.

For the domestic market, some in Congress have begun encouraging USDA to purchase more peanut butter for domestic food programs and for international food aid as a way to increase peanut usage.[32]

Arguments For and Against the Peanut Support Program

The arguments for and against the peanut support programs are the same as those for U.S. farm programs in general. Proponents argue that an income safety net is needed to help producers deal with the substantial price volatility associated with commodity markets. They say a marketing assistance loan program is needed to provide greater marketing options for producers who are at a distinct market-power disadvantage when dealing with a small number of powerful buyers. And in peanut's particular case, proponents argue that farm program support is needed to help offset the substantial market volatility that has emerged since the elimination of the peanut quota system.

In contrast, critics argue that market signals are sufficient to allocate resources within the sector, and that subsidies distort resources away from more efficient uses. Some critics argue that farm subsidies actually keep small, inefficient operators in business and that, in the absence of subsidies, the inefficient operators would not be competitive and the land would be maintained and operated by more efficient, technologically savvy operators who would get better yields and returns from the same acreage. Others argue further that funds allocated to farm support would have greater returns if spent in other sectors.

End Notes

[1] USDA, Production, Supply, and Demand (PSD) database, November 9, 2015.

[2] The average total acreage of all crops on farms growing peanuts was 2,500 acres in 2013, according to USDA's Agricultural Resource Management Survey. See http://www.nass.usda.gov/Surveys/Guide_to_NASS_Surveys/Ag_Resource_Management/ARMS_2014_Peanuts_Highlights.pdf.

[3] Inelastic demand means the percentage change in quantity demanded of a product following a change in its price is less than the percentage change in price.

[4] Economic Research Service (ERS), USDA, Oil Crops Outlook, OCS-15k, Table 8, November 13, 2015.

[5] For details on current farm income support programs, see CRS Report R43448, Farm Commodity Provisions in the 2014 Farm Bill (P.L. 113-79).

[6] For historical peanut policy, see W. C. McArthur, V. N. Grise, H. O. Doty, Jr., and D. Hacklander, U.S. Peanut Industry, AER 493, ERS, USDA, November 1982.

[7] For more on the policy shift, see CRS Report RL30924, Peanut Program: Evolution from Supply Management to Market Orientation, and E. Dohlman, L. Foreman, and M. Da Pra, The Post-Buyout Experience: Peanut and Tobacco Sectors Adapt to Policy Reform, IEB 80, ERS, USDA, November 2009.

[8] Major program crops, referred to as "covered commodities" include wheat, oats, and barley (including wheat, oats, and barley used for haying and grazing); corn, grain sorghum, long grain rice, medium grain rice, and pulse crops (dry peas, lentils, small chickpeas, and large chickpeas); soybeans, other oilseeds (including sunflower seed, rapeseed, canola, safflower, flaxseed, mustard seed, crambe, and sesame seed), and peanuts.

[9] See Table 4 for a comparison of PLC reference prices for selected program crops.

[10] Only PLC is described in this report because it covers 99.7% of eligible peanut acreage. For an explanation of ARC, see CRS Report R43758, Farm Safety Net Programs: Background and Issues.

[11] The 2014 peanut crop marketing season is August 2014 to July 2015.

[12] Table 6 shows program base for peanuts and the other major program crops. Base acres are the historical planted acreage on each FSA farm, using a multi-year average from as far back as the 1980s. Base acre provisions since 1981 are described in C. E. Young, D. W. Skully, P. C. Westcott, and L. Hoffman, Economic Analysis of Base Acre and Payment Yield Designations Under the 2002 U.S. Farm Act, ERS, USDA, September 2005, pp. 36-41.

[13] Generic base acres were included in the 2014 farm bill to address a trade dispute involving Brazil and the U.S. cotton industry. As part of the cotton policy reform, the 2014 farm bill excluded upland cotton from PLC/ARC programs, thus leaving cotton base without any program. To bring cotton base under the new program, it was renamed "generic base" and

opened up to any program crop. See CRS Report RL32571, Brazil's WTO Case Against the U.S. Cotton Program.

[14] If the total number of acres planted to all covered commodities on the entire farm does not exceed the generic base acres on the farm, only the amount of acreage actually planted to a covered commodity is attributed to that covered commodity for payment purposes.

[15] Table 6 summarizes peanut base acres and total generic base under the 2014 farm bill.

[16] See CRS Report R40532, Federal Crop Insurance: Background.

[17] For more information, see http://www.rma.usda.gov/help/faq/peanutrevenue.html.

[18] Federal Crop Insurance Corporation (FCIC), Nationwide Summary of Business—By Commodity, as of November 16, 2015, http://www.rma.usda.gov.

[19] The 2014 farm bill instructed USDA to write regulations that define "significant contribution of active personal management" to more clearly and objectively implement existing law. The proposed rule was issued in March 2015, and the comment period ended May 26, 2015. Issuance of the final rule is pending.

[20] D. Orden and C. Zulauf, "The Political Economy of the 2014 Farm Bill," invited paper, AAEA session The 2014 Farm Bill: An Economic Post Mortem, ASSA Annual Meetings, January 4, 2015, Boston, MA.

[21] Calculations are by CRS using monthly farm price data from the National Agricultural Statistical Service, USDA, from January 2002 through September 2015.

[22] When the effects of domestic subsidies—such as expanded production and exports—spill over into international markets and can be shown to induce price suppression or altered trade patterns, then those subsidy programs may be subject to challenge under WTO dispute settlement proceedings. See CRS Report RS22522, Potential Challenges to U.S. Farm Subsidies in the WTO: A Brief Overview.

[23] ERS, USDA, Oil Crops Outlook, OCS-15k, November 13, 2015.

[24] Farm Service Agency (FSA), USDA, "Table 35—CCC Net Outlays by Commodity & Function, Fiscal Years 2007- 2016E," CCC Budget Essentials, February 2015. USDA's analysis for the President's FY2016 budget includes projections of peanut PLC outlays that rise to $679 million in FY2017 and continue to grow to $799 million in FY2025. In addition, USDA projects substantial peanut storage and handling costs (related to marketing loan forfeitures) that rise from a projected $31.2 million in FY2017 to $85.3 million in FY2025; available at: http://www.fsa.usda.gov/Assets/USDA-FSA-Public/usdafiles/ About FSA/Budget/pdf/pb16_commodity_estimates.pdf.

[25] FAPRI, U.S. Crop Program Fiscal Costs: Revised Estimates with Updated Participation Information, June 2015.

[26] Congressional Budget Office (CBO), "August 2015 Baseline for Farm Programs," August 26, 2015.

[27] An exception occurred in 2012 when record production combined with high prices to push crop value to $2 billion.

[28] PLC payments on peanut base = 0.85 times 2 million acres of base x $135 per ton x 1.5 tons per acre = $344 million.

[29] Both CBO and FAPRI project annual peanut production of 5 to 6 billion pounds over their extended forecast periods: CBO, "August 2015 Baseline for Farm Programs," August 26, 2015; and FAPRI, U.S. Crop Program Fiscal Costs: Revised Estimates with Updated Participation Information, June 2015.

[30] U.S. Department of Agriculture, "USDA Helps Open and Expand Export Markets for U.S. Agriculture Through 2014 Farm Bill Programs," press release, April 16, 2014, http://www.usda.gov/wps/portal/usda/usdamediafb?

contentid=2014/04/0063.xml&printable=true&contentidonly=true. APC is the trade organization that represents all segments of the peanut industry. It operates a number of marketing, research, and other programs for the peanut industry.

31 CRS Report R43696, Agricultural Exports and 2014 Farm Bill Programs: Background and Issues.

32 "House Ag Members Quiz Vilsack on Wide Range of Issues," Hagstrom Report, February 11, 2015.

In: Peanuts and Sugar
Editor: Edith Perez

ISBN: 978-1-63485-487-0

Chapter 2

PEANUT PROGRAM: EVOLUTION FROM SUPPLY MANAGEMENT TO MARKET ORIENTATION*

Remy Jurenas

SUMMARY

The 2002 farm bill radically overhauls the peanut program, by completely replacing the supply and price management system in place for more than 60 years. It repeals the limit set on the amount of peanuts that farmers can sell domestically for food consumption, and substitutes in large part the revenue this "quota" system with its high level of price support had guaranteed them, with an infusion of annual government payments to "historic" peanut producers. The new program's price support and income subsidy features (covering the 2002 to 2007 crops) are similar to those authorized for producers of other crops. These will ensure that "historic" producers receive a return roughly comparable to what they accessed in the past, after taking into account they will no longer have to rent or buy quota. Actual returns will vary among farmers, depending on whether they had produced quota peanuts and had incurred the additional cost of renting quota. As part of this historic change,

* This is an edited, reformatted and augmented version of a Congressional Research Service publication RL30924, prepared for Members and Committees of Congress dated August 8, 2002.

owners of peanut quota will be compensated for elimination of an income-generating asset.

As background, the 1996-2001 peanut program largely kept intact the broad outlines of previous policy except for two changes. Reflecting a compromise between growers and shellers (the marketers of peanuts to food manufacturers) and calls by others for the program's repeal, Congress in 1996 reduced the quota loan rate by 10% to $610 per ton. Other changes were intended to ensure the program operated at "no-cost" to taxpayers. The House during farm bill debate rejected program opponents' efforts to modify the Agriculture Committee-reported package by a 3-vote margin. From 1996 through 1998, program opponents pressed for further change, but failed in securing passage of amendments offered to agriculture spending bills. In other action, three emergency farm aid packages in the 1999-2001 period provided a total of $170 million in supplemental income payments to peanut growers. Another issue that lawmakers addressed in 2000, and may again face, is whether to assist growers to cover their share of program losses.

The new program reflects an approach proposed by many peanut farmers in the Southeast (the largest peanut producing region) and some in the Southwest who had concluded that the quota program could not be sustained for political and economic reasons. They were concerned that the quota system could not be defended much longer against opponents (food manufacturers and those ideologically opposed to government management of a food commodity) who had sought for many years to "reform" the program. These farmers also realized changes were needed to address competitive pressures from increased peanut and related product imports under the terms of current and anticipated trade agreements, and that additional budget resources made available for commodity programs could facilitate a policy change.

With peanuts marketed internationally at a price much lower than the level at which the past program supported the U.S. price of food peanuts, the peanut quota structure and import restrictions (by controlling the supply and significantly affecting the price) placed the cost of the peanut program largely upon the buyers of peanuts (manufacturers and consumers). The new program's changes shift these costs largely to the federal government and taxpayers.

Recent Developments

President Bush on May 13, 2002, signed into law a 6-year comprehensive farm bill (P.L. 107-171, the Farm Security and Rural Development Act) that includes authority to support the price of peanuts, to extend income assistance to historical peanut producers, and to compensate peanut quota holders for the loss of an income-producing asset (sections 1301-1310). This measure authorizes a much different peanut program than that in place for more than 60 years, adds and makes changes to other existing commodity programs, and includes rural development and environmental programs, among other initiatives.

The U.S. Department of Agriculture (USDA) has begun to implement some provisions of the new peanut program. On July 8, USDA announced steps to put into effect a new peanut quality program. Under the 2002 farm bill, all peanuts marketed in the United States (irrespective of whether produced domestically or imported) must be officially inspected and graded by federal inspectors or federally licensed state inspectors. In the interim while the Agricultural Marketing Service (AMS) drafts new grading and handling regulations, USDA announced that *the* requirements of the current peanut marketing agreement and related programs will continue to apply; appointed 18 interim members representing producers and the peanut industry to the newly created Peanut Standards Board (PSB) charged with advising AMS on the details of the new quality program; terminated the existing Peanut Administrative Committee responsible for the expiring marketing agreement; and designated trustees to locally administer the mandatory peanut inspection program until the new regulations are established. On July 19, Secretary of Agriculture Veneman announced that historical peanut producers will be asked to update their peanut acreage history and yield information with the Farm Service Agency (FSA) by August 5. FSA will use this data to determine each producer's peanut base and yield that will serve to calculate the direct and counter-cyclical payments each will receive in the 2002-2007 period. On August 1, AMS issued a notice requesting nominations to the PSB, which is required to be in place by November 9.

U.S. Peanut Market

Peanuts are a regional crop, with most production occurring in three areas. In 1999-2001 period, the Southeast (Georgia, Alabama, Florida, and South Carolina) accounted for 57% of U.S. peanut output; the Southwest (Texas, Oklahoma, and New Mexico), 28%; and the Virginia-North Carolina region, 15%. The largest producer was Georgia, which accounted for 39% of total peanut output, followed by Texas with 22%. Production is geographically concentrated in each state; accordingly, peanuts account for a large share of farm and related agribusiness income earned in a number of peanut-producing counties. According to the *Census of Agriculture*, there were 12,211 peanut producers in the United States in 1997, down from 16,194 in 1992. Production nationwide, while fluctuating from year to year due to variable weather, averaged almost 3.8 billion pounds (1.9 million short tons) annually in the 1999-2001, down from an annual average of 4.3 billion pounds (2.14 million tons) in 1990-92. Peanut output generated $950 million in cash receipts each year from 1999 to 2001 to farmers, nearly a 28% decline from the $1.3 billion annual average in the 1990-92 period.

Lower production and cash receipts in the most recent period reflect the impact of two significant policy changes made by the 1996 farm bill: (1) setting the amount producers can sell domestically (the "poundage quota") equal to projected U.S. food demand,[1] and (2) lowering by 10% the support level for peanuts sold to meet U.S. food demand.[2] Higher imports also have contributed to lower receipts. Imports of peanuts (raw peanuts and the peanut equivalent of peanut butter) in 2000 accounted for 14% of domestic food use, compared to 2% in 1991. Increased imports reflect the market access commitments made by the United States under various trade agreements, and the incentive for other countries to sell into the higher-priced U.S. market compared to other export alternatives.[3]

Just over 46% of the 2000 peanut supply was consumed as food domestically. Of the remainder, 12% was crushed into oil (viewed as a premium cooking oil) and into meal (used as a protein supplement in livestock feed rations). Sales overseas accounted for about 11%, with the European Union, Canada, and Japan being major export markets. Consumption for domestic food use fell an average 2.3% each year from marketing year (MY) 1989/90 to MY1995/96, largely due to changing demographics (primarily smaller numbers of children among the baby-boomer generation), health and dietary concerns about the fat content in peanuts, and competition from other snack foods that had prompted consumers to shift away from higher-priced peanut products toward lower-priced snack products. In a reversal of this trend, starting in MY1996/97, U.S. peanut consumption for food has increased an average 1.8% each year. Observers speculate that this recent trend might reflect a decline in concern over fat in foods, a growing awareness by consumers of studies that show eating peanuts may be beneficial to health, and increased retail promotion by peanut product manufacturers. Of the peanuts used for domestic food use and export in MY2000/01, 46% were processed into peanut butter (a staple in American diets), 22% went into snack peanut products, 22% were used in peanut candy, and 9% were marketed as cleaned in-shell (i.e., ballpark, roasted).

FEATURES OF THE 1996-2001 PEANUT PROGRAM

To support the farm price of peanuts, the USDA for the 1996-2001 crops extended price support benefits to growers, placed a limit on the amount of peanuts allowed to be sold for domestic food use, and generally restricted imports of foreign peanuts. The most significant changes made by section 155 of the 1996 farm bill (P.L. 104-127) reduced the level of minimum price guarantees available on domestically marketed peanuts ("quota" peanuts) and effectively eliminated the program's future budget exposure. The Congressional Budget Office at that time projected that the detailed changes made to key quota provisions would generate more than $400 million in budget savings over the FY1997-2003 period. In 1999, 2000, and 2001, Congress authorized $170 million in supplemental income payments to peanut growers as part of broad financial assistance packages approved for the agricultural sector.[4]

The new program enacted by the 2002 farm bill will first apply to the 2002 peanut crop beginning with harvest, which starts in August, without the price support, poundage quota, and marketing assessment features described below (see *Peanut Program in the 2002 Farm Bill* on pages 12 - 18 for details).

Program Overview

The peanut program's purpose historically has been to support the incomes of peanut producers and ensure ample domestic peanut supplies. Through the 2001 marketing year, it differed from the grains, rice and cotton programs in that USDA did not made direct payments to peanut growers (notwithstanding the supplemental income assistance Congress extended in recent years). Rather, growers' income has been supported primarily through USDA actions taken to manage peanut supplies and by making available the price guarantees set in statute. Unlike the voluntary nature of USDA's grain and cotton programs, the peanut program's features were mandatory on all farmers if those that produced quota peanuts voted to approve poundage quotas. In a referendum held December 1997, 94.8% of those voting favored poundage quotas. As a result, quotas applied to farm marketings of peanuts through the 2001 crop. The following summarizes the main features of the 1996- enacted peanut program.

Price Support. Two levels of price support benefits were available to producers, depending on the end use and destination of the peanuts sold. Benefits were extended in the form of "non-recourse" loans that USDA extended to three area wide marketing associations (see *Program Administration* below). Non-recourse means that an association pledged the peanuts acquired from growers (for which a payment is made) as loan collateral. Peanuts marketed for food use in the United States ("quota" peanuts) were eligible for a high level of price support. Peanuts exported or crushed into peanut oil and meal (referred to as "additionals") were eligible only for a much lower level of support. The higher "quota" support level reflected the historical premium assigned to peanuts sold domestically into the high-value edible use market and covered production costs. The lower support level for additionals reflected the much lower market value of peanuts sold for export or crushing. Operating under complex procedures, each association (under contract with USDA's Commodity Credit Corporation (CCC)) sells and disposes of acquired quota peanuts at not less than specified price levels, and of acquired additionals at market prices. To the extent that sales did not cover loan proceeds extended to growers, the difference ("losses") was made up by tapping association "profits," with the remaining losses absorbed by the CCC (until changed by the 1996 farm bill).

As required by statute, the *quota loan rate* for the 1996-2001 crops was frozen at $610 per ton (30.5 cents per pound). This change effectively reduced quota support by 10.1% from 1995's $678.36/ton (33.92 cents/lb.) level. Also, the 1996 farm bill retained the requirement that USDA set the loan rate for additionals at a level that ensures the CCC does not incur losses from their sale and disposal, and that also takes into account demand for peanut oil and meal, expected prices of other vegetable oils and protein meals, and export demand for peanuts. USDA on February 15, 2001, announced that the *additionals loan rate* for the 2001 crop will be $132 per ton (6.6 cents/lb.), the same as for the 2000 crops, but $43 less than the $175 per ton set for additionals marketed from the 1998 and 1999 crops.

Income Support to Peanut Growers. For the 1999, 2000, and 2001 crops, producers were eligible to receive payments intended to partially compensate growers for continuing low commodity prices and increasing costs of production (Table 1). The 1999 crop payment rates spelled out in FY2000 agriculture appropriations (Section 803(a) of P.L. 106-78) were set equal to

5% of the quota or additional loan rate. USDA accordingly disbursed $55 million to eligible peanut growers. Another emergency farm aid package specified the payment rate for the 2000 crop quota and additional peanuts (Section 204(a) of P.L. 106-224). USDA made $61 million available under this provision in spring 2001. A similar provision was included in the farm aid package (P.L. 107-25), signed into law August 13, 2001. It required USDA to disburse $54 million in supplemental payments to peanut growers by September 30, 2001.

Table 1. Peanut Loan Rates and Market Assistance Payments

	LOAN RATE	PAYMENT RATE	TOTAL PROGRAM BENEFIT[a]
dollars per ton			
1999 CROP			
Quota	$610	$30.50	$640.50
Additionals	$175	$8.75	$183.75
2000 CROP			
Quota	$610	$30.50	$640.50
Additionals	$132	$16.00	$148.00
2001 CROP			
Quota	$610	$25.72	$635.72
Additionals	$132	$13.49	$145.49

[a] Loan rate plus payment rate.

Supply Management. Two mechanisms limited the amount of peanuts allowed to be sold in the domestic market: the national poundage quota and import restrictions. Both tools served to manage the amount of peanuts supplied for primarily U.S. food use.

Poundage Quotas. A national poundage quota limited the quantity of peanuts that producers sold for domestic consumption (see "buyback" exception below). The national quota was distributed among eligible states based on each state's previous year's share of the quota, and then distributed by "farm" to quota holders based largely on past production history. A producer holding or leasing farm quota received price protection at the high price support level, either by selling to commercial buyers or effectively transferring ownership of their unsold peanuts to USDA's designated marketing agent in return for price support benefits. A farmer could sell peanuts produced in excess of his farm quota(s) (referred to as "non-quota" or "additionals") primarily for export or crushing into peanut oil and meal. A farmer without a quota could produce as much as he wanted, but was required to market them as additionals for export or crushing. However, when quota peanuts fell short in meeting domestic food demand (as a result of lower production due to poor weather and/or of changing manufacturer preferences for peanut type), any farmer could sell additionals as quota peanuts under the "buyback" provision. As producers, shellers, and users adjusted to the new market environment created by the 1996 farm bill changes, buybacks in the 1996, 1997 and 1998 marketing years accounted for a much higher share of domestic peanut sales for food than in previous years (about 10- 15% versus 1-3%). Buyback activity in the 1999 and 2000 marketing years fell significantly, apparently in reaction to farmer concern about the losses they were forced to absorb as a result of such activity associated with the 1998 crop.

The 1996 law required USDA to announce a national poundage quota equal to projected U.S. peanut consumption for food and related uses (excluding seed). Use of this quota tool was intended to guard against a surplus, and to eliminate the program's budget exposure. Under previous farm bills, USDA each year was required to set the national quota (defined then to also include seed use) at not less than a specified statutory minimum, even if USDA's projection showed food use would be lower. The 1996 law eliminated the minimum provision. Under the revised definition, USDA on December 13, 2000, announced that the 2001 crop's national poundage quota will be 1.18 million tons (2.36 billion pounds), the same level as set for the 1999 and 2000 quota. USDA's decision to retain the same quota level for the third consecutive year reflected in part its assessment that (1) domestic peanut consumption for food had leveled off, and (2) projected increased peanut imports (allowed to enter under trade agreements) continued to displace domestically-produced peanuts that otherwise would enter U.S. food marketing channels. The 2001 quota level represented a 12.6% reduction from the minimum 1.35 million ton national poundage quota that was in effect for the 1991-1995 crops.

Import Restrictions. With peanuts marketed internationally at a price much lower than the level at which the peanut program supports the U.S. price of food peanuts, the quantity of peanuts and certain products allowed to enter the U.S. market to compete with domestic peanut production is restricted. Under multilaterally and bilaterally negotiated trade agreements, the United States imposes three *tariff-rate quotas* (TRQs) on peanut imports. The TRQ based on General Agreement of Tariffs and Trade (GATT) market access rules permits imports up to a specified level (the in-quota amount) to enter at a "bound," or fixed, tariff. Imports under two bilateral trade agreements enter duty free. Imports above the in-quota in each TRQ also can enter, but are subject to a very high tariff. This high tariff reflects the protective value of the previous small absolute quota. With the high above-quota tariff, foreign-origin peanuts from sources other than Mexico are not expected to be price competitive in the U.S. market for quite some time. Under the three trade agreements, U.S. market access commitments mean that the in-quota amount (compared to the pre-1995 import quota's 1.7 million pounds) is much larger in 2002 — 126 million pounds, rising slightly each year to reach 127.6 million pounds in 2007. Under the GATT agreement, Argentina is allocated an 83% share of the TRQ. Under the North American Free Trade Agreement (NAFTA), Mexico has duty-free access to the U.S. market for Mexican-produced peanuts under a quota that gradually rises through 2008. Afterwards, Mexican-origin peanuts will be allowed to enter in unlimited quantities. Israel had duty-free access for domestically produced peanuts under a small TRQ that expires, unless extended, at year-end 2002.

A separate GATT-based import quota also caps U.S. imports of peanut butter and paste at slightly above the 1993 level. However, imports of peanut butter and paste from Mexico under NAFTA are exempt from this quota, as long as peanuts used in these products are grown in Mexico. In general terms, the GATT-based import quotas are in effect indefinitely; the NAFTA provisions also apply indefinitely unless the United States or Mexico were to withdraw, upon notice, from the agreement.

The 1996- and 2002-enacted peanut programs did not amend peanut import policy under these trade agreements, which continue to be administered under existing Presidential authority.

Marketing Assessments. A budget deficit marketing assessment applied only to marketings of domestically produced peanuts. Imports were not subject to this levy. Assessments collected from growers and "first purchasers" represented the peanut sector's contribution to budget deficit reduction targets, imposed in the early 1990s. The assessment rate for the 1997-2002 crops was 1.2% of the "quota" or "additionals" loan rate, whichever applied. Growers paid 54.2% of the assessment rate; the first buyers' share was 45.8%. Under this requirement, USDA collected about $10-$12 million annually since FY1996 in assessments. As "directed" by Congress in report language in the FY 1999 agriculture appropriations measure, the Secretary of Agriculture in January 2000 decided to apply assessments already collected against the 1996, 1997, and 1998 crops to cover part of the Southeast area marketing association's losses as prescribed under a loss sharing mechanism included in the 1996 enacted program (see *Activation of Loss Sharing Provisions*).

Program Administration and Costs

Three area marketing associations are involved in administering the peanut program, acting as agents for the Commodity Credit Corporation (CCC) — the entity that finances USDA farm programs. These regional associations have kept track of quota and additional peanuts that are sold, offered price support loan benefits to farmers, and arranged for warehousing peanuts brought under loan. The CCC has financed each association's price support operations and overhead costs with funds borrowed from the U.S. Treasury. Separately, county offices of the Farm Service Agency (FSA) have administered poundage quotas, maintained farm data, and performed other functions by dealing directly with producers and quota holders. USDA estimated that FSA field administrative costs associated with loan making and quota management totaled $5.3 million in FY1999.

1995-96 Debate on the Peanut Program

The peanut program enacted as part of the 1996 farm bill largely kept intact the broad outlines of prior U.S. peanut policy, but addressed two issues – the level of price support available for quota peanuts and program cost. In hearings held by the House and Senate Agriculture Committees, growers argued that the program supported rural economies, urged that its basic structure be maintained, and suggested a few changes. Peanut shellers and some peanut product manufacturers, though, argued for significant reductions in the quota price support level. These two groups argued such a change was critical to the long-term survival of the peanut industry, and was needed to reverse declining consumer demand for peanut products. Other food manufacturers and their coalition partners favored outright repeal of the program, arguing government should not play a role in managing supplies and dictating prices. Reflecting these divergent views, House floor debate in February 1996 was particularly intense. The Agriculture Committee's proposed modifications to the existing program were retained by only a 3-vote margin (212-209). The closeness of this vote energized program opponents to press for further change in the floor amendments they offered later in 1996, and again in 1997 and 1998 (see next section).

The final provisions included aspects of the peanut growers' proposal, and a split-the-difference compromise between the 1995 crop's $678/ton quota loan rate and peanut shellers' call for a support level around $550/ton. Reflecting this, the enacted measure reduced price support on quota peanuts marketed domestically 10% to $610/ton. While growers in late 1995 had opposed any support reduction, manufacturers argued that the Committee-proposed reduction was not deep enough to reverse the decline in domestic peanut consumption. Some food manufacturers had argued for an even steeper cut - down to $450/ton.

PEANUT PROGRAM LEGISLATION IN 1997-2001

Bills Introduced in 105th Congress

Representatives Shays and Lowey on June 11, 1997, and Senator Santorum on November 13, 1997, introduced H.R. 1864 and S. 1535, respectively, to phase out the current peanut program at the end of the 2001 crop year. The House bill was similar to the amendment that Representative Shays offered during 1996 farm bill floor debate in February 1996 that was rejected on a 212-209 vote. Both bills proposed to reduce the $610 per ton price support level for peanuts marketed for domestic food use (quota peanuts) to $550 for the 1998 crop, $515 in 1999, $480 in 2000, and $445 in 2001. S. 1535 also required USDA to add carryover stocks to projected domestic food use in determining each year's national poundage quota level, taking into account imports, government purchases, and "buyback" activity. Other provisions permitted the unlimited sale, lease, and transfer of quota across county and state lines; the sale of additionals also for seed, to U.S. government agencies, and for domestic food use to offset projected imports; capping the initial disbursement of loan proceeds to producers at 80% in 1998-2001; and revising the process for sharing loan losses. Beginning with the 2002 crop, both bills would have made available non-recourse loans at not more than $350 per ton. H.R. 1864 would also have authorized loan deficiency payments to be made to producers who choose not to take out non-recourse loans. With both bills proposing to repeal the current supply management system effective October 1, 2001, there would no longer have been any distinction between quota and additional peanuts in administering all price support operations.

Supporters of both bills pointed out that the "Depression-era" program was anti-competitive, and restricted who can grow and sell peanuts to a small number of farmers at the expense of consumers. They argued that these proposals provided for a "fair transition period" for farmers and lenders to adjust to a new market, following which the peanut program would operate like most other commodity programs. Supporters of the peanut program countered that changes made by the 1996 farm bill reduced the quota support level by 10% and eliminated all government costs. They questioned the impetus to debate the program each year and argued that the 1996-enacted provisions should be given an opportunity to work.

Another measure (H.R. 1875), introduced by Representative Crane on June 12, 1997, proposed to permit U.S. firms to import Mexican peanuts into free trade zones (FTZs), to be processed into peanut butter and paste for sale in the U.S. market. Duty-free imports of Mexican peanuts are capped under NAFTA, but there is no limit on the amount of peanut butter produced from Mexican peanuts that can enter. According to an AP wire story, the president of the peanut shelling company (which also operates a peanut butter plant) seeking this change said this proposal would have put American companies on equal footing with Mexican peanut butter manufacturers, without forcing them to move to and build new plants in Mexico. Peanut growers countered, saying that the plan would cost farm jobs because Mexican peanuts entering a FTZ would displace American-grown peanuts. Their spokesman pointed out that peanut shellers and manufacturers not located in a proposed FTZ would also have been at a disadvantage.

House Floor Amendments Debated During 105th Congress

In the late 1990s, opponents of the peanut program turned to the appropriations process to pursue their objectives. In House floor debate on the *FY1998* agriculture appropriations measure (H.R. 2160), Representative Neumann on July 24, 1997, offered an amendment that effectively would have required USDA to administer a peanut program for the 1998 crop with a loan rate for quota peanuts not higher than $550 per ton. If enacted, this proposal would have reduced the quota price support level $60 (or almost 10%) from the minimum $610 per ton then available. This amendment drew from a provision in H.R. 1864 that called for the same amount of reduction in quota price support. The House rejected this amendment on a vote of 185-242.

During floor debate, supporters of the amendment argued that the "quota" features of the program limited the supply of peanuts and thus kept the price of peanuts paid by consumers higher than would be otherwise. Members mentioned that the domestically-supported price was almost twice the world price of peanuts, in part because of the added costs that producers incurred in acquiring and/or renting quota. Two members added that USDA's implementation of the 1996 farm bill's program had "created an artificial government-induced shortage" of peanuts — an example of "Government price fixing" that ignored consumer interests. Others argued that the program benefitted an "elite few" — those who owned 68% of the quota nationwide (according to GAO's 1993 report) due to inheritance or purchase but that did not farm peanuts themselves. As a result, they claimed the program supported quota holders at the expense of consumers and taxpayers.

The amendment's opponents countered that the 1996 changes ended direct taxpayer support of the peanut program (saving $434 million over 7 years) and made it market oriented. Several mentioned that the government's "contract" made in the 1996 farm bill provided peanut growers with a safety net that should not be violated and should be allowed to work as enacted. It was pointed out that growers already had to adjust to a 10% reduction in their support price and must live with that level now for 7 years without any adjustment for inflation. Several argued that the proposal represented an effort by large "greedy" food corporations to increase their profits at the expense of small family farmers and rural communities, claiming that consumers would not see cheaper peanut butter and candy bars. It was further noted that even though farmers have already experienced a price cut, manufacturers have not "passed on one penny" of savings to household consumers.

During House floor debate on the *FY1999* agriculture appropriations measure (H.R. 4101) on July 23, 1998, Representative Neumann again offered an amendment that would have required USDA to administer a peanut program for the 1999 crop with a loan rate for quota peanuts not higher than $550 per ton. In the debate that followed, many of the arguments made in 1997 were again presented. The House rejected this amendment on a 181- 244 vote.

Legislative Activity in 106th Congress

Bills Introduced. Senator Santorum on April 14, 1999, introduced S. 802 (slightly different from S. 1535 offered in the 105th Congress) to phase out the current peanut program at the end of the 2001 crop year. Representative Shays introduced an identical bill (H.R. 2571) on July 20, 1999. These measures would have reduced the authorized $610 per ton price support level for peanuts marketed for domestic food use (quota peanuts) to $550 for the 2000 crop and $500 for the 2001 crop. Quotas would have been eliminated for the 2002 and subsequent year crops. Starting in 2002, all peanuts produced would have been eligible for non-recourse loans at not more than $350 per ton. A new section would have amended the National School Lunch Act to require (upon enactment) that peanuts and products purchased by USDA for donation under six nutrition programs be bought at prevailing world market prices, and that such purchases be only of additional (non-quota) peanuts. The bill's supporters argued that the proposed changes would "correct the inequities of the peanut quota system," result in a price support program similar to that available for other crops, and enable USDA to purchase lower-priced peanuts for its nutrition programs. Another measure (H.R. 2598, introduced by Representative Wu on July 22, 1999) proposed to end the peanut program, effective October 1, 1999.

Peanut growers and product manufacturers met in May 1999 and reportedly agreed to not battle out their differences in Congress. Reflecting this truce, no amendment to alter the peanut program was offered during House and Senate consideration of their respective *FY2000* agriculture appropriations bills (H.R. 1906; S. 1233). A similar agreement affecting consideration of the *FY2001* agriculture spending bill reportedly also was struck between growers and manufacturers.

Floor Action. The FY2000 agriculture appropriations measure included as part of a broad farm aid package, payments for producers of the 1999 peanut crop as compensation for low commodity prices and continued increases in peanut production costs (section 803(a) of P.L. 106-78). Payments were made to producers on produced quota or additional peanuts equal to 5% of the loan rate set for each peanut category. A similar provision to provide payments to growers harvesting the 2000 crop was included in the 2000 farm aid package approved by Congress (section 204(a) of P.L. 106-224).[5] Taxpayers rather than peanut product manufacturers covered the cost of these income transfers; the payments made by the U.S. Treasury to producers had no direct impact on the price that peanut shellers and food manufacturers paid for peanuts. Separately, to address the impact of 1999 program losses on Southeast growers, section 2102 of P.L. 106-246 provided a mechanism for USDA to cover the balance of these losses, to be paid back by growers in future years (see next section).

Activation of Loss Sharing Provisions

Producer concern about the financial impact that activation of the 1996-enacted loss-sharing provisions would have on their returns from the 1999 peanut crop led USDA and Congress to adopt remedies in 2000. More recently, the expectation that Congress will enact a much different peanut program effective with the 2002 crop affected the marketing of 2001 quota peanuts. This development is expected to result in a substantial reduction in the returns that peanut growers receive for the 2001 crop, and may prompt some to again seek comparable relief.

As background, losses in the Southeast associated with a higher-than-average portion of the 1999 crop placed under quota loan triggered all eight of the peanut program's loss sharing provisions.[6] Because these losses were substantial (projected to reach $60 million), USDA in late 1999 faced pressure from growers to apply the marketing assessment funds collected in the 1996-98 period to cover in part these losses. Growers of quota peanuts expressed concern that if the last loss sharing provision was triggered, they would face paying an assessment of up to $95 per ton for every ton of 2000 crop quota peanuts marketed, according to USDA estimates. Further, language in the FY2000 agriculture appropriations conference report "expect[ed]" USDA to use funds collected but not yet transferred to the U.S. Treasury to offset these losses. To address this issue, Secretary of Agriculture Dan Glickman on January 10, 2000, approved the use of $28 million to reduce projected 1999 losses, which in turn, reduced the assessment that Southeast growers faced paying later in 2000. Even with this decision, assessment funds collected during FY2000 were not expected to cover the balance of expected 1999 quota peanut losses ($32 million). As a result, quota growers in the Southeast region faced the prospect of paying an additional assessment in 2000/01. Because such a payment would have cut into grower income received in the 2000/01 marketing year, some groups advocated the option of designating the assessments collected in future years to cover 1999 losses. This approach was reflected in a provision included in P.L. 106-246 (section 2101 of Title II, chapter 1) that directed USDA to borrow from the Commodity Credit Corporation to cover the balance of these losses. At that time, growers were expected to pay off this "loan" as the CCC collected marketing assessments from them in 2000, 2001, and 2002 until the entire amount was repaid.

A similar situation has again developed with respect to the 2001 crop. High peanut yields contributed to a 30% increase in production compared to 2000. Though USDA expects domestic food consumption (primarily filled by quota peanuts) to recover somewhat in the 2001/02 marketing year, the prospect of much lower peanut prices under the new program anticipated last fall to be authorized in the 2002 farm bill (see below) encouraged buyers to minimize their inventory. Anticipating that prices in the 2002/03 season could be about half of this year's level, shellers cut back on purchases of 2001 crop quota peanuts. Reflecting the decline in the price of quota peanuts, farmers in the Southeast as of late January 2002 had placed about 20% of their quota peanuts under loan. With no buyers for this sizable quantity of high-priced peanuts, the prospect has increased that producers will experience a loss as the area wide marketing associations sell these peanuts at much lower prices into the export or crushing markets. As the loss sharing provisions take effect, available resources (including the marketing assessments collected and intended to repay 1999 crop losses) will not be sufficient to cover projected losses. According to one estimate, the financial loss that growers in the Southeast face ranges between $140 to $180 per ton, if the eighth loss sharing provision is activated. Peanut producers in other producing regions also reportedly face absorbing losses, which are expected to be much lower – under $10 per ton.

LEGISLATIVE ACTIVITY IN 107TH CONGRESS

Peanut Program in the 2002 Farm Bill

The 2002 farm bill provides for a radically new peanut program framework (sections 1301-1310 of P.L. 107-171, the Farm Security and Rural Investment Act of 2002). The completely overhauled program repeals the quota system in place since the 1930s that limited the amount of peanuts allowed to be marketed for domestic food use, replacing it with an approach similar to that found in the programs available for other crops that extend price and income support to producers. The new peanut program replaces the revenue that the prior supply management structure (using farm-level quotas) with its high level of price support had guaranteed farmers, with a large infusion of direct government payments. The Congressional Budget Office (CBO) has estimated that the new program will cost almost $2.9 billion over the farm bill's authorized six-year period.

The enacted peanut program effectively transfers the cost of the peanut program from consumers (primarily food manufacturers) to the federal government. Under the pre-2002 policy, manufacturers paid higher prices for food-use peanuts because of the program's two-tier price support structure, a restrictive import quota that protected the peanut production sector from foreign competition, and the restriction on the sale of domestically produced peanuts for U.S. food use by farmers with no quota.

Major Provisions of the New Program. The 2002 farm bill completely restructures the previous peanut program to make available to growers of peanuts the same type of price support and income subsidy benefits that producers of wheat, feed grains, cotton, rice, and soybeans will also receive. The three components of the redesigned peanut program are:

- marketing loan benefits (non-recourse loans or corresponding payments),
- fixed direct payments, and
- counter-cyclical deficiency payments.

Table 2 provides the level of program benefits available under each component. Benefit eligibility and additional details on each component are described in the following sections. According to the farm bill's timetable, USDA will make the first direct and counter-cyclical payments to historic peanut producers this fall.

Another significant program feature are the peanut program payment limits that will apply per farm or per individual. These are separate and in addition to the limits that apply to payments made per farm on the production of other eligible crops. All but one of the enacted provisions apply to the 2002 to 2007 crops.

As part of this historic restructuring, the 2002 farm bill will compensate owners of the peanut quota, many of whom are not peanut farmers, for the loss of an income-producing asset.

Table 2. Program Benefit Levels Available to Peanut Farmers and Historical Peanut Producers: 2002 Farm Bill, for the 2002-2007 Crops

POLICY OBJECTIVE / PROGRAM TOOL	$ per ton	q per pound
Price Support / Loan Rate	355	17.75
Basic Subsidy / Direct Payment	36	1.80
Supplemental Income Subsidy / derived relative to *Target Price* of	495	24.75

Eligibility for Program Price and Income Support Benefits. Under the new program, all producers of peanuts will be eligible to receive marketing loan benefits on each year's crop. However, only historical peanut producers (e.g., those who were actively involved in planting and harvesting peanuts in the 1998-2001 period) will be eligible to receive direct payments and counter-cyclical assistance each year, irrespective of whether or not they continue to produce peanuts. These payments will be made on past production on historical acreage, not on current production (see *Formula for Calculating Payments* below).

Marketing Loan Benefits. Any peanut farmer will be eligible for non-recourse marketing assistance loans and loan deficiency payments, calculated against a loan rate of $355 per ton for *all* peanuts produced. In practice, a producer would pledge harvested peanuts as collateral to obtain a non-recourse loan at this rate from the Farm Service Agency or other designated entities. The availability of such a loan effectively provides operating capital to the producer until the loan is repaid one of three ways: (1) with interest within 9 months if the market price is above the loan rate, (2) without interest at a USDA-determined price ("loan repayment rate") if market prices are below the loan rate, or (3) by the transfer (forfeit) by the producer of the pledged peanuts to the CCC as full settlement of the loan at the end of the loan term with no penalty. Under the second option, the difference between the USDA-determined price and the loan rate received by the producer is called a marketing loan gain. Provisions stipulate that USDA must set this loan repayment rate at a level that minimizes loan forfeitures, the accumulation of peanut stocks, and USDA storage costs; and allows U.S.-produced peanuts to be marketed freely and competitively both domestically and internationally. Alternatively, instead of taking out a non-recourse loan, a producer may elect to receive a loan deficiency payment that is equal to the marketing loan gain.[7]

Fixed Direct Payments. A producer with a history of producing quota and/or additional peanuts will receive annual fixed direct, payments of $36 per ton. These payments (not linked to either current production or prices) will be similar to the production flexibility contract payments first made to producers of wheat, corn and other feed grains, cotton and rice under the 1996 farm bill,[8] and modified somewhat by the 2002 farm bill. Payments will be made only to a farmer who grew peanuts in 1998-2001, even if he now or in the future decides not to produce peanuts and/or shifts to grow other permitted crops. The amount of the payment made to an eligible farmer will be the same each year for the program's duration, and be based on a statutory formula (see Table 3 and *Formula for Calculating Payments*).

Counter-Cyclical Income Assistance. A producer with a history of producing quota and/or additional peanuts will also receive supplemental income subsidies in the form of "counter-cyclical" payments each year when the "effective price" is less than the "target" price of $495 per ton. These payments are designed to provide more government support when peanut prices decline, and less income support when prices improve. They are intended to automatically supplement other subsidies available under the new program, such as marketing loan benefits and fixed direct payments. Counter-cyclical payments (subject to a reduction for direct payments received) will be triggered when the national average market price for peanuts is below $495 per ton. Payments will be made only to a farmer who grew peanuts in 1998-2001, even if he now or in the future decides not to produce peanuts and/or shifts to grow other permitted crops. The amount of the deficiency payment made to an eligible farmer will be the same each year for the program's duration, and be based upon a statutory formula (see Table 3 and *Formula for Calculating Payments*).[9]

Formula for Calculating Payments. Three factors will be used to calculate the amount of fixed direct and counter-cyclical payments that each historic peanut producer will receive. Payments will be equal to a recipient's farms' payment yield, multiplied by 85% of his farms' average peanut acres (defined as "payment acres"), further multiplied by the program component's payment rate (Table 3). USDA will derive each recipient's average yield and acreage factors, using available data showing the peanut yield and acreage planted to peanuts or prevented from being planted for each of a producer's farms in the 1998-2001 crop years. Once calculated, each historical producer will have a one-time opportunity through March 31, 2003, to assign these yield and acreage results to cropland on a farm of his choice. Payments based on this formula will be made only to historic peanut producers, even if they decide not to grow peanuts or shift to producing another permitted crop.

Quota Compensation. Holders of peanut quota in 2001 will be compensated at the annual rate of 11¢ per pound, or $220 per ton. Over the five years of authorized compensation, quota holders will receive 55¢ per pound, or $1,100 per ton. These payments are intended to compensate owners for the loss of an income-producing asset that they either inherited or purchased. The conference agreement permits any holder the option to receive this compensation in the form of one lump sum payment. About two-thirds of the quota compensation is expected to be paid out to individuals and entities that did not themselves produce peanuts, but instead rented quota in 2001 to other farmers.[10]

Table 3. Factors for Calculating Annual Payments to a Historical Peanut Producer

	Recipient's Payment Yield[a]	
X	Recipient's Payment Acres (Peanut Acres[b] x 85%)	
X	Payment $36 per ton	Rate Equal to the Effective Price, derived as: (1) the difference between the target price of $495 per ton, and (2) the national average market price, *or* $391,[c] *whichever is higher*
=	DIRECT FIXED PAYMENT	COUNTER-CYCLICAL PAYMENTS

[a] The average of the peanut yield (pounds per acre) associated with each of a producer's farms in the 1998-2001 crop years, excluding any year in which production did not occur.

[b] The average of the planted acreage associated with each of a producer's farms in the 1998- 2001 period, including any acres prevented from planting because of a natural disaster or condition beyond the producer's control.

[c] Equal to the loan rate ($355) per ton plus the fixed decoupled, or direct, payment rate of $36 per ton.

Payment Limitations. Because the new peanut program replaces the high market prices guaranteed by the quota feature of the previous peanut program with marketing loan benefits and payments, the issue of payment limits received considerable attention as conferees sought to resolve differences between House and Senate provisions. Since many peanut producers also grow other crops in rotation with peanuts and receive payments under these other commodity programs, the terms of and the payment limit level set in the 2002 farm bill affected their view of how they might fare under a radically restructured peanut program. In other words, decisions legislated on these matters would affect the maximum amount of government payments and loan benefits that farm operations that grow peanuts would receive under any policy change.

The House peanut program explicitly provided (section 169 of H.R. 2646) that the limits on peanut program payments to an individual and/or entity would be *separate and in addition to* the aggregate limit now in place on payments made under all of the grains, cotton, and oilseeds programs. Recipients of peanut program payments would be subject to the same rules and eligibility criteria (i.e., the three entity rule, spouse allowance, use of marketing certificates) that applied to producers receiving payments for other crops. The

Senate farm bill (section 169 of S. 1731), by contrast, proposed to subject the payments of all eligible crops (including peanuts) to *one combined* annual limit per individual and/or entity. It also would have tightened the rules and eligibility criteria for receiving program payments. Both measures explicitly stipulated that the quota compensation payments proposed for peanut quota owners would not be subject to either set of payment limits and conditions.

The House approach calling for a separate peanut payment limit acknowledged that some larger farm operations (e.g., those that grow both cotton and peanuts) would very quickly reach the current payment limit. To ensure that the peanut producing portion of these large farms could fully benefit from payments available under the proposed new program, proponents succeeded in including a separate limit for peanut payments. Senate-approved provisions, however, included a lower aggregate limit and more stringent eligibility criteria on payments made to an individual/entity or married couple under all commodity programs (including the new peanut program). The Senate position reflected the philosophical view that the raising of payment caps and liberalizing of eligibility rules over time (i.e., to circumvent them, according to supporters of limits) has encouraged the growth of large farms and helped to drive small- and mid-sized farms out of business. Those opposed to this trend further argued that farm programs have benefitted most a small group of large producers and a large number of absentee landlords who need aid the least.[11] To counter the Senate provisions, House opponents argued the lower limits would make the new peanut program "ineffective." Their view is that large peanut/cotton operations would not be able to fully maximize benefits under both programs if the Senate provisions become law.

In final action, farm bill conferees agreed to make the payment limits *separate and in addition to* the same limits that will also apply to payments made under the grains, cotton, and oilseeds programs that a peanut producer can receive if eligible for them. The limit on peanut program payments, and also separately under the other "program" crops, is $180,000 per person, per year (or $360,000 under the 3-entity and spouse allowance rules). Benefits are higher for those operations that use commodity certificates and loan forfeiture gains to access additional marketing loan benefits. Table 4 provides a breakdown of the newly-authorized payment limitation (by category), and compares them to the prior law's limits for program crops.[12]

Program Cost. Converting the pre-2002 peanut program to one designed to operate similar to the price and income support programs for other crops will involve considerable budgetary expense. The Congressional Budget Office (CBO) projects that the 6-year cost of the enacted peanut program (relative to the April 2001 baseline) will be $2.87 billion (Table 5). Over the 10-year budget period used to score the farm bill, CBO projects the new program will cost $3.9 billion.

Table 4. Commodity Program Payment Limits and Peanuts: Comparison of Previous Law to the 2002 Farm Bill Conference Agreement

	PREVIOUS LAW	CONFERENCE AGREEMENT
Overview	Not applicable to peanuts	Peanut payment limit is separate and in addition to the limit on grains, cotton, and oilseed program payments.
Marketing Loan Benefits[a]	$150,000	$75,000[b]
Fixed Decoupled, or Direct, Payments	$80,000	$40,000
Counter-Cyclical Payments		$65,000
Total Per Person	$230,000	$180,000
3 Entity Rule / Spouse Allowance	$230,000	$180,000
Total Limit	$460,000	$360,000[c]

Note: See footnotes 10 and 11 for sources of additional information

[a] Marketing loan gains and loan deficiency payments.

[b] There is no practical limit, in that a producer can use commodity certificates and loan forfeiture gains to bypass the stated limitation.

[c] To illustrate, a large peanut and cotton farm would be eligible for payments equal to double the amount shown for each type of payment and rule. A very large operation producing both crops (and organized to maximize the receipt of program benefits) would be eligible for $720,000 in payments. However, with no effective limit on marketing loan benefits (see footnote b), payments under the cotton and peanut programs can be higher than this limit.

Over the farm bill's authorized 6-year period, the quota compensation component will account for 45% of the peanut program's entire cost. If the amount authorized to compensate quota owners is excluded from this cost projection, current and historic peanut producers will receive an average $249 million annually in payments and marketing loan benefits. Concerned that growers would have to absorb the storage costs associated with peanuts placed under loan, farm bill conferees addressed this issue by directing USDA to use CCC funds to pay storage, handling, and related costs through the 2006 peanut crop. CBO estimates budget outlays for such storage costs will total $74 million.

Table 5. Cost of Enacted Peanut Program (compared to April 2001 Baseline)

	SIX YEARS (FY2002-2007)	TEN YEARS (FY2002-2011)
millions of $		
Marketing Assistance Loans	287	495
Counter-Cyclical Payments	828	1,435
Direct Payments	378	628
Storage Costs	74	74
Treatment of Crop Insurance Policies for 2002	3	3
SUBTOTAL, PROGRAM BENEFITS	1,570	2,635
Quota Compensation	1,300	1,300
TOTAL	2,870	3,935

Source: Congressional Budget Office, May 1, 2002 estimate.

Note: Peanut program costs (excluding quota compensation payments) are expected to be about $500 million more during the FY2002-2006 period than shown in this table, according to an estimate prepared by CBO using its most recent (March 2002) baseline.

Rationale for Policy Change. The enacted peanut program is based on the approach offered by a coalition of peanut farmers from the Southeast and west Texas who had concluded that the program structure in place for more than 60 years could not be sustained for political and economic reasons. This group was concerned that the quota system could not be defended much longer against opponents (food manufacturers and those ideologically opposed to government management of a food commodity) who had sought for many years to "reform" the program. These farmers also realized changes were needed to address competitive pressures from increased peanut and related product imports under U.S. commitments made in current trade agreements (particularly under NAFTA, which has opened the U.S. market to Mexican origin peanuts, peanut butter, and peanut products). Peanut shellers and food manufacturers supported this change, viewing the coalition's proposal as accomplishing their longstanding objective of reforming the peanut program and gaining access to lower-priced peanuts.

Peanut growers from the Southeast, central Texas and the Virginia-North Carolina region opposed to the marketing loan concept, however, advocated another approach they felt would better stimulate consumption of U.S.-produced peanuts. They favored continuing a two-price system, and making a few changes to the quota program. Under their proposal, producers that sell quota peanuts would have received price support at a higher level than available under the quota program. Purchasers, though, would have been able to buy these peanuts at the much lower world price, and USDA would have made up the difference. To illustrate, if the farm bill set the support price at $650 per ton and the world price was $350 per ton, USDA would have covered the difference with a $300 per ton payment to the farmer.[13]

Both groups developed their respective proposals to facilitate their desired policy change seeing the opportunity to tap the additional $73.5 billion in multi-year budget resources made available by the FY2002 budget resolution for agricultural commodity programs.

Adding pressure for change, House opponents of the program signaled in mid-June 2001 they would introduce their proposal (H.R. 2164) during farm bill debate if the House Agriculture Committee did not "reform" the peanut program. Their bill proposed to reduce the loan rate for all peanuts to not more than $350 per ton by 2004 (i.e., 43% below the $610 per ton loan rate for quota peanuts), repeal the quota system altogether starting with the 2004 crop (with no compensation to quota holders), and require the Secretary of Agriculture to purchase peanuts and peanut products for nutrition programs at a lower price. H.R. 2164 would have substantially reduced the level of program benefits available to peanut farmers and quota owners, and thereby benefitted consumers (primarily food manufacturers), who would pay a lower price for peanuts. Other changes proposed in H.R. 2164 would have largely eliminated program costs after 2004.

Floor Consideration. Members offered five amendments during floor consideration to modify the House and Senate Agriculture Committee's reported farm bill (H.R. 2646; S. 1731). Some addressed regional issues, one focused on the divisive issue in Georgia over whether quota owners were being fairly compensated for the loss of their quota, while others sought to clarify the future relationship between peanut growers and other key participants in the peanut industry. One Senate amendment proposed to terminate the peanut program after 2005.

The House by voice vote on October 3, 2001, agreed to an amendment offered by Representative Stenholm to retain a role for the area marketing associations[14] in administering the new program. Representative Etheridge on

October 4 proposed to raise the target price against which counter-cyclical payments would be calculated from \$480 to \$500 per ton. He subsequently withdrew his amendment. Senator Inhofe on February 12, 2002, proposed to start the new program with the 2003 rather than 2002 crop; he later withdrew his amendment. The Senate by voice vote also on February 12 agreed to an amendment offered by Senator Miller to increase the quota compensation rate from 10 to 11 cents per pound (modified from an earlier proposal to raise the rate to 12 cents/lb.), to clarify the role of area marketing associations with respect to peanut storage and the handling of peanut "marketing pools," to subject the imposition by these associations of certain overhead expenses and by other loan servicing agents of storage costs to a state-level referendum vote by historic producers, and to require that all peanuts placed under a marketing assistance loan be subject to state or federal inspection and grading, among other changes.[15]

Senator Lugar offered an amendment that would have completely phased out the peanut program (together with the current income and price support provisions for other commodities) after the 2005 crop. The level of price support would have been "progressively and uniformly" lowered starting with the 2003 crops and reach zero in 2006. During this period, USDA would have increased the quota in phases to anticipate its elimination effective with the 2006 crop. Price support would have been replaced with vouchers of up to \$30,000 made available annually through 2006 to any producer who signed a "risk management contract," and undertook specified risk management activities. Examples include buying whole farm revenue insurance and/or contributing to a whole farm stabilization account. This voucher system would have applied to all commodity (and not just peanut) producers. His proposal was defeated (70-30) during Senate farm bill floor debate on December 12, 2001.

Conference Action. House and Senate negotiators charged with resolving differences between the peanut provisions in their respective farm bills considered them in an atmosphere of mounting pressure in March and April 2002 that they also reach decisions on various far-reaching issues so that final provisions apply to the 2002 crops. Farmers and their lenders, facing planting and financing decisions, expressed concern over whether the quota program or the radically different new program would apply to the 2002 crop that was about to be planted. In south Georgia, this usually begins in early May. Further, program-specific issues that conferees debated included settling upon the level of budget resources to allocate for the proposed peanut program change, reaching agreement on differences over the level of program benefits (i.e., price support, income assistance, and quota compensation levels) to provide, and determining the payment limits and accompanying terms that should apply to the financial benefits that peanut producers receive under the new program.

House and Senate conference leaders on March 19, 2002, reportedly agreed to allocate $2.6 billion for the peanut, sugar, and dairy program provisions added by the Senate's farm bill. Of this total, one account mentioned that they had set aside $500 million for the higher 10-year costs associated with the Senate's peanut program.[16] This issue of budget resources for the new peanut program remained in flux until conferees reached final agreement on a multitude of farm bill provisions on April 30.

Analyses of New Program. A General Accounting Office (GAO) analysis of the House Agriculture Committee's approved peanut program showed that new and existing producers would benefit more from the new support mechanisms than they would under a continuation of the quota program and its relatively high support level. Its report stated that peanut shellers, food manufacturers, and consumers would pay less because of the much lower support level. The lower prices, though, would be offset by a substantial increase in USDA outlays to maintain producer income. GAO also expected that the new support measures will reduce incentives for increased imports.[17]

An initial analysis by USDA's Economic Research Service similarly points out that the production incentives created by the 2002 farm bill's peanut and other commodity programs "will vary among different types of producers" (e.g., whether a farmer had produced primarily quota peanuts or produced additional peanuts, or whether the farmer has no history of peanut production).[18] The factor identified as key in influencing if a farmer plants peanuts is whether expected program benefits and/or the projected peanut market price cover the variable costs associated with producing peanuts.[19] Another issue some farmers will consider (looking at both market prices and program benefits) is whether producing peanuts results in higher returns compared to producing other crops.

Some observers expect that peanut producers, shellers, and food manufacturers will proceed cautiously in adapting to the peanut program changes. Since sales of peanuts in the United States have never been subject to the same market forces that other crops have been for years, analysts can only speculate at this time what the farm and wholesale price of food-use peanuts might be, and how that will over time affect producers' and users' decisions on producing and purchasing peanuts, respectively. Observers will also be watching to see the extent to which food manufacturers (operating in a new program and marketing environment) pass on savings from paying much less for peanuts to retail consumers.

Other Legislative Action

The FY2001 emergency farm aid package enacted by Congress and signed by the President on August 13, 2001, authorized market loss payments to peanut farmers. Section 3 of P.L. 107-25 (H.R. 2213) provided $54.21 million in supplemental payments to growers that had produced 2001 crop quota and additional peanuts. Section 11 required USDA to make these supplemental payments by September 30, 2001. The impact of these payments on overall support of peanut producers is reflected in Table 1.

ADDITIONAL READING

Farm Foundation. The 2002 Farm Bill: Policy Options and Consequences. "Peanut Policy" by Stanley M. Fletcher and Nathan B. Smith. September 2001. (Available on the Web in pdf format at [http://www.farmfoundation.org/2002_farm_bill/fletcher.pdf])

Food and Agricultural Policy Research Institute. *The House and Senate Farm Bills: A Comparative Study*, FAPRI Policy Working Paper #01-02, March 2002, pp. 14-16.

Presentations made at a conference entitled "The New Farm Bill-Peanuts and More" held May 15, 2002, in Tifton, Georgia. "Legislative Background of the 2002 Farm Bill," by Evans Plowden, American Peanut Shellers Association; "Peanut Provisions of the Farm Security and Rural Investment Act of 2002" by Nathan Smith, University of Georgia College of Agricultural and Environmental Sciences; and "Opportunities Under the New Marketing Loan Program for Peanuts" by Richard Pasco, American Peanut Product Manufacturers, Inc. (Available on the Web at [www.gapeanuts.com] - scroll down to see list)

U.S. Department of Agriculture. Economic Research Service (ERS). Commercial Agriculture Division. *Peanuts: Background for 1995 Farm Legislation*, by Scott Sanford and Sam Evans. Agricultural Economic Report No. 710. Apr. 1995. 34 p. (Available on the Web at [http://ewg.org/farm/peanuts/docs/ERS_Peanuts1995.pdf])

——. Agricultural Outlook. "Peanut Consumption Rebounding Amidst Market Uncertainties." March 2002. Pp. 3-5 (available on the Web in pdf format at [http://www.ers.usda.gov/publications/agoutlook/Mar2002/ao289a.pdf]).

——. "Analysis of Peanut Program Provisions in 2002 Farm Bill," by Erik Dohlman (available on the Web at [http://www.ers.usda.gov/Features/FarmBill/Analysis/peanut2002act.htm]).

U.S. General Accounting Office. *Peanut Program: Potential Effects of Proposed Farm Bill on Producers, Consumers, Government, and Peanut Imports and Exports*. GAO-01- 1135R. September 26, 2001. (Available on the Web in pdf format at [http://www.gao.gov/new.items/d011135r.pdf])

End Notes

[1] For more explanation, see Poundage Quotas on page 5.

[2] For additional information, see Price Support on pages 3-4.

[3] For details, see Import Restrictions on pages 5-6.

[4] See Income Support to Peanut Growers on page 4.

[5] See Income Support to Peanut Growers on page 4 for details.

[6] The pre-1996 "area cross-compliance" provision served to reduce the program's cost to the federal government (i.e., as area association and/or CCC-owned peanut inventories were sold) by requiring producers to offset some of this cost under a complex process. In practice, sharing losses had pitted regions against each other, as well as growers of additionals against those that primarily sold quota peanuts. The eight-step process added by the 1996 farm bill expanded upon and re-prioritized the order in which any losses in an area quota pool were to be covered. These provisions are found in section 155(d) of the 1996 farm bill (P.L. 104-127; 110 Stat. 924-925; 7 U.S.C. 7271(d)). Though complex, these changes in the process to be followed to cover losses within and between associations were intended to place greater responsibility for absorbing losses on those individual producers and regions that actually generate them. Depending on other decisions that USDA makes, the cumulative impact of this prioritized loss-sharing mechanism was intended to bring program costs down to zero.

[7] For additional background on this price support mechanism, see CRS Report 98-744 ENR, Agricultural Marketing Assistance Loans and Loan Deficiency Payments.

[8] The Agricultural Market Transition Act (AMTA, Title I of P.L. 104-127) offered multi-year production flexibility "contracts" to producers with land previously enrolled in a target price deficiency payments program for these crops. AMTA earmarked a specific amount of funds for contract payments to be made over 7 years in fixed but declining annual amounts, and was intended to stabilize and constrain commodity program entitlement spending. The objective was to break the tie between payments and: market prices, the planting of a specific crop, or annual cropland diversion requirements. Payments to an individual participant were based on his established acreage and yield (per-acre output) under the old

programs. The rules allowed a participant starting in 1996 to plant almost any combination of crops on contract acreage. The only other restrictions affecting producer eligibility were that contract land must be used for agricultural purposes, that fruits and vegetables generally cannot be produced on such land, and that conservation rules must be followed.

[9] For additional background on this policy tool, see CRS Report RS20913, Farm "Counter-Cyclical Assistance".

[11] For additional information, see CRS Report RS21138, Farm Commodity Payment Limits: Comparison of Proposals, and CRS Report RL31272, A New Farm Bill: Comparing the House and Senate Proposals with Current Law, April 12, 2002, pp. 9-11.

[12] For more on this issue, see the CRS Agriculture Policy and Farm Bill Electronic Briefing Book page entitled "Commodity Program Payment Limits Under the 2002 Farm Bill."

[13] This description is based on "Peanut Policy Update," May 7, 2001, by Nathan B. Smith, University of Georgia Cooperative Extension Service.

[14] See Program Administration and Costs on pages 6-7 for background on these associations.

[15] In the farm bill conference, negotiators retained the Stenholm amendment, accepted Miller's increase in the quota compensation rate to 11 cents per pound, and addressed the other issues raised in the Miller amendment by authorizing CCC funding to cover storage costs for peanuts placed under loan, and subjecting all peanuts marketed in the United States to one uniform set of inspection and grading standards.

[16] AgWeb.com, Inside Washington Today, "Update: Several steps back for farm bill 'progress'" by Jim Wiesemeyer, March 27, 2002.

[17] Peanut Program: Potential Effects of Proposed Farm Bill on Producers, Consumers, Government, and Peanut Imports and Exports, GAO-01-1135R, September 26, 2001.

[18] USDA, ERS, "Farm Bill 2002: Analysis of Selected Provisions: Peanuts," June 21, 2002 (available on the Web at [http://www.ers.usda.gov/Features/FarmBill/Analysis/peanut2002act.htm]).

[19] Variable costs are the out-of-pocket cash expenses paid for inputs unique to the commodity being produced. Variable expenses depend on production practices and on quantities and prices of inputs. These include inputs such as seed, fertilizer, feed, chemicals, and hired labor.

In: Peanuts and Sugar
Editor: Edith Perez

ISBN: 978-1-63485-487-0

Chapter 3

U.S. SUGAR PROGRAM FUNDAMENTALS*

Mark A. McMinimy

SUMMARY

The U.S. sugar program provides a price guarantee to producers of sugar beets and sugarcane and to the processors of both crops. The U.S. Department of Agriculture (USDA), as program administrator, is directed to administer the program at no budgetary cost to the federal government by limiting the amount of sugar supplied for food use in the U.S. market. To achieve both objectives, USDA uses four tools—as reauthorized without change by the 2014 farm bill (P.L. 113-79) and found in chapter 17 of the Harmonized Tariff Schedules of the United States— to keep domestic market prices above guaranteed levels. These are:

- price support loans at specified levels—the basis for the price guarantee;
- marketing allotments to limit the amount of sugar that each processor can sell;
- import quotas to control the amount of sugar entering the U.S. market;
- a sugar-to-ethanol backstop—available if marketing allotments and import quotas are insufficient to prevent a sugar surplus from

* This is an edited, reformatted and augmented version of a Congressional Research Service publication R43125, prepared for Members and Committees of Congress, dated

developing, which in turn could result in market prices falling below guaranteed levels.

To supplement these policy tools in supporting sugar prices above government loan levels, while avoiding costly loan forfeitures, important administrative changes were adopted in late 2014. These included imposing limits on U.S. imports of Mexican sugar and establishing minimum prices for Mexican sugar imports, actions that fundamentally recast the terms of bilateral trade in sugar. Most recently, two U.S. sugar refiners are pressing for the withdrawal of these changes, so although this new regime is in effect, there is a measure of uncertainty about its future.

Under the U.S. sugar program, nonrecourse loans that may be taken out by sugar processors, not producers themselves, provide a source of short-term, low-cost financing until a raw cane sugar mill or beet sugar refiner sells sugar. The "nonrecourse" feature of these loans means that processors—to meet their repayment obligation—can exercise the legal right to forfeit sugar offered as collateral to USDA to secure the loan, if the market price is below the effective support level when the loan comes due.

Sugar marketing allotments limit the amount of domestically produced sugar that processors can sell each year. In a 2008 farm bill provision, retained by the 2014 farm bill, USDA each year must set the overall allotment quantity (OAQ) at not less than 85% of estimated U.S. human consumption of sugar. The OAQ is intended to ensure that permitted sales of domestic sugar, when added to imports under U.S. trade commitments, do not depress market prices below loan forfeiture levels for refined beet sugar and raw cane sugar.

The United States imports sugar in order to meet total food demand. The amount of foreign sugar supplied to the U.S. market reflects U.S. commitments made under various trade agreements. The most significant import obligation is the World Trade Organization (WTO) quota commitment, which requires the United States to allow not less than 1.256 million tons of sugar (almost all raw cane) to enter the domestic market from 40 countries. The United States also grants much smaller import quotas to the nine countries covered by four free trade agreements. At the same time, a 2008 farm bill provision, also retained in the 2014 farm bill, directs USDA to manage overall U.S. sugar supply, including imports, so that market prices do not fall below effective support levels.

If market prices fall below levels guaranteed by the sugar program, USDA must administer a sugar-for-ethanol program in which it purchases domestically produced sugar from the market and sells it to ethanol producers as feedstock for fuel ethanol production.

SUGAR POLICY OVERVIEW

The U.S. sugar program is singular among major agricultural commodity programs in that it combines a floor price guarantee with a supply management structure that encompasses both domestic production for human use and sugar imports. The sugar program provides a price guarantee to the processors of sugarcane and sugar beets, and by extension, to the producers of both crops. The U.S. Department of Agriculture (USDA) is directed to administer the program at no budgetary cost to the federal government by limiting the amount of sugar supplied for food use in the U.S. market. To achieve both objectives, USDA uses four tools to keep domestic market prices above guaranteed levels. Measures one through three below were reauthorized through crop year 2018 without change by the 2014 farm bill (P.L. 113-79). The fourth measure is found in long-standing trade law. The four are:

1. price support loans at specified levels—the basis for the price guarantee;
2. marketing allotments to limit the amount of sugar that each processor can sell;
3. a sugar-to-ethanol (feedstock flexibility) backstop—available if marketing allotments and import quotas fail to prevent a price-depressing surplus of sugar from developing (i.e., fail to keep market prices above guaranteed levels);
4. import quotas to control the amount of sugar entering the U.S. market.

In addition to the foregoing policy tools, two agreements signed by the U.S. Department of Commerce (DOC) in late 2014—one with the government of Mexico and another with Mexican sugar producers and exporters—impose annual limits on Mexican sugar exports to the United States and establish minimum prices for imported Mexican sugar.

The current sugar program has its roots in the Agriculture and Food Act of 1981 (P.L. 97-98), according to the USDA.[1] The sugar program that Congress enacted in the 1981 farm bill required the Secretary of Agriculture to support prices of U.S. sugarcane and sugar beets at minimum levels—initially through purchases of processed sugar, and subsequently by offering nonrecourse loans. The legislation also encouraged the President to impose duties, fees or quotas on foreign sugar to prevent domestic prices from moving below established support levels to avoid imposing budgetary costs on the government. In its report on the 1981 farm bill, the Senate Committee on Agriculture, Nutrition and Forestry cited the importance of sugar imports to U.S. sugar supplies, pointing out that volatile world market prices of sugar contributed to sharp fluctuations in U.S. sugar prices, while adding that the United States was alone among sugar producing nations in being without an effective government price support program.[2]

The sugar program has long been a source of political controversy over the degree of government support and market intervention it involves with sharply differing perspectives on the balance of benefits and drawbacks to the program. Critics of the program, including the Coalition for Sugar Reform, which represents consumer, trade and commerce groups, manufacturing associations and food and beverage companies that use sugar, argue the sugar program acts to keep domestic prices far above world sugar prices. In so doing, the Coalition contends the sugar program imposes a hidden tax on consumers that has led to the loss of jobs in the food manufacturing sector by encouraging imports of sugar-containing products and by providing manufacturers an incentive to move facilities abroad to gain access to lower priced sugar. The American Sugar Alliance, consisting of sugarcane and sugar beet producers, including farmers, processors, refiners, suppliers and sugar workers, is a leading advocate for the U.S. sugar program. It points out that the price support feature of the sugar program fosters a reliable supply of sugar at reasonable prices at no cost to the government. The sugar program, it argues, is necessary to shield the domestic sugar industry from unfair competition from sugar imports at world market prices that are distorted by heavily subsidized foreign sugar that is dumped on the world market at prices that are below production costs.

PRICE SUPPORT LOANS

Nonrecourse loans taken out by a processor of a sugar crop, not producers themselves, provide a source of short-term, low-cost financing until a raw cane sugar mill or beet sugar refiner sells sugar. The "nonrecourse" feature means that processors—to meet their loan repayment obligation—can exercise the legal right to forfeit sugar offered as collateral to USDA to secure the loan, if the market price is below the effective support level when the loan comes due. *Figure 1* and *Figure 2* illustrate the repayment options available to beet sugar refiners and raw cane sugar mills, respectively, and show loan rates and effective support levels for FY2015.

The price levels at which processors can take out loans are referred to as "loan rates." The raw cane sugar loan rate (18.75¢/lb) is lower than the refined beet sugar loan rate (24.09¢/lb) to reflect its unprocessed state. The raw sugar loan rate is lower because raw sugarcane must be further processed by a cane refinery to have the same value and characteristics as refined beet sugar for food use. These loan rates are national averages. Actual loan rates are adjusted by region to reflect marketing cost differentials.

The minimum market price that a processor wants to receive in order to remove the incentive to forfeit sugar and instead repay a price support loan, though, is higher than the loan rate. This "effective support level," also called the loan forfeiture level, represents all of the costs that processors need to offset to make it economically viable to repay the loan. These costs equal the loan rate, *plus* interest accrued over the nine-month term of the loan, *plus* certain marketing costs. The effective support level for 2014-crop (FY2015) raw cane sugar is 20.95¢/lb; for refined beet sugar, it ranges from 24.4¢ to 26.1¢/lb, depending on the region.

If market prices are below these loan forfeiture levels when a price support loan usually comes due (i.e., July to September), and a processor hands over sugar earlier pledged to obtain this loan rather than repaying it, USDA records a budgetary expense (i.e., an outlay). If this occurs, USDA gains title to the sugar and is responsible for disposing of this asset.

Two suspension agreements the DOC signed in December 2014—one with the Government of Mexico and another with Mexican sugar producers and exporters—have substantially modified the terms for importing sugar from Mexico and may have the practical effect of raising the effective support level.[3] For one, Mexican sugar is an important source of the U.S. sugar supply, with imports of Mexican sugar averaging 15% of the sum of U.S. production plus imports during the three most recent marketing years from 2011/2012 to 2013/2014. The agreements (see "Suspension Agreements Recast Sugar Trade with Mexico" below) establish minimum prices for Mexican sugar imports that are at, or above, effective U.S. support levels. These minimum prices are calculated at Mexican plants, so transportation costs to the U.S. processor or end user would add several cents per pound to the delivered cost of Mexican sugar. As a result, prices of imported Mexican sugar should track well above levels that would encourage U.S. loan forfeitures.

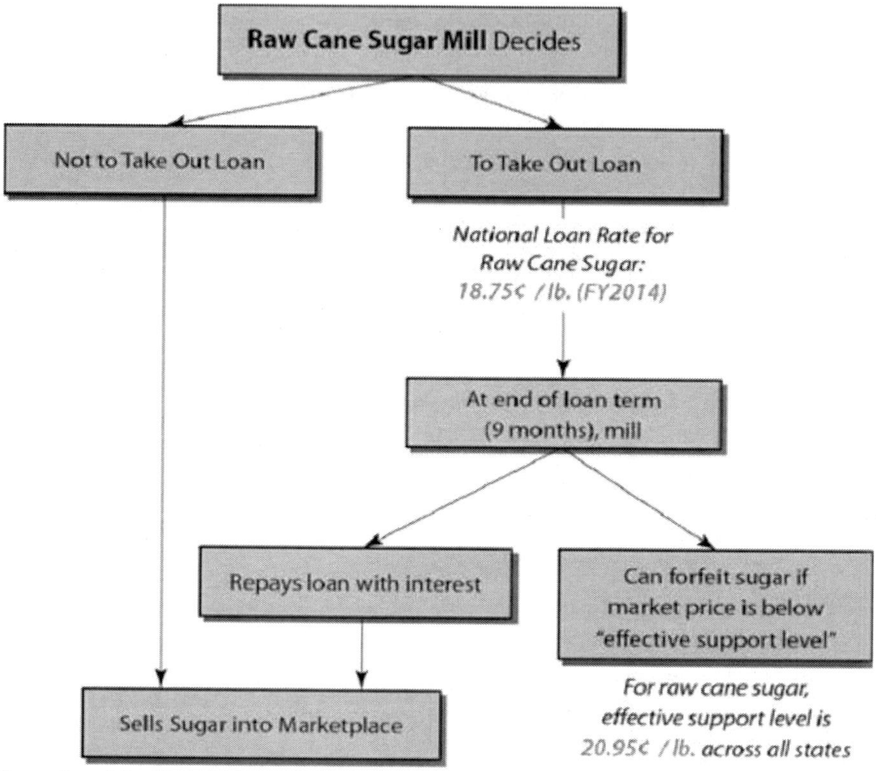

Note: As of April 7, 2015, mills that process sugarcane had 696,314 tons of 2014-crop raw cane sugar under loan, valued at $265.1 million. This represents 18.4% of USDA's March 2015 estimate of raw cane sugar production from the 2014 sugarcane crop.

Figure 1. Price Support Loan Making Process for Raw Cane Sugar.

Market prices for raw cane sugar and refined beet sugar since the 2008 farm bill provisions took effect were higher than loan forfeiture levels until mid-year 2013 (*Figure 3* and *Figure 4*, respectively). Toward the end of FY2013, market prices that were below these effective support levels prompted processors to forfeit, or hand over, to USDA 381,875 tons of sugar (4.3% of FY2013 U.S. sugar output valued at almost $172 million). USDA actions taken to avert these forfeitures, and then to dispose of sugar acquired as a result of these forfeitures, are detailed below in "Sugar Purchases and Exchanges for Import Rights" and "Feedstock Flexibility Program for Bioenergy Producers."

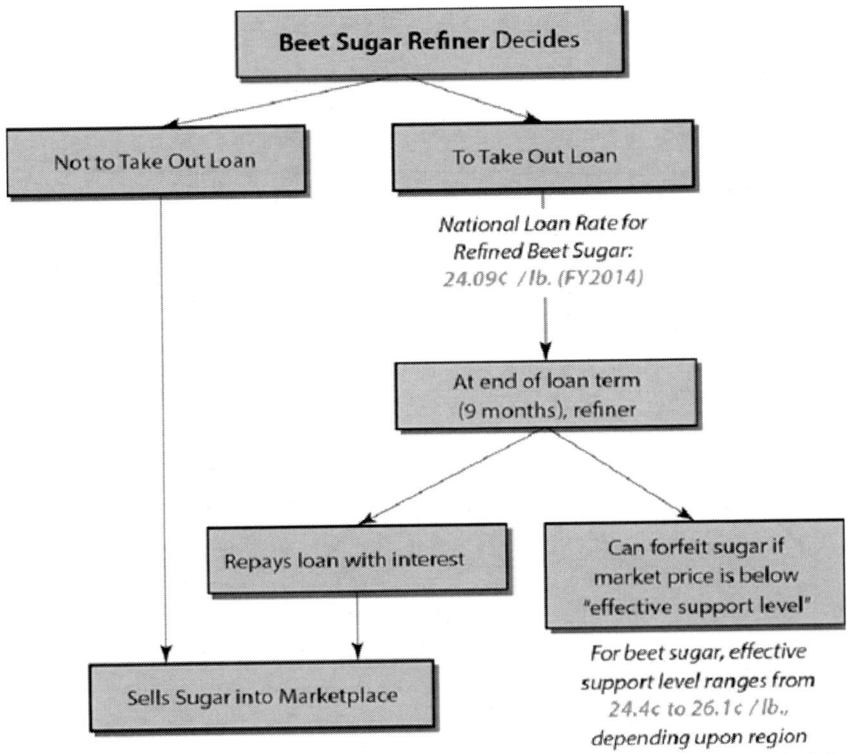

Note: As of April 7, 2015, processors of sugar beets had 884,000 tons of 2014 beet sugar and in-process beet sugar under loan, valued at $396.2 million. This represents 18.2% of USDA's March 2015 estimate of refined beet sugar production from the 2014 sugar beet crop. Sugar beet processors also still had under loan 12,500 tons of beet sugar from the 2013 crop valued at $5.9 million.

Figure 2. Price Support Loan Making Process for Refined Beet Sugar.

TOOLS FOR BALANCING SUPPLIES AND SUPPORTING PRICES

The government sets annual limits on the quantity of domestically produced sugar that can be sold for human use. It also restricts the level of imports that may enter the domestic market through tariff-rate quotas and via an import limitation agreement with Mexico. This is done to avoid costs during times when an imbalance between sugar supplies and demand could lead to low prices and sugar forfeitures under the loan program.

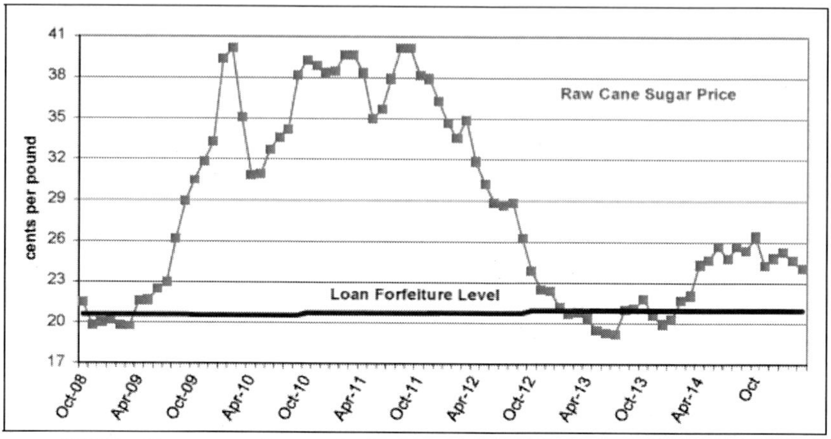

Source: USDA, Economic Research Service, for price data; USDA, Farm Service Agency, for loan forfeiture level.

Note: Raw cane sugar market price is the average futures price for the nearby month contract for domestic #16, traded in New York City on the Intercontinental Exchange (ICE).

Figure 3. Raw Cane Sugar Prices Have Been Above Loan Forfeiture Level Since the 2008 Farm Bill Except in Early FY2009, Late FY2013, and Early FY2014.

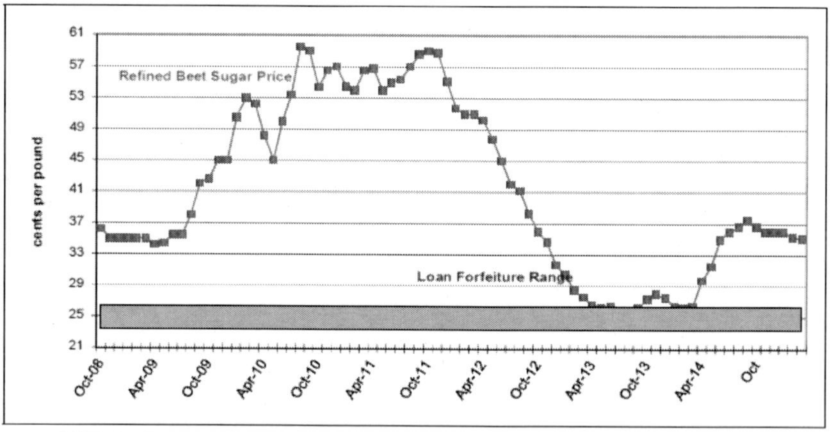

Source: USDA, Economic Research Service, for price data; USDA, Farm Service Agency, for loan forfeiture range.

Note: The market price for refined beet sugar is the quoted price for wholesale refined beet sugar in Midwest markets, as published by Milling and Baking News.

Figure 4. Refined Beet Sugar Prices Have Stayed Above Loan Forfeiture Range Since the 2008 Farm Bill Until March 2013.

MARKETING ALLOTMENTS

Sugar marketing allotments limit the amount of domestically produced sugar that processors can sell each year. They do not, however, limit how much beet and cane farmers can produce, nor do they limit how much sugar beets and sugarcane that beet refiners and raw sugar mills can process. In a 2008 farm bill provision that was retained in the 2014 farm bill, USDA is required each year to set the overall allotment quantity (OAQ) at not less than 85% of estimated U.S. human consumption of sugar for food. This task is carried out by the USDA's Commodity Credit Corporation (CCC) at the beginning of each fiscal year. The OAQ is intended to ensure that permitted sales of domestic sugar, when added to imports under U.S. trade commitments, do not depress market prices below loan forfeiture levels for refined beet sugar and raw cane sugar. Sugar production that is in excess of a processors' marketing allotment may not be sold for human consumption except to allow another processor to meet its allocation or for export.

In recent years, U.S. sugar production has consistently fallen short of the OAQ, averaging 89% of the OAQ threshold during the most recent three completed years from FY2012 through FY2014. Over this same period, U.S. sugar production has amounted to 75% of U.S. human use of sugar. .

Figure 5 illustrates the persistent gap between domestic sugar production, the higher levels of the OAQ, and U.S. domestic consumption for human use. Substantial quantities of sugar have been imported to cover shortfall between domestic output and human consumption. For this reason, market participants view USDA's decisions on setting import quotas rather than marketing allotments as having more of an impact on market price levels (see "Import Quotas").

The national OAQ is split between the beet and cane sectors and then allocated to processing companies based on previous sales and production capacity. If either sector is not able to supply sugar against its allotment, USDA has authority to reassign such a "shortfall" to imports.

Import Quotas

The United States imports sugar in order to meet total food demand. From FY2012 through FY2014, imports accounted for 31% of U.S. sugar used in food and beverages. The amount of foreign sugar supplied to the U.S. market reflects U.S. commitments made under various trade agreements. At the same time, a 2008 farm bill provision—one retained in the 2014 farm bill— directs USDA to manage overall U.S. sugar supply, including imports, so that market prices do not fall below effective support levels. The most significant import limit is the World Trade Organization (WTO) quota commitment, which requires the United States to allow not less than 1.256 million tons of sugar (almost all raw cane) to enter the domestic market from 40 countries. The United States also grants much smaller import quotas to the six countries covered by the Dominican Republic-Central American Free Trade Agreement (DR-CAFTA), and to Colombia, Panama, and Peru under separate free trade agreements. For instance, the tariff-rate quota (TRQ) for calendar year 2015 totals 138,100 metric tons raw value for the DR-CAFTA countries and 52,250 million tons raw value for Columbia. Panama and Peru have smaller TRQs.

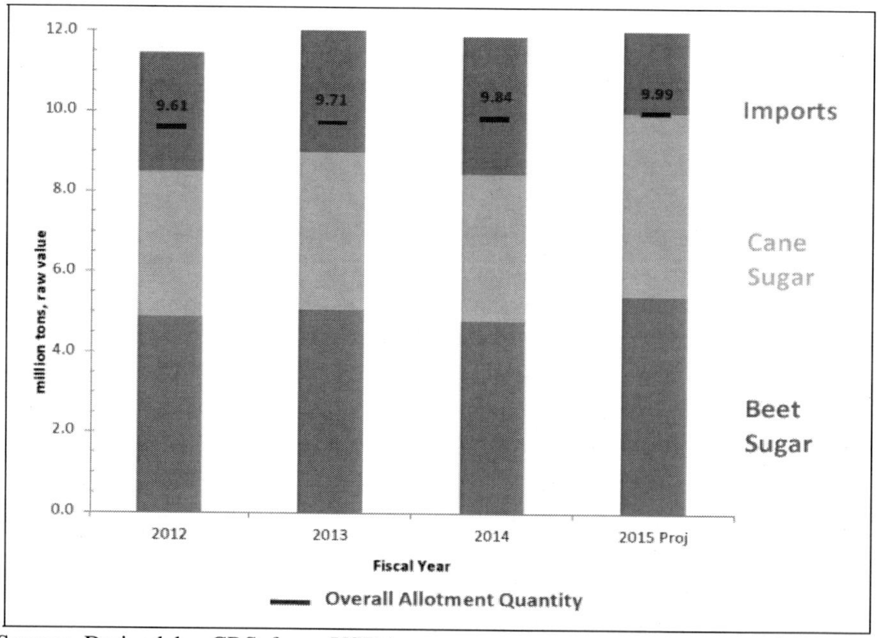

Source: Derived by CRS from USDA sugar program announcements and USDA's World Agricultural Supply and Demand Estimates reports.

Note: Imports shown occur under terms of U.S. trade commitments and are discussed in more detail in the next section.

Figure 5. Overall Allotment Quantity Compared to Total U.S. Sugar Supply.

Beyond these defined import commitments, unrestricted, duty-free access to Mexican sugar under the North American Free Trade Agreement (NAFTA) introduced uncertainty over how much sugar Mexico would ship north in any year. To illustrate, U.S. imports of Mexican sugar since 2008 have ranged from a low of about 800,000 tons in FY2010 to a high of almost 2.1 million tons in FY2013. This variability (*Figure 6*) in part reflects large swings in the amount of Mexican sugar available for export in any year, depending on the impact of drought in some years in Mexico's sugarcane-producing regions, and the degree to which U.S. exports of cheaper high-fructose corn syrup displace Mexican consumption of Mexican-produced sugar.

During the three most recently completed marketing years, FY2012-FY2014, Mexico was by far the largest source of U.S. sugar imports, supplying 50% of total U.S. sugar imports on average over this period. Reflecting Mexico's unique status as an unrestricted supplier, its annual shipments varied from a high of 2.1 million short tons, raw value (STRV)[4], comprising 66% of U.S. sugar imports in FY2013, to a low of 1.1 million STRV status, comprising 29% of U.S. imports in FY2012. Sugar entering the United States under tariff-rate quota programs during these three years amounted to 37% of all imports, with DR-CAFTA countries supplying a subtotal of nearly 4% of total sugar imports (*Figure 6*).

To address the market uncertainty expected from imports of Mexican sugar once it achieved unrestricted access in 2008, the 2008 farm bill introduced a new policy to regulate imports, and this policy was retained by the 2014 farm bill. The farm bill directed that at the beginning of each marketing year (October 1) USDA was required to set the WTO quotas for raw cane and refined sugar at the minimum level—1.256 million tons—necessary to comply with this trade commitment (*Figure 6*). In case of an emergency shortfall of sugar prior to April 1, due to either weather or war, USDA was directed to increase these quotas. Absent such a supply emergency, USDA must wait until April 1 (the midpoint of the marketing year) before deciding whether or not to increase the WTO raw sugar quota. Any increase in the import quota is temporary in that it applies only until the beginning of the next marketing year, which begins on October 1.

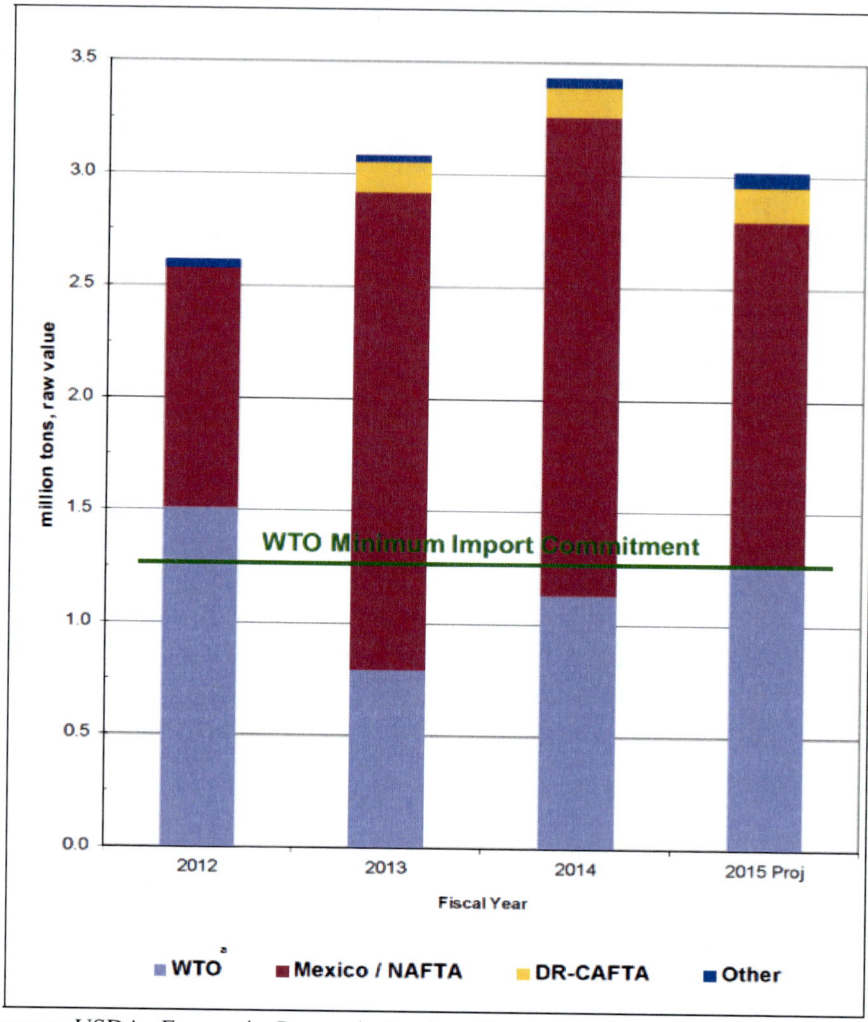

Source: USDA, Economic Research Service, Foreign Agricultural Service, and the World Agricultural Outlook Board.

Notes: Imports for domestic food/beverage consumption only; excludes sugar imported for the sugar re-export program.

[a] FY2014 imports under the WTO commitment reflect a shortfall of 236,841 tons (i.e., the cumulative amount of sugar that eligible countries with a quota can sell, but did not ship, to the U.S. market for various reasons). For FY2015, USDA projects a shortfall of 99,208 tons as of March 2015.

Figure 6. U.S. Sugar Imports, by Trade Agreement. (Raw Cane and Refined Sugar)

SUSPENSION AGREEMENTS RECAST SUGAR TRADE WITH MEXICO

While the 2014 farm bill reauthorized the sugar program intact for five years through 2018 crops, events since enactment of the farm bill have materially altered the program. A recent, major change with substantial repercussions for the U.S. sugar program concerns treatment of imported sugar from Mexico. From 2008 until December 2014, Mexican sugar exports were accorded unrestricted, duty-free access to the U.S. market under NAFTA. Two suspension agreements that the U.S. government signed with the Government of Mexico and with Mexican sugar producers and exporters in December 2014 have fundamentally altered trade in sugar with Mexico while creating ripple effects for the sugar program and for sugar users. The two suspension agreements stem from parallel countervailing duty (CVD) and antidumping (AD) investigations initiated in the spring of 2014 by the International Trade Commission (ITC) and the International Trade Administration (ITA) of the DOC in response to a petition filed by the American Sugar Coalition (ASC). The ASC represents sugarcane and sugar beet producers, processors, refiners, and sugar workers. Sections 704 and 734 of the Tariff Act of 1930 (19 U.S.C. §1671(c) and §1673(c)), as amended, provide the legal authority for the CVD and AD suspension agreements.

Preliminary findings in the CVD investigation determined that the Mexican government was subsidizing Mexican sugar exports.[5] The AD investigation concluded as a preliminary matter that Mexican sugar was being dumped into the U.S. market, that is, sold at less than fair value— defined as below the sale price in Mexico, or below the cost of production.[6] The investigations determined these actions had injured the U.S. sugar industry, and based on these preliminary findings, the DOC imposed cumulative duties on U.S. imports of Mexican sugar to be deposited by U.S. importers of sugar, ranging from 2.99% to 17.01% under the CVD order, and from 39.54% to 47.26% under the AD order.

In December 2014, the U.S. Department of Commerce (DOC) entered into suspension agreements with the Government of Mexico and with Mexican sugar industry interests. Under the CVD agreement that DOC entered into with the Government of Mexico and the AD order that DOC signed with Mexican sugar producers and exporters, the DOC agreed to suspend both the CVD and AD investigations and to remove the duties it had imposed on imports of Mexican sugar. In return, the Government of Mexico agreed to relinquish the unrestricted access to the U.S. sugar market it had negotiated under NAFTA. Further, the Mexican government and Mexican producer groups and exporters also agreed to observe the certain restrictions on Mexican sugar exports to the United States.

The two suspension agreements have substantially recast U.S. sugar trade with Mexico by imposing three fundamental changes on Mexican sugar exports to the United States.

- Mexico's previously unlimited sugar exports to the U.S. market are henceforth limited to an assessment of U.S. needs, defined as the residual of projected U.S. human use less domestic production and imports from tariff-rate quota countries.
- Refined sugar exports from Mexico are limited to 53% of Mexico's allowable quantity in any given marketing year (October 1 to September 30), whereas previously no such restriction was in place.
- Mexican sugar is subject to minimum reference prices of $0.26 per pound for refined sugar and $0.2225 for all other sugar.[7] Prior to the agreements, no floor price was imposed.

To determine the quantity of Mexican sugar that may be imported into the United States in a given marketing year under the suspension agreements, USDA is tasked with making an initial calculation of the domestic requirement for Mexican sugar in July. This quantity is subject to a recalculation in September, December, and March that may result in increases in quantity from the initial calculation.

In addition to imposing limits on the quantity of Mexican sugar that may be imported into the U.S. market, the agreements limit the concentration of Mexican sugar imports over the course of the marketing year to not more than 30% of the assessment of U.S. needs from October 1 through December 31 and not more than 55% from October 1 through March 31. For instance, in the wake of the agreement the initial export limit on Mexican sugar of 1,162,604.75 metric tons raw value for the 2014/2015 marketing year was subsequently increased to 1,383,969.68 metric tons raw value, which became effective on March 30, 2015.

Potential Effects on Government Outlays and Sugar Prices

In practice, the changes ushered in by the suspension agreements should greatly facilitate the USDA's task of operating the sugar program at no cost to the government, as Congress directed in the 2014 farm bill. Prior to the suspension agreements, imports of sugar from Mexico represented the only unmanaged source of supply under the sugar program. The USDA's ability to administer the sugar program at no net cost has been at issue since the 2012/2013 crop year, when net government outlays for the sugar program spiked to $259 million. That year, large quantities of domestic sugar under loan were forfeited in the face of excess supplies and low market prices. This obligated USDA to dispose of the forfeited sugar at a significant loss under the Feedstock Flexibility Program (FFP) and via exchanges in which the agency provided swapped forfeited domestic sugar for the right to import certain quantities of sugar.[8]

In an analysis issued in March 2015, the Food and Agricultural Policy Institute (FAPRI) at the University of Missouri projected net government outlays for the sugar program under two scenarios: with the suspension agreements, and without them. FAPRI concluded that under the suspension agreements net government outlays for sugar would be zero over marketing years 2016 through 2024. Without the agreements, FAPRI projected that annual outlays would average $16 million a year during marketing years 2016 through 2018, declining to $8 million a year on average from 2019 through 2024.[9] In its March 2015 Baseline for Farm Programs, the Congressional Budget Office (CBO) projects government outlays for the sugar program at zero over the period FY2015 through FY2019. From FY2020 through FY2025 CBO projects outlays totaling $115 million, reflecting a likely re-examination of the agreement after five years and the potential for policy uncertainty over Mexican sugar imports thereafter.[10]

Assessing the potential for the suspension agreements to add to costs borne by sugar-using industries and consumers, the Coalition for Sugar Reform, representing consumer, trade, and commerce groups; manufacturing associations; and food and beverage companies that use sugar, contends that the suspension agreements will result in higher sugar prices for U.S. users and consumers. Following the signing of the suspension agreements in December 2014, the Coalition asserted, "These agreements will ensure that any Mexican sugar needed to adequately supply the U.S. market must be priced well above world market prices—prices that are even higher than mandated by the U.S. sugar program."[11]The American Sugar Alliance, a coalition of sugar producers, including farmers, processors, refiners, sugar suppliers and workers, has expressed support for the agreements, contending they will foster free and fair trade in sugar, while benefiting U.S. sugar farmers, workers, consumers, and taxpayers.[12]

Considering that Mexican sugar is a significant source of U.S. sugar supplies that can vary in quantity from one year to the next, and considering also that minimum prices of Mexican sugar are at U.S. loan levels, or above them, without including transportation costs to U.S. destinations, it is evident that pricing on Mexican sugar should be well above U.S. loan levels as long as the suspension agreements remain in effect. Transportation from Mexican mills adds several cents per pound to the cost of sugar delivered to U.S. plants—as much as $0.03 to $0.06 per pound, according to FAPRI.

Two Sugarcane Refiners Challenging Suspension Agreements

Whether the new framework around trade in Mexican sugar imposed by the suspension agreements will remain in effect is not entirely certain. The agreements have no termination date, but the signatories may terminate them at any time. The suspended CVD and AD investigations are subject to a review after five years. More immediately, two U.S. sugarcane refiners—Imperial Sugar Company and AmCane Sugar LLC—are attempting to challenge the agreements. In January 2015, the two companies petitioned the U.S. International Trade Commission (ITC), contending the agreements do not eliminate completely the injurious effect of sugar imports from Mexico as the law permitting such agreements requires.[13] In a unanimous decision issued in March 2015, the ITC concluded the agreements do eliminate entirely the injurious effect of Mexican sugar imports.[14] In late April 2015, the two sugar-refining companies indicated their intention to appeal the ITC's decision on injury to the United States Court of International Trade, according to press reports.[15]

The companies also have petitioned the DOC to continue the CVD and AD investigations to final determinations. In early May 2015, the DOC determined the two sugar-refining companies have standing under the law to make such a petition. As such, the agency announced it would resume the CVD and AD investigations with the intention of issuing final determinations within 135 days of the May 4, 2015, notice date—roughly mid-September 2015.[16]In the meantime, the terms of the suspension agreements remain in force.

Looking ahead, if DOC were to issue final affirmative findings (similar to their preliminary findings) that subsidization and dumping of Mexican sugar occurred, and if ITC were to issue a final determination that the U.S. sugar industry was injured as a result, then the suspension agreements would remain in effect. Alternatively, if either agency were to issue a negative final determination—that is, concluding that subsidization, dumping, or injury did not occur—then the investigations would be ended, and the suspension agreements that limit Mexican sugar imports and set minimum reference prices would be terminated.

MECHANISMS AIMED AT COUNTERING LOW PRICES

In addition to domestic marketing allotments and import quotas and limits, USDA has two policy mechanisms to help prevent prices from slipping below effective loan forfeiture levels, thereby limiting program costs that might otherwise accrue to the government as a result of substantial loan forfeitures. These include offering CCC sugar to processors in exchange for surrendering rights to import tariff-rate quota sugar; purchasing sugar from processors in exchange for surrendering tariff-rate quota sugar; and removing sugar from the human food market by purchasing sugar from processors for resale to ethanol producers for fuel ethanol production.

Sugar Purchases and Exchanges for Import Rights

To dispose of sugar owned by CCC without increasing the risk of loan forfeitures, the farm bill authorizes USDA to transfer ownership of CCC-owned sugar in exchange for rights to purchase tariff-rate quota sugar, or certificates of quota entry, which carry a low tariff rate or zero tariff. From July to September 2013, USDA completed four sugar "exchanges" in an effort to bolster market prices and forestall loan forfeitures of some 2012 crop sugar. Two exchanges involved bids made by refiners and brokers for sugar acquired by USDA from processors as a result of loan forfeitures in return for surrendering import rights. Two other exchanges involved USDA purchasing sugar from processors, which then was exchanged for import rights that cane refiners and brokers surrendered to USDA. The latter two initiatives were taken to reduce the amount of sugar expected to be supplied to the U.S. market and were implemented by USDA using 1985 farm bill authority. This cost reduction provision authorizes USDA to purchase a supported commodity deemed to be in surplus if such action results in program savings.

Feedstock Flexibility Program for Bioenergy Producers

If market prices fall to levels that threaten to result in loan forfeitures, the Secretary of Agriculture may purchase surplus sugar and sell it to bioenergy producers to avoid forfeitures. In the event that forfeitures of sugar loans do occur, the Secretary is required to administer a sugar for-ethanol program using domestic sugar intended for food use. The objective of this Feedstock Flexibility Program (FFP) is to permanently remove sugar from the market for human consumption by diverting it into a non-food use—ethanol. When the Secretary activates this program, USDA will purchase surplus and other sugar acquired from processors and then sell that sugar to bioenergy producers for processing into fuel-grade ethanol and other biofuels. Competitive bids would be used by USDA to purchase sugar from processors and also to sell that sugar (together with any sugar forfeited by processors) to ethanol producers. An exception to the requirement to activate this program is that forfeited sugar may be sold back into the market for human food use in the event of an emergency shortfall of sugar. In August and September 2013, USDA activated this program as remaining loans came due and sugar prices headed below effective support levels (*Figure 3* and *Figure 4*).

Administrative Year in the Sugar Program

The text box below sets out specific dates, and calendar windows, for undertaking key administrative actions that are integral to managing the U.S. sugar program.

U.S. Sugar Program Calendar of Administrative Actions

In July, USDA is to calculate the "export limit" for Mexican sugar for the U.S. market for the upcoming marketing year (October-September), which is to be 70% of the projection of the "target quantity of U.S. needs" for Mexican sugar based on the USDA's July World Agricultural Supply and Demand Estimates (WASDE) report. The export limit becomes effective October 1.

On September 1, the Secretary of Agriculture is to announce the amount of sugar (if any) that the Commodity Credit Corporation (CCC) is to purchase prior to the end of the current marketing year (September 30) to avoid loan forfeitures. Any purchases are to be resold for ethanol production under the Feedstock Flexibility Program (FFV).

In September, a subsequent calculation of the target quantity of U.S. needs is to be carried out based on the September WASDE with the export limit to remain at 70% of the target quantity. The new export limit quantity cannot be below the export limit announced in July.

By September 30, USDA must announce sugar loan rates for the year beginning October 1.

By October 1, USDA is to establish domestic human consumption of sugar for the new marketing year (October-September) and also establish domestic marketing allotments for sugarcane and sugar beet processors.

By October 1, the Secretary of Agriculture sets initial sugar import quotas for the new marketing year (October-September) at the minimum levels that are required to comply with international trade agreements, except for refined sugar.

By October 1, USDA is to announce the amount of sugar, if any, the CCC is to purchase in current crop year that is to be made available for sale under the FFV, and to re-estimate this amount and provide notice by Jan. 1, April 1, and July 1.

From October 1 to March 31, the Secretary of Agriculture may increase the import quota for refined sugar, but only in the event of war or natural disaster.

In December, USDA is to recalculate the target quantity for Mexican sugar for the current marketing year based on the December WASDE report. The export limit is to be raised to 80% of target quantity as of January 1. The new export limit quantity cannot be below the September export limit.

In March, USDA is to recalculate the target quantity for Mexican sugar based on the March WASDE report. The export limit is to be raised to 100% of target quantity as of April 1. The new export limit quantity cannot be below the December export limit.

Prior to April 1, USDA may increase the export limit on Mexican sugar to address potential shortages in the U.S. market.

From April 1, the Secretary may increase the Overall Allotment Quota and the tariff rate quotas that restrain imports of sugar in the event of an emergency shortfall of sugar.

From April 1, tariff rate quotas on imported sugar may be increased as long as doing so will not threaten to result in forfeitures under the sugar loan program.

After April 1, The Department of Commerce may increase the export limit on Mexican sugar in response to a written request from USDA citing the need for additional imports of Mexican sugar.

End Notes

[1] USDA, ERS Sugar & Sweeteners at http://www.ers.usda.gov/topics/crops/sugar-sweeteners /policy.aspx.

[2] Report of the Senate Committee on Agriculture, Nutrition, and Forestry to accompany S. 884, May 27, 1981.

[3] See Agreement Suspending the Countervailing Duty Investigation on Sugar from Mexico at http://enforcement.trade.gov/agreements/sugar-mexico/CVD-Agreement.pdf; also, Agreement Suspending the Antidumping Duty Investigation on Sugar from Mexico at http://enforcement.trade.gov/agreements/sugar-mexico/ADAgreement.pdf.

[4] A short ton is equivalent to 2,000 pounds. Raw value is a factor of 1.07 of refined value, according to USDA, except for Mexican sugar for which raw value is a factor of 1.06 of the actual weight of the shipped product.

[5] See U.S. Department of Commerce Fact Sheet of August 26, 2014, at http://enforcement.trade.gov/download/factsheets/factsheet-mexico-sugar-ad-prelim-082614.pdf.

[6] See U.S. Department of Commerce Fact Sheet of October 27 at http://enforcement.trade.gov/ download/factsheets/ factsheet-mexico-sugar-ad-prelim-102714.pdf.

[7] Prices are based on dry weight, commercial value, f.o.b. at Mexican plants.

[8] See U.S. International Trade Commission publication 4467, Sugar from Mexico, p. 27, http://usitc.gov/publications/ 701_731/pub4467.pdf.

[9] Impacts of the U.S.-Mexico Antidumping and Countervailing Duty Suspension Agreement, FAPRI, March 27, 2015, at http://www.fapri.missouri.edu/wp-content/uploads/2015/03/ FAPRI-MU-Bulletin-07-15.pdf.

[10] Telephone conversation of April 1, 2015, with Dave Hull, Congressional Budget Office.

[11] Coalition for Sugar Reform press release of December 22, 2014, at http://sugarreform.org/wp-content/uploads/2011/ 07/CSR-AD-CVD-Agreements-Signed-12-22-14-FINAL.pdf.

[12] American Sugar Alliance press release of March 19, 2015, at http://www.sugaralliance.org/ itc-suspensionagreements-remove-the-injury-caused-by-unfairly-traded-mexican-sugar-5245/.

[13] CVD: 19U.S.C. §1671c(c); AD: 19 U.S.C. §1673c(c).

[14] See U.S. ITC press release of March 19, 2015, at http://www.usitc.gov/press_room/news_ release/2015/ er0319ll436.htm.

[15] Reuters article of April 24, 2015, at http://af.reuters.com/article/commodities News/idAFL1N0XL1QY20150424.

[16] Federal Register notice of May 4, 2015, at https://www.federalregister.gov/ articles/ 2015/05/04/2015-10253/sugarfrom-mexico-continuation-of-antidumping-and-countervailing-duty-investigations.

In: Peanuts and Sugar
Editor: Edith Perez
ISBN: 978-1-63485-487-0

Chapter 4

SUGAR PROVISIONS OF THE 2014 FARM BILL (P.L. 113-79)*

Remy Jurenas

SUMMARY

The 2014 farm bill (Agricultural Act of 2014, P.L. 113-79) continues the sugar and the sugar-to ethanol programs without change for another five years (i.e., through FY2019). The sugar program provides a minimum price guarantee to sugar crop processors and is structured to operate at no cost to the federal government using two tools: marketing allotments that limit the amount that sugar processors can sell, and import quotas that restrict the quantity of foreign sugar allowed to enter the U.S. market. The sugar-to-ethanol program is intended to be used if marketing allotments and the administration of import quotas do not succeed in keeping market prices for sugar above minimum guaranteed levels. If activated, it ensures that stocks of sugar are not carried over to the following marketing year so as to continue to depress prices.

During farm bill debate, Members of Congress engaged in vigorous debate on future sugar policy on behalf of both sides. Sugar producers/processors and food manufacturers also waged aggressive media campaigns to influence the outcome of amendments offered during floor debate. Producers of sugar beets and sugarcane, and the processors of

* This is an edited, reformatted and augmented version of a Congressional Research Service publication R42551, prepared for Members and Committees of Congress, dated March 21, 2014.

these crops into sugar, favored retaining the current program without change. They highlighted the jobs and economic activity created by the domestic sugar sector. Food manufacturers that use sugar in their products sought flexibilities in how the U.S. Department of Agriculture (USDA) administers the program, with an eye toward paying lower prices as a result. In advocating changes, they pointed to the higher wholesale refined sugar prices paid since the 2008 farm bill provisions took effect (twice the level compared to the previous 2002 farm bill period), and to the jobs that their firms create.

The enacted provisions reflect those agreed to by the House and Senate Agriculture Committees in reporting out their respective farm bills. During the period that Congress considered this latest farm bill (2012-2014), opponents of the sugar program offered five floor amendments to change both committees' reported provisions and to instruct House conferees. All were defeated. In the 112th Congress, S.Amdt. 2393 to S. 3240 would have phased out the program within three years. S.Amdt. 2433 to S. 3240 would have reverted most program authorities to those in effect prior to the 2008 farm bill changes and repealed the sugar-to-ethanol program. In the 113th Congress, S.Amdt. 925 to S. 954 and H.Amdt. 227 to H.R. 1947 would have lowered price support levels to those in effect in FY2008, and made a number of changes to require USDA to administer sugar marketing allotments and sugar import quotas so that sugar would be available "at reasonable prices." It also would have repealed the sugar-for-ethanol program. These amendments were nearly identical to the freestanding Sugar Reform Act (S. 345 and H.R. 693).

In scoring the farm bill, the Congressional Budget Office (CBO) estimated that if current sugar policy continued, a 10-year total of $188 million in outlays would occur for FY2014-FY2023, all of it associated with the sugar-to-ethanol program. CBO scored the Sugar Reform Act as reducing these outlays by $82 million over this period. Separately, USDA actions taken in late FY2013 to reduce sugar supplies and activate the sugar-to-ethanol program to prop up market prices did not boost prices sufficiently above program-guaranteed levels. Consequently, these, together with subsequent USDA actions to dispose of sugar pledged as collateral for loans by processors and then forfeited, resulted in $259 million in federal outlays associated with the 2012 sugar crops.

Although existing sugar policy remains intact in the 2014 farm bill, the debate between sugar program supporters and opponents, which largely revolves around the level of domestic sugar prices, is expected to continue. Sugar growers and processors seek the highest price possible, with backstops in place to ensure they receive the benefits of the current price guarantee. Users of sugar in manufactured food products want as low a price as possible within the basic structure of the current program.

OVERVIEW OF SUGAR PROGRAM

The U.S. sugar program provides a price guarantee to producers of sugar beets and sugarcane and to the processors of both crops. The U.S. Department of Agriculture (USDA) further is directed to administer the program at no budgetary cost to the federal government by limiting the amount of sugar supplied for food use in the U.S. market. To achieve both objectives, USDA has four available tools—as reauthorized by the 2014 farm bill (Agricultural Act of 2014, P.L. 113-79, Section 1301 of Title I and Section 9009 of Title IX), and by Chapter 17 of the Harmonized Tariff Schedules of the United States—to keep domestic market prices above guaranteed levels. These are:

- extending price support loans to processors at specified levels (the basis for the price guarantee);
- setting marketing allotments to limit the amount of sugar each processor can sell;
- establishing import quotas to restrict the amount of sugar allowed to enter the U.S. market; and
- making a sugar-to-ethanol backstop available if marketing allotments and import quotas are insufficient to keep market prices above guaranteed levels.

SUPPORTERS OF SUGAR PROGRAM

During farm bill debate, producers of sugar beets and sugarcane, and the beet refiners and raw sugar mills that process these crops into refined sugar and raw cane sugar, respectively, supported extending the U.S. sugar policy as contained in the enacted 2008 farm bill. They argued that the program had succeeded in ensuring "reliable supplies of high-quality, safe, responsibly-produced sugar at reasonable prices" for consumers, and that it provided producers with "an economic safety net." They emphasized that these objectives had been achieved at "zero cost to American taxpayers."[1] Sugar crop producers and processors are represented by the American Sugar Alliance (ASA).

Two large general farm organizations supported continuing the current sugar program without any change. The American Farm Bureau Federation stated that while other commodities will be faced with reduced government support in the next farm bill, "the sugar program should be left intact as efforts to generate savings would require convoluted policy structures." The National Farmers Union supported continuing the sugar program and encouraged "Congress to work with ... sugar producers to adopt a strong sugar program in future farm bills." Also, a coalition of 17 developing countries that benefit from preferential quota access to the U.S. sugar market favored continuing current U.S. sugar policy, arguing that it "provides a guaranteed level of access ... at fair, predictable prices."[2]

OPPONENTS OF SUGAR PROGRAM

Sugar users (i.e., manufacturers of sugar-containing food products and beverages) supported making changes to the U.S. sugar program. In their view, the sugar program "was made worse by the 2008 farm bill" and had operated as "a textbook example of the consequences of excessive government intrusion in the marketplace." They argued that the program, "by overly restricting the supply of sugar in the U.S. market," had kept U.S. market sugar prices "far above" world sugar prices. This development, they contended, resulted in U.S. consumers and food manufacturers paying more for sugar than foreign users pay, and encouraged the relocation of food processing jobs offshore, led to the elimination of thousands of U.S. jobs, and created a "dramatic inequity of the benefits provided to sugar growers over other agricultural producers" supported by other commodity programs.[3]

Sugar users are primarily represented by the Coalition for Sugar Reform (CSR). CSR includes the food and beverage companies that use sugar (e.g., confectionery firms, bakeries, cereal manufacturers, beverage makers and dairy companies, and the trade associations for these industries), consumer and trade advocacy groups, and business organizations. Three trade associations representing food manufacturing firms where sugar is a principal input also placed U.S. sugar policy at the top of their legislative agenda. They are the American Bakers Association, the National Confectioners Association, and the Sweetener Users Association.[4]

In 2013, congressional opponents of current U.S. sugar policy introduced identical bills to revise U.S. sugar policy (H.R. 693 and S. 345, Sugar Reform Act of 2013). These were intended to be used as amendments to be offered on the floor when each chamber debated the farm bill. These measures proposed to retain the current structure of the sugar program but modify various price support, marketing allotment, and import quota provisions. They were crafted to authorize flexibility in how USDA uses the two program tools that limit sugar supplies but still meet the statutory directive that the program operate at no cost (i.e., maintain market prices above support levels so that processors have no incentive to forfeit price support loans, and if attained, not record any budget outlays). Both bills also would have repealed the sugar-for-ethanol program.

LEGISLATIVE ACTIVITY IN THE 112TH CONGRESS

Sugar Program Extension

Efforts within Congress to complete action on an omnibus farm bill after the November 2012 elections did not succeed. In late December, attention shifted to finding a legislative vehicle to extend existing authorities for agricultural commodity programs, including sugar. In the final days of the 112th Congress, congressional leadership decided to use the "fiscal cliff" bill to simply extend many 2008 farm bill provisions through September 30, 2013. Among its provisions, Section 701(a) and (b) of P.L. 112-240 extended the 2008 farm bill's commodity program authorities for one year. This meant that 2008-enacted sugar program authority applied to the 2013 sugar crops (i.e., most of FY2014, as beets and cane are harvested and processed and sugar is subsequently marketed). Separately, Section 701(f)(9) provided authority, if triggered, for USDA to implement the sugar-to-ethanol program for the 2013 sugar crops.

Earlier Action

Earlier in 2012, the Senate approved a farm bill (S. 3240) that would have continued existing sugar program authorities. Two floor amendments offered to change the Senate Agriculture Committee-reported measure were defeated. S.Amdt. 2393 (tabled, or rejected, on a 50-46 vote) would have phased out the program within three years. S.Amdt. 2433 (defeated on a 46-53 vote) would have reverted most program authorities to those in effect prior to the 2008 farm bill changes and would have repealed the sugar-to-ethanol program. This amendment served as the basis for the Sugar Reform Act bills introduced early in 2013. The House Agriculture Committee-approved farm bill (H.R. 6083) also would have reauthorized the sugar program without change. The House, though, never considered this measure.

LEGISLATIVE ACTIVITY IN THE 113TH CONGRESS

The Senate-passed farm bill (S. 954) and the House-passed farm bill (H.R. 1947) proposed to continue 2008-enacted U.S. sugar policy without change. An amendment (identical to S. 345, Sugar Reform Act) to reflect the interests of sugar users and consumers was offered by program opponents during Senate floor debate on May 22, 2013, but was defeated. On June 20, 2013, the House debated future sugar policy when it considered an amendment to H.R. 1947, the first farm bill. This proposal, similar to H.R. 693 (Sugar Reform Act), was defeated.

Table 1 provides a side-by-side comparison of the enacted 2008 farm bill sugar program provisions with those enacted in the 2014 farm bill. For comparison, the table also lays out the provisions of the defeated Sugar Reform Act offered as floor amendments during the debate on the 2014 farm bill.

Senate Farm Bill Activity

The Senate Agriculture Committee, when reporting out its farm bill (S. 954) on May 14, 2013, proposed to reauthorize the 2008 farm bill sugar program without any change through crop year 2018 (§1301 of the Agriculture Reform, Food, and Jobs Act of 2013). The committee's measure also called for reauthorizing the sugar-for-ethanol program in the bill's Energy title (§9008).

During floor debate on S. 954, the Senate considered one amendment to revise the committee-approved sugar program provisions. This amendment was defeated on a 45-54 vote. Offered by Senator Shaheen on May 22, 2013, S.Amdt. 925 proposed to reduce price support levels (from 18.75¢/lb. for raw cane sugar, and 24.09¢/lb. for refined beet sugar) to those in effect just prior to enactment of the 2008 farm bill (FY2008, i.e., 18.0¢/lb. for raw cane sugar; 22.9¢/lb. for refined beet sugar), and to make a number of changes to require USDA to administer sugar marketing allotments and sugar import quotas in ways that would result in sugar being available "at reasonable prices." The amendment would have granted USDA discretionary authority to suspend or modify any marketing allotment provision, taking into account the interests of consumers, those employed in the food production sector, businesses, and agricultural producers. It also would have required USDA to exercise discretion in administering the sugar import quota—for example, by allowing for adjustments in quota levels to provide for adequate sugar supplies at reasonable prices. Another provision would have required USDA to set the ending sugar stocks-to-use ratio at about 15.5%, but with authority to adjust this target to prevent "unreasonably" high prices or loan forfeitures. Sugar users argued that having USDA use this stocks-to-use level in implementing the sugar program would result in much lower prices than in the 2009-2011 period. This amendment also would have repealed the sugar-to-ethanol program.

House Farm Bill Activity

The House Agriculture Committee, in reporting its farm bill (H.R. 1947) on May 14, 2013, similarly proposed to reauthorize the enacted 2008 farm bill sugar program without any change through crop year 2018 (§1301 of the Federal Agriculture Reform and Risk Management Act of 2013). The House-reported bill also called for reauthorizing the sugar-for-ethanol program in the Energy title (§9009). Representative Goodlatte filed an amendment to revise the sugar program with an eye to offering it during committee markup, but withdrew it from consideration.

On June 20, 2013, the House considered one amendment to revise the committee-approved sugar program provisions. This amendment was defeated on a 206-221 vote. Offered by Representative Pitts, its text was identical to H.R. 693 (Sugar Reform Act) introduced earlier in 2013, and to the amendment offered during Senate floor debate. With the defeat of this farm bill (H.R. 1947), the House subsequently considered a scaled-back farm bill without a nutrition title (H.R. 2642) that would have reauthorized current sugar program authorities on an indefinite basis (i.e., no expiration date). The sugar-for-ethanol program, however, would have only been authorized through the 2018 crop. This measure passed the House on July 11 by a 216-208 vote.

On October 11, 2013, the House debated H.Res. 378 to instruct House farm bill conferees to "advance provisions to repeal" one sugar program requirement added by the 2008 farm bill and proposed to be continued by both the House and Senate farm bills. This requirement stipulates that USDA can increase imports of sugar under a sizeable import quota only after the midpoint of the marketing year (i.e., April 1), unless an emergency sugar shortage surfaces earlier. Prior to 2008, USDA had discretion to increase this quota at any time of the year if it determined market circumstances warranted such action. H.Res. 378 was introduced by Members who supported the position of food manufacturers that use sugar. Their intent was to have House conferees advocate for a return to the discretionary authority that the Secretary of Agriculture previously exercised "to manage supplies of sugar throughout the marketing year to meet domestic demand at reasonable prices." The resolution would have been non-binding if passed. The House defeated this measure by a 192-212 vote.

Reaction to Conference Agreement

With the sugar and sugar-to-ethanol program provisions identical in both the House- and Senate- passed measures, farm bill conferees concurred and focused instead on resolving differences elsewhere in the commodity and nutrition titles. Sugar producers and processors applauded continuation of current policy that they said will enable the sector to deal "with the dual threat of increasing foreign subsidies and falling sugar prices." Food manufacturers expressed disappointment that conferees failed to reform the sugar program that they maintain costs taxpayers "nearly $300 million last year," puts "bakers, consumers, and other food manufacturers at a disadvantage," and sends "thousands of jobs overseas."[5]

Other Bills

During the 113th Congress, supporters of maintaining current sugar policy introduced a measure that urges the President to seek the elimination of other countries' subsidies that support the production or export of sugar (H.Con.Res. 39). If the President determines that all covered countries have eliminated these subsidies, the resolution calls for the President to propose legislation to Congress to implement a "zero for zero" sugar subsidy policy. In other words, once other countries eliminate their market-distorting sugar programs, the U.S. sugar production sector also would advocate for an end to U.S. sugar policy.[6]

Opponents introduced other measures to eliminate current sugar policy. Sections 101 and 102 of H.R. 1567 would eliminate the sugar price support, marketing allotment, and import quota provisions. S. 956 would permanently suspend price support and related authorities for specified agricultural commodities, including those that provide price support and marketing allotments for sugar.

COST ESTIMATES

The Congressional Budget Office (CBO) projected in its May 2013 baseline that the continuation of current sugar policy as approved by the Senate, and reported by the House Agriculture Committee, would result in budget outlays of $39 million over 5 years (FY2014-FY2018) and $188 million over 10 years (FY2014-FY2023). While CBO scored the operation of the sugar price support program at zero in each of these time periods, its projection assumed that USDA will in some years need to activate the sugar-to-ethanol program. In scoring the 2014 farm bill conference agreement, CBO did not change this budget projection.

In a more recent projection, the Food and Agricultural Policy Research Institute (FAPRI) estimates that sugar policy as enacted by the 2014 farm bill and accounting for expected market conditions would result in outlays of $133 million over 5 years (FY2014-FY2018) and $446 million over 10 years (FY2014-FY2023).[7]

CBO also projected that the Sugar Reform Act amendment would have achieved total 5-year savings of $27 million (FY2014-FY2018) and 10-year savings of $82 million (FY2014-FY2023) from the above baseline that assumed the continuation of current sugar policy. Since the amendment would have repealed the sugar-to-ethanol program, this score implied that USDA in some years would record outlays in administering the sugar program's price support operations.

FY2013 PROGRAM COSTS

Opponents pointed to the federal outlays incurred to support sugar prices in the last quarter of FY2013 and the first quarter of FY2014 to defend their view that the sugar program does not operate at "no cost" and needs to be reformed. Countering, program supporters pointed out that the enacted 2008 farm bill directs USDA to administer the program at no cost to taxpayers, and if that cannot be achieved, to take steps to minimize costs. Further, they noted that the non-recourse price support loans available to sugar processors are designed to guarantee them minimum prices for their sugar when market prices fall below these minimums. Accordingly, forfeiting on loans is an option that the authorized program allows them to exercise when this occurs.

With the actions that USDA took to head off loan forfeitures of 2012-crop processed sugar, and its subsequent decisions to implement the sugar-to-ethanol program using sugar that processors forfeited, the sugar program recorded $259 million in budget outlays (i.e., $141 million in FY2013, $118 million in FY2014). Of this total, 67% ($174 million) represents the cost of the sugar-to-ethanol program (i.e., purchases of sugar by USDA from processors, and offering forfeited sugar, for sale to ethanol producers at a substantial discount). The remaining 33% ($85 million) is attributable to sugar purchased by USDA and then exchanged for import rights that cane refiners and brokers surrendered to USDA.

Sugar Market Price Is Key Issue

The main issue in sugar policy debate over the last few years revolved around the price level for domestic sugar. Sugar growers and processors sought the highest level possible, so long as the program's minimum price guarantee was met. Users of sugar in manufactured food products sought as low a price as possible within the basic structure of the 2008-enacted program. Processors sought to retain the program's minimum price guarantees. Users sought to reduce them by 4% to 5%. Processors sought to retain all other details of the current program, designed in large part to accommodate the uncertainties surrounding how much sugar Mexico ships north in any year. Users sought to grant USDA more flexibility in how program tools are administered, by repealing certain prescriptions added in 2008 designed to reduce its discretionary authorities to manage the program. Their objective was to have USDA manage the program in ways that could result in U.S. market prices for raw cane and refined sugar being lower and closer to what they were in the years leading up to the 2008 farm bill period (see *Figure 1* and *Figure 2*).

MARKET AND POLICY OUTLOOK

Domestic sugar prices are expected to remain close to current levels (*Figure 2*) for the remainder of FY2014 as the 2013 sugar crops continue to be processed and marketed. USDA expects that over the next several months, U.S. prices will stay above loan forfeiture levels due to lower U.S. sugar production, reduced imports of sugar from Mexico, and an increase in demand from food manufacturers. A top USDA official confirmed this outlook in an interview, stating "he believes the department will be able to comply with Congress' mandate to run the program without taxpayer expense if possible."[8]

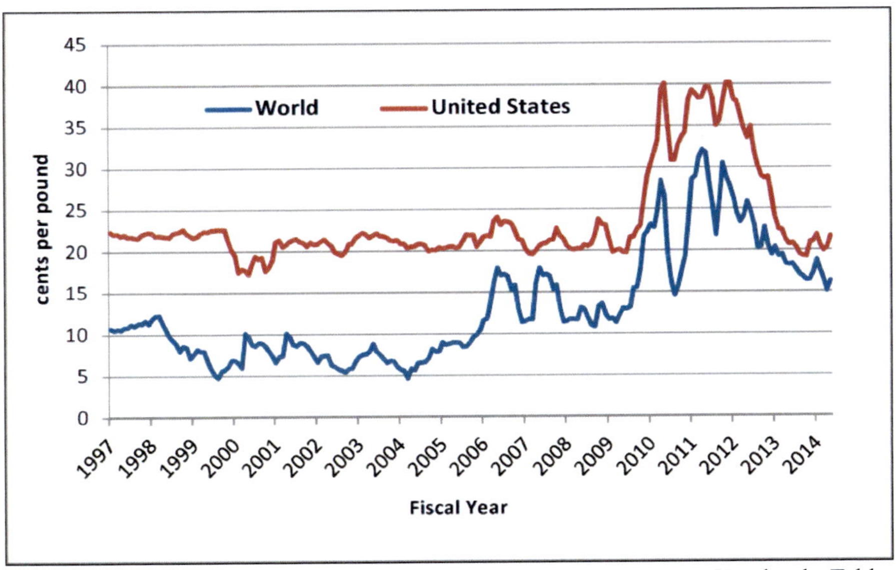

Source: USDA, Economic Research Service, Sugar and Sweeteners Yearbook, Tables 3b and 4.

Note: Covers period during which 1996, 2002, and 2008 farm bill sugar provisions applied.

Figure 1. Raw Sugar Prices: United States Compared to World.

In reacting to final farm bill action, food manufacturers that use sugar signaled their intent to continue to fight for reform by working with House and Senate leaders to make sure the sugar program "is on the table, even if those legislative efforts must take place outside of the Farm Bill process." These opponents note that congressional supporters "gained substantial momentum during the past year with the close votes that occurred on their floor amendments, and that efforts will continue for program modifications." Program supporters also expect the "battle" over the sugar program's future to continue.[9]

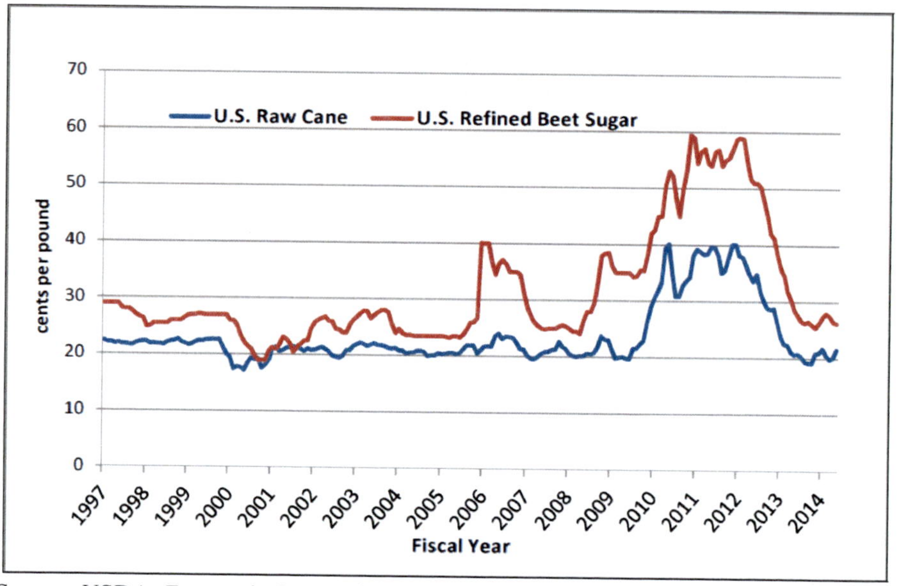

Source: USDA, Economic Research Service, Sugar and Sweeteners Yearbook, Tables 4 and 5.

Note: Covers period during which 1996, 2002, and 2008 farm bill sugar provisions applied.

Figure 2. U.S. Sugar Prices: Raw Compared to Refined.

Sugar farmers and processors continue to emphasize that foreign sugar subsidies make U.S. sugar policy necessary, and that trade-distorting policies used by Brazil, India, Mexico, and Thailand, among others, need to be eliminated. Once these policies are disciplined through multilateral trade negotiations under the auspices of the World Trade Organization (WTO), the U.S. sugar production sector would advocate for an end to current U.S. sugar policy. Sugar industry spokesmen point to H.Con.Res. 39 as a roadmap to accomplish this (see "Other Bills" for details). Observers of the longstanding WTO Doha Round negotiations note that trade negotiators have tried since 2001 to discipline trade-distorting agricultural policies but have not yet succeeded.[10] Further, WTO member countries have not yet agreed upon any timetable to go beyond the limited deals covering agriculture agreed to at the December 2013 Bali Ministerial.[11]

Table 1. Sugar Program Provisions in 2014 Farm Bill Compared to 2008 Farm Bill and to Sugar Reform Act of 2013 Offered as Floor Amendments and Defeated

2008 Farm Bill & One-Year Extension (P.L. 110-246 & P.L. 112-240, Title VII)	2014 Farm Bill (P.L. 113-79)	*Sugar Reform Act of 2013 (S. 345 and H.R. 693) as Modified by Defeated Floor Amendments to the 2014 Farm Bill*
	Time Period Covered	
2008-2013 crops of sugarcane and sugar beets.	2014-2018 crops of sugarcane and sugar beets.	Would apply to 2014-2018 crops of sugarcane and sugar beets.
	No-Net Cost Directive	
Continued no-cost requirement found in 2002 farm bill.	Continues current policy.	Would continue 2008 farm bill authorities, except for changes shown below. Would maintain no-cost directive.
Required USDA to operate sugar-for-ethanol program *(see below)* to ensure this no-cost directive is met.	Continues sugar-for-ethanol program as a backstop to ensure this directive is met.	Would repeal sugar-for-ethanol program *(see below)*.
	Price Support Levels and Loans	
Gradually raised raw cane sugar loan rate to 18.75¢/lb. by FY2012, in 1/4¢ increments beginning in FY2010, as follows: *¢ / lb.* FY2009—18.00 FY2010—18.25 FY2011—18.50 FY2012—18.75 FY2013—18.75 FY2014—18.75	Maintains 18.75¢/lb. raw cane sugar loan rate for entire farm bill period (through the 2018 crop year, or FY2019).	Would reduce raw cane sugar loan rate to 18.0¢/lb. for 2014 through 2018 crop years (i.e., FY2015 through FY2019).
Set refined beet sugar loan rate at 22.9¢/lb. in FY2009. Starting in FY2010, setbeet sugar rate equal to 128.5% of the raw cane loan rate in effect (e.g., rising to 24.09¢/lb. in FY2012), as follows: *¢ / lb.* FY2009—22.90 FY2010—23.45 FY2011—23.77 FY2012—24.09 FY2013—24.09 FY2014—24.09	Maintains 24.09¢/lb. refined beet sugar loan rate for entire farm bill period.	Would reduce effective refined beet sugar loan rate to 22.9¢/lb. through 2018 crop year (i.e., through FY2019).
Continued other price support provisions enacted in 2002 farm bill.	Continues all other 2008 farm bill price support provisions.	Would continue all other 2008 farm bill price support provisions.

2008 Farm Bill & One-Year Extension (P.L. 110-246 & P.L. 112-240, Title VII)	2014 Farm Bill (P.L. 113-79)	*Sugar Reform Act of 2013 (S. 345 and H.R. 693) as Modified by Defeated Floor Amendments to the 2014 Farm Bill*
	Payment-in-Kind Authority	
Continued in-kind authority and added stipulation that planted beets or cane diverted from production can be used only as bioenergy feedstock.	Maintains provision.	Would maintain provision.
	Storage Payments	
Increased (only through crop year 2011) the minimum storage rates to be paid by USDA to processors that forfeit loans at 10¢/cwt. for raw cane sugar and 15¢/cwt. for refined beet sugar. These rates reverted back to pre-2008 farm bill levels for the 2012 and 2013 sugar crops.	Continues minimum storage rates in effect before temporary 2008 farm bill change.	Would continue minimum storage rates in effect before temporary 2008 farm bill change.
	Storage Facility Loans	
Retained financing authority, and added stipulation that loans shall not require any prepayment penalty.	No change.	No change.
	Marketing Allotments and Allocations	
Restored mandatory sugar marketing allotments as a tool to be used by USDA to avert loan forfeitures. Required USDA to set the national "overall allotment quantity" (OAQ – the total amount of U.S.-produced sugar that can be sold in the domestic market each year) using five specified factors *(see below)*. Stipulated that the OAQ be split between beet and cane sectors on a 54.35% and 45.65% basis, respectively. Required each sector's allotment to be allocated to states (in the case of cane) and to individual processors (both beet and cane sectors). Stipulated that the OAQ had to accommodate WTO and NAFTA import commitments (1.532 million short tons (ST)).	Maintains all provisions without change through the 2018 crop year for sugar (i.e., FY2019).	Would maintain most provisions, except for changes noted below, through the 2018 crop year for sugar (i.e., FY2019).

Table 1. (Continued)

2008 Farm Bill & One-Year Extension (P.L. 110-246 & P.L. 112-240, Title VII)	2014 Farm Bill (P.L. 113-79)	*Sugar Reform Act of 2013 (S. 345 and H.R. 693) as Modified by Defeated Floor Amendments to the 2014 Farm Bill*
Required USDA to estimate for each year the quantity of sugar that will be consumed as food by humans, the quantity of sugar that provides for reasonable carryover (ending) stocks, the quantity of sugar that will be available from carry-in (beginning) stocks for human food use, the quantity of sugar that will be processed from U.S. production of sugarcane and sugar beets, and the quantity of sugar that will be imported for human food use.	Maintains current requirement on the supply and demand components that USDA must estimate each year.	Would maintain current requirement on what USDA must estimate, with one additional requirement: that USDA estimate the quantity of sugar that provides for reasonable carryover (or ending) stocks at reasonable prices.
Required USDA to use two criteria to set the OAQ at a level sufficient to maintain raw and refined sugar prices that result in no loan forfeitures to the CCC but not less than 85% of USDA's estimate of human food and beverage use. Stipulated that USDA must adjust upward or downward the OAQ to reflect re-estimates in any of the factors specified above, but could not reduce the OAQ to an amount less than 85% of estimated U.S. human food use.	Maintains current authorities.	Would repeal the second requirement that the OAQ be set at not less than 85% of USDA's estimate of human food and beverage use. Would replace that with requirement that USDA set the OAQ at a level that is appropriate to maintain adequate supplies at reasonable prices, taking into account all sources of domestic sugar supply, including imports. Would remove provision that USDA may not adjust the OAQ below the 85% estimate of U.S. human food use.
Made no changes to current U.S. import quota commitments found in various trade agreements and laws. On January 1, 2008, Mexico became eligible to ship duty free an unlimited amount of sugar to the U.S. market.	Continues current U.S. trade commitments without any change.	Would continue current U.S. trade commitments without any change.
Repealed requirement for USDA to reallocate sugar import quota shortfalls.	No comparable provision.	Would require USDA to establish a process for any country with a share of the U.S. sugar import quota to temporarily transfer all or part of its share to any other country with a U.S. sugar import quota share. Stipulates that any such transfer shall be valid only if voluntarily agreed to between the two countries.
Required USDA to set initial import quotas for raw cane and refined sugar at the minimum level necessary to comply with U.S. trade agreement obligations. Laid out steps to be followed to increase imports in the event of an emergency sugar shortage. In case of such a shortage before April 1 of a marketing year, required USDA to increase supplies *first* by reassigning allotment deficits to imports of raw cane sugar (i.e., increase the raw sugar quota), and *second* to the refined sugar quota, if certain conditions are met. On or after April 1, allows USDA only to increase the raw cane sugar quota, if specified conditions are	Continues current policy.	Would maintain requirement that USDA set import quotas for raw cane sugar and refined sugar at not less than the minimum level necessary to comply with U.S. trade agreement obligations. Modifies criteria to be used to adjust imports as follows: Would require USDA to adjust the quotas for raw cane sugar and refined sugar to provide for adequate sugar supplies at reasonable prices in the U.S. market. Would require USDA to set and adjust these quotas so that ending sugar stocks will be about 15.5% of total sugar use at the end of each fiscal year. Would allow for

2008 Farm Bill & One-Year Extension (P.L. 110-246 & P.L. 112-240, Title VII)	2014 Farm Bill (P.L. 113-79)	*Sugar Reform Act of 2013 (S. 345 and H.R. 693) as Modified by Defeated Floor Amendments to the 2014 Farm Bill*
met.		USDA to adjust the ending sugar stocks ratio target if necessary to prevent unreasonably high prices or forfeitures of loans taken out by processors if market prices fall below effective support levels. In setting and adjusting quotas, would require USDA to consider their impact on consumers, workers, businesses (including small businesses), and agricultural producers.
Sugar-for-Ethanol Program (Feedstock Flexibility Program)		
Required USDA (for FY2008-FY2013) to purchase sugar from those firms that sell sugar (equal to the quantity of imports that USDA estimates exceeds U.S. food demand), and to resell such sugar as a biomass feedstock to produce bioenergy, in a way to ensure that sugar price support program provisions *(see above)* operate at no cost and avoid loan forfeitures. Required USDA to use competitive procedures in entering into contracts with sellers and buyers of sugar, and to sell any sugar held in CCC's inventory, for this purpose. Required USDA to use CCC resources, including "such sums as are necessary," to implement this authority. Prescribed how CCC-inventory sugar is to be disposed for this Program and other purposes, and allowed for the sale of CCC-inventory sugar in the case of emergency shortages of sugar for food use caused by war, flood, hurricane, other natural disaster, or other similar event.	Continues current policy through the 2018 crop year for sugar (i.e., FY2019).	Would repeal program upon enactment.

Source: Public laws and bills cited in table headers.

Note: The Senate approved the sugar program provisions of the Senate Agriculture Committee-reported bill (S. 954) without change on June 10, 2013. The Senate considered the Sugar Reform Act as S.Amdt. 925 to S. 954 during floor debate on May 22, 2013. This amendment was defeated on a 45-54 vote. The House considered the Sugar Reform Act as H.Amdt. 227 to revise the House Agriculture Committee-reported sugar program provisions during floor debate on its farm bill (H.R. 1947) on June 20, 2013. That amendment was defeated on a 206-221 vote. With the subsequent defeat of H.R. 1947, the House passed a farm bill without the nutrition title (H.R. 2642) on July 11, 2013. This included the Agriculture Committee-reported sugar program provisions found in H.R. 1947 with changes that would authorize the sugar program (except for the sugar-to-ethanol program) on a permanent basis (i.e., no expiration date). The farm bill conference report (H.Rept. 113-333 to accompany H.R. 2642) reauthorized the enacted 2008 farm bill's sugar program without any changes, and will be in effect for another five years (through the 2018 crops and for sugar processed in FY2019). Although S.Amdt. 925 and H.Amdt. 227 were defeated, their provisions are included in this table for comparison, and because some provisions could resurface in future legislative debate.

This outlook suggests that the U.S. sugar production sector's roadmap would not yield any results for quite some time, and likely not in the time period covered by the newly reauthorized sugar program (i.e., through FY2019). Looking at the near term, sugar industry spokesmen note that any efforts to change the program require addressing the impact of large unrestricted sugar imports from Mexico. Specifically, the industry seeks joint management of sugar by both the United States and Mexican governments to balance supply and demand. To address the criticism made that the sugar program no longer operates on a no-cost basis (as seen in FY2013), the industry notes that the $258 million spent was less than 3% of commodity program spending and the first time in a decade that the program had not operated at no net cost to the taxpayer.[12]

End Notes

[1] American Sugar Alliance, statement submitted to the House Agriculture Committee's Subcommittee on General Farm Commodities and Risk Management, hearing on "Formulation of the 2012 Farm Bill: Commodities & Crop Insurance," May 17, 2012, accessed at http://www.sugaralliance.org/images/stories/PapersAndTestimony/ASA-HAC-testimony-5- 12.pdf.

[2] American Farm Bureau Federation, "Policy Recommendations for the 2012 Farm Bill," September 28, 2011, p. 5, accessed at http://www.fb.org/issues/FarmBureau Recommendations110928.pdf; National Farmers Union, 2012 NFU Policy, adopted by delegates at their March 2012 convention, accessed at http://www.nfu.org/policy-nfu/218-article-i/ 973-e-commodities#anchor5; ASA, "Developing Nations Reaffirm Sugar Policy Support, Praise Farm Bill," May 21, 2012, accessed at http://www.sugaralliance.org/ newsroom/developing-nations-reaffirm-sugar-policy-support-praisefarm-bill.html.

[3] Coalition for Sugar Reform, statement submitted to the House Agriculture Committee's Subcommittee on General Farm Commodities and Risk Management, hearing on "Formulation of the 2012 Farm Bill: Commodities & Crop Insurance", May 17, 2012, accessed at http://sugarreform.org/wp-content/uploads/2011/06/CSR-House-Ag-Testimony-May-17-2012-FINAL-.pdf.

[4] American Bakers Association, "Sugar Program Reform," accessed at http://americanbakers. org/issues/sugar/; CSR, "Message from the Chairman"—President, National Confectioners Association, accessed at http://sugarreform.org/ about/message-from-the-chairman/; Sweetener Users Association, "Sweetener Users Urge Policymakers to Reform U.S. Sugar Policy," accessed at http://www.sweetenerusers.org/SUA% 20Press%20Release% 20FINAL%202-12- 13.pdf.

[5] American Sugar Alliance, "Sugar Comments on Farm Bill Approval in Senate," February 4, 2014, accessed at http://sugaralliance.org/newsroom/sugar-comments-on-farm-bill-approval-in-senate.html; Coalition for Sugar Reform, "Farm Bill Conference Report Leaves Congress with Unfinished Business on Sugar Subsidies," January 28, 2014, accessed at http://sugarreform.org/wp-content/uploads/2011/07/CSR-Farm-Bill-01-28-14-FINAL.pdf; American Bakers Association, "Bakers Disappointed that Sugar Subsidy Program Remains

in Farm Bill," February 4, 2014, accessed at http://americanbakers.org/2014/02/bakers-disappointed-that-sugar-subsidy-program-remains-in-farm-bill/.

[6] American Sugar Alliance, "Momentum Building for 'Zero-for-Zero' Sugar Policy," August 6, 2013, accessed at http://www.sugaralliance.org/newsroom/momentum-building-for-zero-for-zero-sugar-policy.html.

[7] FAPRI – University of Missouri, U.S. Baseline Briefing Book: Projections for Agricultural and Biofuel Markets, March 2014, pp. 25, 48, accessed at http://www.fapri.missouri.edu/outreach/publications/2014/ FAPRI_MU_Report_02_14.pdf. FAPRI is an independent organization that applies its comprehensive analytical models to make market projections and evaluate the consequences of government policies for agricultural producers, consumers and taxpayers. CBO plans to issue its new baseline later this spring that will reflect its assessment of the budgetary consequences of the enacted 2014 farm bill.

[8] The Hagstrom Report, "Scuse: No sugar expenditures expected in 2014," February 24, 2014, http://www.hagstromreport.com/2014news_files/2014_0224_scuse-no-sugar-expenditures-expected-2014.html.

[9] See footnote 5; The Hagstrom Report, "Stallman: Not sure Republicans have votes for SNAP bill," September 13, 2013, http://www.hagstromreport.com/2013news_files/2013_0913_stallman-not-sure-republicans-have-votes-for-snapbill.html; Politico Pro, "Sugar industry fears appropriations attack," March 13, 2014.

[10] For background, see CRS Report RS22927, WTO Doha Round: Implications for U.S. Agriculture, and CRS Report RL32060, World Trade Organization Negotiations: The Doha Development Agenda.

[11] For background, see WTO documents on the Bali Ministerial Declaration and decisions at http://wto.org/english/ thewto_e/minist_e/mc9_e/balipackage_e.htm.

[12] The Hagstrom Report, "Sweetener Users: Sugar program still needs to change," February 26, 2014, http://www.hagstromreport.com/2014news_files/2014_0226_sweetener-users-sugar-program-still-needs-tochange.html. See also ASA, The Sugar Beat, "What 8 Cents a Year Buys You," Volume 2014 Issue 8, February 25, 2014.

In: Peanuts and Sugar
Editor: Edith Perez
ISBN: 978-1-63485-487-0

Chapter 5

PROJECTING WORLD RAW SUGAR PRICES*

Stephen Haley

ABSTRACT

Three factors are critical to the long-term outlook for U.S. sugar supply and use: the U.S. sugar program, the availability of sugar imports from Mexico, and the level of sugar prices in the world market. This report presents a modeling framework that can be used to generate world sugar price projections. In addition to using the traditional world supply and demand analysis, the modeling framework emphasizes the role of Brazil, the world's largest producer of sugarcane, sugar, and sugarcane-based ethanol. The resulting model is intended to improve USDA's world sugar price forecasts and enhance scenario analyses to derive implications for future world prices and U.S. sugar policy. Analysis of alternative Brazil scenarios illustrates impacts on the U.S. budgetary cost of loan forfeitures for sugar under current U.S. policies. The report includes documentation, analysis, and model projections for world sugar markets through 2024/25.

Keywords: world raw sugar prices, Intercontinental Exchange No. 11 raw sugar futures contract, world sugar model, Brazil, Center/South Brazil, Brazil ethanol supply and demand, long-term USDA sugar price forecasting

---

* This is an edited, reformatted and augmented version of report number SSSM-317-01, issued by U.S. Department of Agriculture, Economic Research Service, January 2015.

INTRODUCTION

The most important factors affecting U.S. sugar supply and use are the U.S. sugar program, the availability of sugar imports from Mexico, and the level of sugar prices in the world market. This last factor has recently become of increased interest to market participants, analysts, and policy-makers. In the past, interest has been limited because world sugar prices have been far below levels at which the U.S. sugar program supports domestic prices. However, during the period August 2009 through July 2012, world prices for raw sugar averaged more than 5 cents/pound (lb) above the U.S. raw sugar loan rate. Although world prices have since fallen below loan-rate levels, changes in U.S. raw sugar prices have remained strongly correlated with changes in world prices. In fiscal year 2013 (2012/13), weakness in world raw sugar prices contributed notably to sugar loan forfeitures and USDA purchases of sugar for ethanol and livestock-feed resale and trade-license exchanges, costing the Commodity Credit Corporation (CCC) more than $250 million.[1]

Due to Brazil's large percentage share of world sugar production and trade, long-term upward trends in Brazilian sugar production costs are expected to keep world sugar prices from descending to the low levels of the early-to-mid 2000s (which ranged between 6.44 and 9.99 cents/lb).[2] Higher world prices, along with normal year-to-year volatility, will affect U.S. sugar policy analysis and projections of future USDA budget expenditures.[3]

ERS has developed a model that generates world sugar price forecasts for timelier forecasting and improved scenario analyses to derive implications for future world prices and U.S. sugar policy. The model emphasizes the large influence of Brazilian sugar production and exports on world sugar pricing. Unlike all other sugar-producing countries and regions, Brazil's sugarcane sector supplies large quantities of both sugar and sugarcane-based ethanol. It is important for the price-projection framework to capture the factors influencing the choice of how much sugar and ethanol to produce, and this report describes and documents the resulting model.

USDA MODELING OF THE WORLD SUGAR MARKET

In addition to monitoring and analyzing supply/demand balances in the United States and Mexico, the monthly ERS *Sugar and Sweetener Outlook* examines developments in world sugar markets based on data and analysis by the Foreign Agricultural Service (FAS), LMC International, the International Sugar Organization, and others. At least twice a year (in May and/or June and December), ERS evaluates world production, trade, and pricing prospects for the current and out-marketing year.

ERS has done previous research on the structure of world sugar pricing. McConnell, Dohlman, and Haley (2010) emphasized the role of Brazil in determining the long-term course of world prices. As the world's largest exporter of sugar, Brazil has the dominant role in meeting the growing world demand for sugar, but its world market competitiveness is vulnerable to exchange rate volatility and uncertain developments in the domestic ethanol market.

The growth of flex fuel vehicles (FFVs) in Brazil has made its transportation sector the sugar industry's main competitor. FFVs give Brazilian drivers the option of using either gasoline, which has a minimum anhydrous ethanol blend requirement set by the Government, or hydrous ethanol (no blending with gasoline). Because ethanol in Brazil is derived from sugarcane, the price relationship between sugar and ethanol is fundamental to the supply of both products. At the same time, ethanol producers must keep their prices competitive with gasoline in energy-equivalent terms. Government-determined gasoline prices heavily influence ethanol prices and the subsequent return to sugar/ethanol producers. State governments impose different tax rates on ethanol, changing the economics of ethanol regionally within Brazil. Therefore, changes in gasoline and oil prices and tax policy can have major implications for domestic use of ethanol and producer profitability. These effects are transmitted to the world sugar market and directly influence world sugar prices.

Haley (2013) investigated trends in world raw sugar prices and concluded that there are three basic determinants of medium-to-long-term world raw sugar pricing. The first is the long-term equilibrium between world raw sugar prices and costs of producing sugar in Brazil, the world's largest sugar producer and exporter. The relationship between the Brazilian currency exchange rate and the U.S. dollar has an important impact on costs. The second determinant is medium-term world sugar supply/demand conditions. Two important measures from the U.S. Department of Agriculture's world sugar Production, Supply, and Distribution (PSD) database were derived to show that stockholding relative to levels of sugar consumption has an important effect on the sensitivity of the world sugar prices to changes in overall world sugar availability. Results also supported findings of the aforementioned 2010 sugar price volatility report that Government policies in

India, Pakistan, and China, along with short sugarcane production cycles in those countries, lead to volatility in the world sugar supply as these countries can swing from net exporting to net importing and back over a relatively short period. The third determinant, a risk-related component, is errors in forecasting supply and demand balances of previous years due to unanticipated events.

Traditional analysis of the world sugar market has stressed comparisons of supply with demand. Demand is relatively inelastic in the short to medium term, implying that consumers reduce demand only when world sugar prices move to very high levels. Over the same time span, sugar production has also often been considered unresponsive to prices because of the 1-year planting-harvesting-processing cycle for sugarcane and sugarbeets. Supply/demand conditions are reflected in stockholding, with prices the signal for market participants to allocate supplies between usage and stocks.

In recent decades, the structure of the world sugar market has changed fundamentally because of sugar/ethanol production tradeoffs in Brazil. The emergence and rapid growth of FFVs in Brazil has motivated large investments in sugarcane in the Center/South region. Already the world's largest sugarcane producer, Brazil has very large tracts of unimproved livestock pasture that can be developed for sugarcane cultivation. Because of good long-term prospects for continued population and income growth, large increases in the country's automotive fleet—and the subsequent demand for transportation fuel, both ethanol and gasoline—are expected.

These developments will be primary determinants of world sugar pricing. Any effort to make projections will have to carefully model Brazil's sugarcane and transportation energy sectors, emphasizing analyses of the sugarcane, sugar, ethanol, energy, and automotive industries.

There are reliable data with which to examine sweetener and transportation energy markets. Sources include FAS's Production, Supply, and Distribution (PSD) database (global supply and use data); FAS's Global Agricultural Information Network (GAIN) Reports (current policy and medium-term forecasts); Brazil's Ministério da Agricultura Pecuária e Abastecimento (MAPA); UNICA (Brazil's sugarcane industry association); Agencia Nacional do Petróleo, Gás Natural e Biocombustiveis (ANP) (Brazil energy statistics); Departmento Nacional de Trânsito (Deantran) and Associação Nacional dos Fabricantes dos Veiculos Automotores (ANFAVEA) (Brazil's automotive industry); Economic Research Service (world macroeconomic projections for USDA long-term projections); and LMC

International (sugar production cost estimates and production data for sugarcane, sugar-beets, and sugar).

MODELING BRAZIL'S SUGAR SECTOR

There are three primary tasks for developing this modeling framework. In each, simplifying assumptions are made to keep the overall approach as basic as possible. The tasks are:

1) ***Specifying how ethanol prices are determined (that is, within the framework).*** This poses the question of how ethanol is actually used, which involves consideration of fuel, export, and nonfuel demand, with fuel demand—because of its relative size—the most important. Relevant factors include consumer gasoline pricing and the ratio at which anhydrous ethanol is required for blending with gasoline. In a dynamic setting, we would need to project how underlying fuel demand will evolve over time. In a more complex exercise (not pursued here), much attention would be paid to national, regional, and local taxing policies and the vast array of other policies that favor or tax ethanol production and consumption. Further, export demand may influence domestic producer pricing. However, development of a model of the world ethanol market—though potentially important— is beyond the scope of the present study.
2) ***Determining net returns for sugarcane products.*** Ethanol prices come from the first task, and world sugar prices are determined simultaneously in the world sugar market. Because Brazil is the world's largest sugar producer and exporter, trends in long-run world sugar prices follow trends in Brazil's dollar costs of producing sugar.[4] Exchange rate changes, as well as agronomic and macroeconomic conditions in Brazil and other sugar-trading countries, have a strong effect on returns. Brazilian costs of producing sugar are the lowest among major producers and are likely to continue lower because of the country's infrastructural ability to produce sugar and ethanol from a single sugarcane crop. Also important, but harder to model, are the sugarcane sector's contributions to domestic energy production from the burning of bagasse (sugarcane plant residue left after sucrose extraction) and the sale of power in excess of factory needs to the energy grid.

3) ***Projecting area for sugarcane cultivation and the proportional split between sugar and ethanol by using net return estimates.*** Annual fuel demand for an automotive fleet composed of ever-increasing FFVs is projected to expand, perhaps as much 5 percent per year. With a very large area of land suitable for sugarcane production that faces low opportunity costs (mainly cattle grazing), a core rate of projected expansion may not seem unreasonable. The important element is to account for deviations from the core rate proportional to modeled sugarcane sector returns. Projected returns not consistent with the expected long-term path of those returns could have a very strong effect on estimates of overall production of sugar and ethanol. Also, the expansion of milling, refining, and distilling facilities could affect the technological potential for tradeoffs between sugar and ethanol. According to Brazil's Agricultural Ministry (MAPA), over the last 10 years, ethanol's share of the sugarcane crop has varied between 50 and 60 percent. A shift in investment incentives could boost this share above the 60-percent level.

Brazil's Demand for Ethanol

Table 1 shows Brazil's marketing-year ethanol supply and use from 2003/04 through 2012/13. Total supply, including imports, reached its peak in 2010/11 at 27.812 million cubic meters (m3) and has leveled off in the last 2 years. The growth of FFVs helped propel fuel demand for hydrous ethanol to 15.437 million m3 in 2009/10, but demand has since decreased to only 9.885 million m3 as falling gasoline prices have proven more attractive to consumers. Demand for anhydrous ethanol has grown in line with increased use of gasoline for Brazil's automotive fleet. Export and nonfuel ethanol demand have been much smaller than fuel demand but have been variable. In the years before hydrous ethanol demand increased, combined export and nonfuel uses constituted over 30 percent of total demand. The combined ratio has varied inversely with hydrous fuel demand, topping 30 percent in 2012/13 when hydrous demand fell below the 10.0 million m3 level but falling below 20 percent in the years of greatest demand for hydrous ethanol.

Table 1. Brazil ethanol supply and use, May/April, 2003/04-2012/13

	Anhydrous ethanol production	Hydrous ethanol production	Imports	Total supply	Exports	Anhy-drous fuel	Hy-drous fuel	Nonfuel ethanol plus stocks	Ex-ports/ Prod ratio	Non-fuel/ Prod ratio	Com-bined/ Prod ratio
2003/04	8,768	5,872	2	14,642	926	5,505	3,628	4,583	6.33	31.30	37.63
2004/05	8,172	7,035	0	15,208	2,539	5,817	4,464	2,388	16.69	15.70	32.40
2005/06	7,663	8,145	0	15,808	2,511	5,729	5,089	2,480	15.88	15.69	31.57
2006/07	8,078	9,861	4	17,943	3,846	5,143	6,960	1,995	21.43	11.12	32.55
2007/08	8,465	13,981	1	22,447	3,631	6,085	10,774	1,956	16.18	8.71	24.89
2008/09	9,630	18,051	2	27,684	4,689	6,307	14,450	2,238	16.94	8.09	25.02
2009/10	6,938	18,801	41	25,780	2,940	6,429	15,437	973	11.40	3.78	15.18
2010/11	8,027	19,577	207	27,812	1,896	7,811	14,594	3,511	6.82	12.62	19.44
2011/12	8,624	14,113	1,401	24,138	1,916	8,091	10,460	3,671	7.94	15.21	23.14
2012/13	9,695	15,749	216	25,661	3,480	7,988	9,885	4,308	13.56	16.79	30.35

Source: Production: MAPA; Trade: GTIS; Fuel demand: ANP; Nonfuel plus stocks: residual.

The course of projecting export and nonfuel demand is beyond the scope of this modeling effort. Because overall fuel (that is, gasoline and hydrous ethanol) demand is expected to rise strongly through 2024/25, it is assumed that the combined demand for export and nonfuel ethanol will average about 20 percent of the total.

The steps taken to model ethanol fuel demand, including producer pricing projections, are detailed in Appendix 1, table 1. The first step employs the Brazilian macroeconomic data used in ERS's International Macroeconomic Database (table 2) for projecting growth in Brazil's automotive fleet. This report uses a simple method of projecting population per automotive vehicle as a function of changes in real per capita Gross Domestic Product (GDP).

Table 2. Brazil macroeconomic projections through 2025

	Population (1,000)	Per capita GDP (US dollars)	Real/dollar exchange rate	Inflation rate
2000	176,320	4,360	1.83	7.0
2001	178,870	4,355	2.36	6.8
2002	181,418	4,408	2.92	8.5
2003	183,960	4,397	3.08	14.7
2004	186,489	4,585	2.93	6.6
2005	188,993	4,667	2.43	6.9
2006	191,469	4,789	2.18	4.2
2007	193,919	5,016	1.95	3.6
2008	196,343	5,210	1.83	5.7
2009	198,739	5,114	2.00	4.9
2010	201,103	5,433	1.76	5.0
2011	203,430	5,517	1.67	6.6
2012	205,717	5,538	1.95	5.4
2013	207,965	5,626	2.14	6.0
2014	210,174	5,761	2.25	5.5
2015	212,346	5,931	2.35	3.6
2016	214,479	6,106	2.45	3.9
2017	216,572	6,289	2.53	3.9
2018	218,622	6,480	2.61	3.8
2019	220,633	6,677	2.67	3.8
2020	222,608	6,883	2.74	3.7
2021	224,546	7,096	2.81	3.5
2022	226,443	7,318	2.88	3.5
2023	228,299	7,549	2.95	3.5
2024	230,113	7,789	3.02	3.5
2025	231,887	8,039	3.10	3.5

Source: USDA, Economic Research Service, Long-term International Macro Database.

Estimates of inhabitants per vehicle through 2011 are shown in figure 1, along with comparisons with ratios for the United States, Mexico, and Argentina. The United States has the lowest ratio, which has not varied much over the observation period. Brazil's rate has been higher than either Mexico's or Argentina's, but has been consistently declining as per capita GDP has increased. As the first data column of table 3 indicates, Brazil's population per vehicle declines to Mexico's and Argentina's 2011 level (3.9) by 2022/23, and the projected level for 2024/25 is 3.6. The implication for Brazil's automotive fleet is strong growth, from 35.0 million vehicles in 2011/12 to over 64.0 million vehicles in 2024/25. As figure 2 shows, practically all new automotive vehicle registrations in Brazil since 2008 have been for FFVs, implying near-perfect substitutability between gasoline and hydrous ethanol through 2024/25.

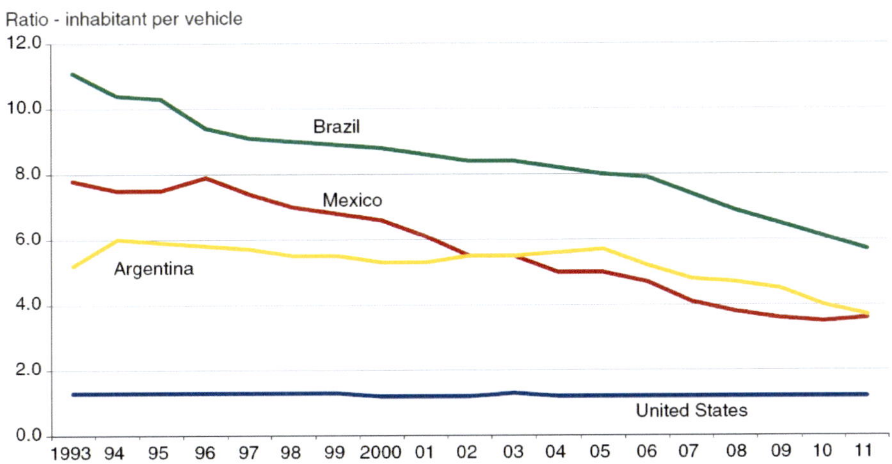

Source: Associação Nacional dos Fabricantes dos Veiculos Automotores.

Figure 1. Inhabitants per vehicle: United States, Brazil, Mexico, Argentina, 1993-2011.

The third data column of table 3 shows average fuel use per vehicle since 2000/01. Because there do not seem to be clear use trends through 2012/13 and because average fuel use stabilized between 2007/08 and 2012/13, the 2012/13 level of 1,286 liters per vehicle is assumed to hold throughout the projection period. (Fuel demand is somewhat responsive to energy prices, but no clear relationships could be discerned for use in the model.) The fourth data column shows calculated annual fuel requirements.

Figure 3 shows the modeling of automotive fuel supply and use. As explained, the number of vehicles and average unit fuel use determine demand. Fuel supply is constituted of gasoline C and hydrous ethanol. Gasoline C is a mixture of pure gasoline (referred to as "A") and anhydrous ethanol. The mix ratio is policy-determined. Because hydrous ethanol has only about 70 percent of the fuel mileage capacity of gasoline, the quantity for use must be adjusted downward by 30 percent to make it comparable with Gasoline A. The mix ratio determines the respective shares of hydrous and anhydrous ethanol in the total.

Table 3. Brazil automotive fuel requirements, estimated and projected through 2024/25

	Population per vehicle (calendar yr)[1]	Automotive vehicles (Adj. to Apr/Mar crop year)	Average fuel per vehicle (liters)	Fuel: gasoline C plus hydrous ethanol (gas basis) (1,000 liters)
2000/01	9.164	19,505,750	1,307	25,486,371
2001/02	8.934	20,262,000	1,221	24,730,154
2002/03	8.766	20,916,000	1,179	24,660,601
2003/04	8.643	21,560,750	1,150	24,798,802
2004/05	8.439	22,384,750	1,183	26,473,346
2005/06	8.236	23,284,500	1,169	27,210,191
2006/07	7.980	24,450,750	1,176	28,764,024
2007/08	7.600	26,067,250	1,215	31,666,853
2008/09	7.166	28,021,500	1,252	35,091,236
2009/10	6.724	30,248,500	1,250	37,801,624
2010/11	6.290	32,712,500	1,259	41,198,914
2011/12	5.887	35,013,454	1,255	43,950,016
2012/13	5.716	36,427,606	1,286	46,861,748
2013/14	5.569	37,856,063	1,286	48,699,366
2014/15	5.390	39,564,289	1,286	50,896,888
2015/16	5.195	41,496,915	1,286	53,383,085
2016/17	4.995	43,588,784	1,286	56,074,139
2017/18	4.801	45,780,947	1,286	58,894,214
2018/19	4.615	48,078,384	1,286	61,849,718
2019/20	4.435	50,486,528	1,286	64,947,638
2020/21	4.261	53,010,625	1,286	68,194,725
2021/22	4.093	55,655,439	1,286	71,597,106
2022/23	3.932	58,426,124	1,286	75,161,412
2023/24	3.776	61,328,735	1,286	78,895,433
2024/25	3.626	64,338,729	1,286	82,767,595

[1]Population per vehicle: percent change = -0.0219-0.564*(per capita GDP:percent change), adj R2=0.492, 1994-2010.

Source: Associação Nacional dos Fabricantes dos Veiculos Automotores; ANP, and USDA, Economic Research Service.

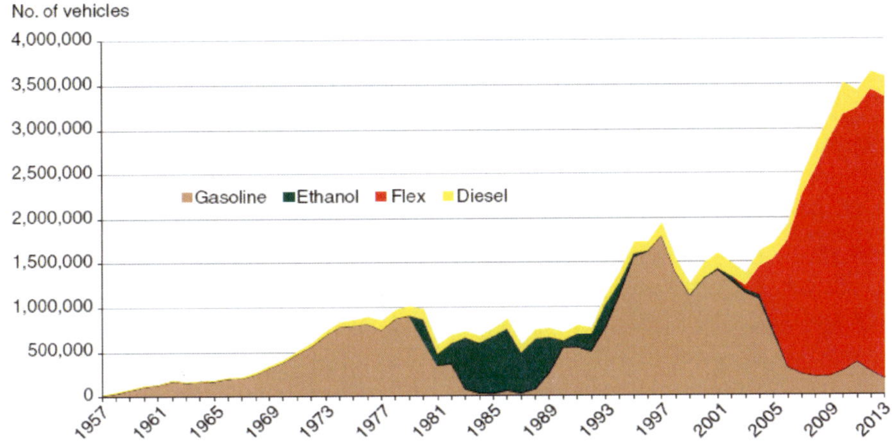

Source: Associação Nacional dos Fabricantes dos Veiculos Automotores.

Figure 2. Total vehicle registrations, by fuel type, 1957-2013.

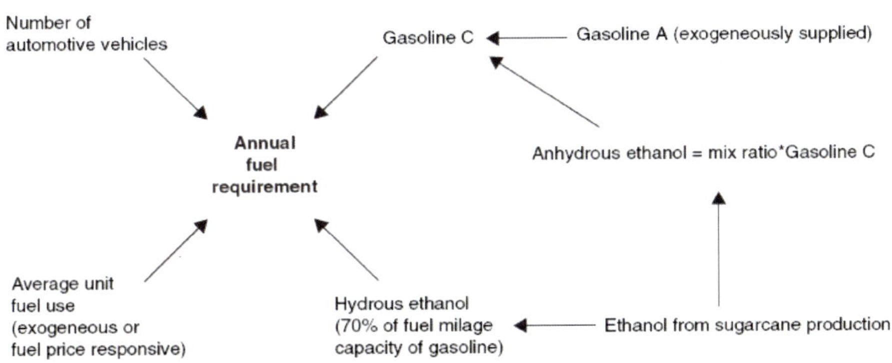

Source: USDA, Economic Research Service.

Figure 3. Modeling of Brazil automotive fuel supply and use.

The total amount of ethanol available in a particular year is recursively determined by expected prices and realized investments from the prior year. This means that technological constraints of time period t, along with expected prices for $t+1$ formed in t, fix the proportion of sugar and ethanol that can be produced in $t+1$. Although the quality of the sugarcane crop can affect this ratio, this cannot be known in advance.

The price of gasoline is currently policy-determined. Its monthly price ranged narrowly between 2.70-2.90 reais ($1.40-1.50) per liter in 2011-13. It is assumed that the price will continue to be determined by policy, but will grow in line with the overall inflation rate. An alternative specification could make price changes proportional to changes in real-denominated oil prices.

The relationship of percentage changes of the hydrous ethanol-gasoline price ratio as a function of the proportion of hydrous ethanol use to gasoline use is estimated (see Appendix 2, table 1). A statistically significant coefficient value of -0.2764 is used in the model to derive an annual pump price for hydrous ethanol.

Figure 4 shows the close correspondence of producer and pump-level hydrous ethanol prices. An estimated long-term co-integrating relationship between these prices is used for mapping the pump price to the producer price. Figure 4 also illustrates the close relationship between anhydrous and hydrous producer prices. Because an additional step is required to produce anhydrous ethanol from hydrous ethanol, its price is higher by approximately the additional cost of that step.

Net Returns to Sugarcane Production in Brazil

Table 2 in Appendix 1 outlines the stages for determining the economic benefits and costs of sugarcane and its products. These returns are necessary for projecting production.

Brazil produces sugarcane in two distinct areas: the Center/South and the North/Northeast. The Center/South area is the larger of the two and is where all sugarcane area expansion is expected. Center/South sugar production costs are among the lowest of those in all sugar-producing countries. The North/Northeast is the traditional base for Brazilian sugar production. Its costs are much higher, and its facilities are not as new or efficient as in the Center/South. Returns must be projected for both regions.

The source of production cost estimates is LMC International; ERS estimates these costs forward through the projection period for both regions. Costs are affected by sugarcane sector yields and other factors, including exchange rate movements, inflation, crop sizes, energy costs, and wage rates (USDA/ERS, May 2014).

Dollar-denominated world sugar prices are determined in the world sugar market. Because most sugar-producing countries have an October/September marketing year, the larger world sugar model uses the price averaged over October of one year through September of the next year. More relevant for Brazil is the April/March world sugar price that more nearly coincides with the

May/April crop year of the Center/South. ERS projects this price as a weighted function of the current and one-year-lagged October/September price and also converts it into real-denominated terms.

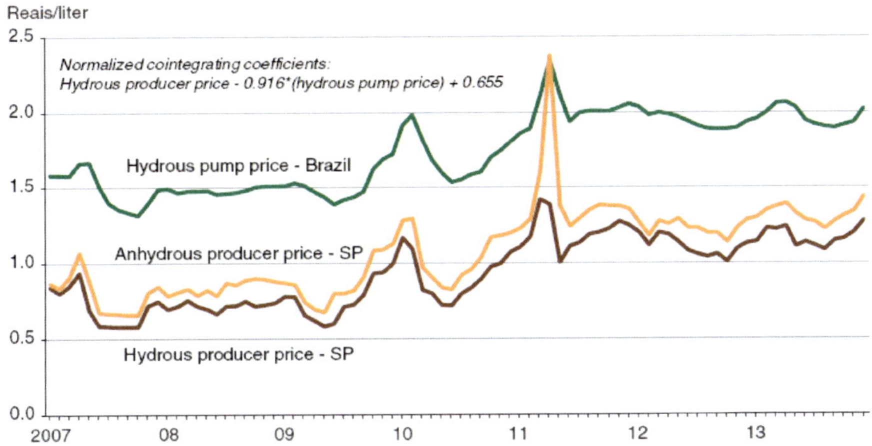

Source: MAPA (www.agriculture.gov.br).

Figure 4. Ethanol prices in Brazil Reais/liter.

Two closely followed Brazilian price series are the Very High Polarity (VHP) export price and the crystal sugar price, both in São Paulo. Both these prices are strongly correlated with real-denominated world raw sugar prices. ERS projects both these prices and combines them in a sugar-blend price using proportional weighting. ERS does the same for ethanol and then follows with a blend price, with sugar and ethanol expressed in terms of total recoverable sugars (TRS)[5] TRS is commonly used to refer to the sugar-solids content of sugarcane. In countries where only sugar is processed from sugarcane, the usual reference is sucrose content. Because other sugar solids besides sucrose contribute to ethanol production, the TRS measure is used instead.

Differencing of the TRS blend price and costs produces the net return, which can also be expressed in percentage terms.

Sugarcane Production and Use in Brazil

Figure 5 shows a diagram of Brazil sugarcane supply and use for any particular year. Sugarcane and TRS yields in both the Center/South and North/Northeast sugarcane production regions are variable from year to year, with no discernable trends. ERS uses averaged values for both types of yield in both regions and projects them as remaining flat through the entire projections period.

Appendix 1, table 3 shows the stepwise development of the production and use framework. Base area expansion is an exogenous assumption: 3 percent in the Center/South and 1 percent in the North/Northeast. These growth rates, especially in the Center/South, reflect the optimism of expanded ethanol fuel demand. Realization of these rates, however, is dependent on sector returns. In the absence of data to estimate a relationship, and in recognition of the need to allow for expansion, ERS incorporates into the framework a linear (straight-line) relationship between each region's average cash cost and average total cost of production (fig. 6). For revenues in excess of average total cost, the expansion rate is greater than the base rate, as shown in the figure. If the revenue equals the average total cost, the realized rate is equal to the base rate. Revenues between the average total and cash costs indicate an expansion greater than zero but less than the base, as per the linear schedule. For a revenue equal to the average cash cost, the expansion rate is zero, while a revenue below cash costs indicates area contraction.

Figure 7 shows the division of TRS for sugar production. The current-year ratio of the sugar-blend price to the ethanol price determines the next year's proportion of the TRS split between sugar and ethanol. Capital can be allocated between uses prior to the start of the producing season but cannot be adjusted after production has started. It is assumed, at least initially, that there is a low share (40 percent) of Center/South TRS that can only be used for producing sugar. This minimum reflects installed capital constraints on switching between sugar and ethanol production. As the sugar-ethanol price ratio increases, Center/South production capital is reconfigured to allow increased sugar production according to the schedule illustrated in the figure. With determination of their proportions, sugar and ethanol production can be projected in the next period.

ERS analysis could discern no income or own-price elasticity for Brazil sugar demand. Per capita sugar consumption is, therefore, fixed at the 2012/13 level for all projection years; that is, sugar consumption increases at the same rate as population. The framework assumes sugar imports equal to zero and a constant ending stocks level. Sugar exports are projected as the difference between production and consumption.

Appendix 2, table 1 provides more detail regarding the structure and the equations discussed thus far.

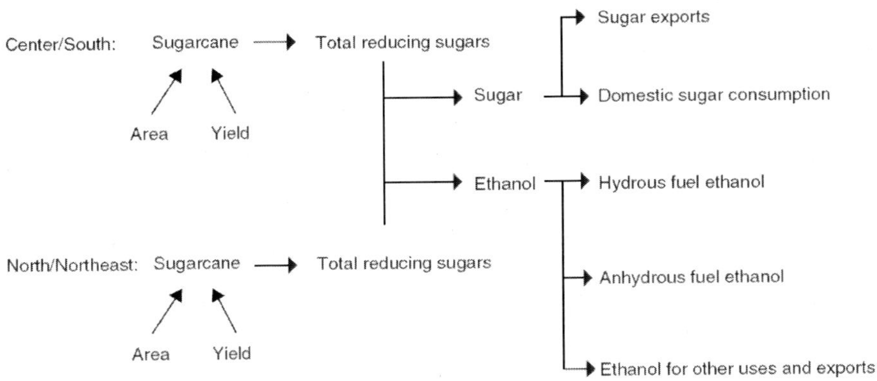

Source: USDA, Economic Research Service.

Figure 5. Brazil sugarcane sector - production and use.

Note: C/S = Center/South; N/NE = North/Northeast.
Source: USDA, Economic Research Service.

Figure 6. Brazil model: Area expansion as function of net production return.

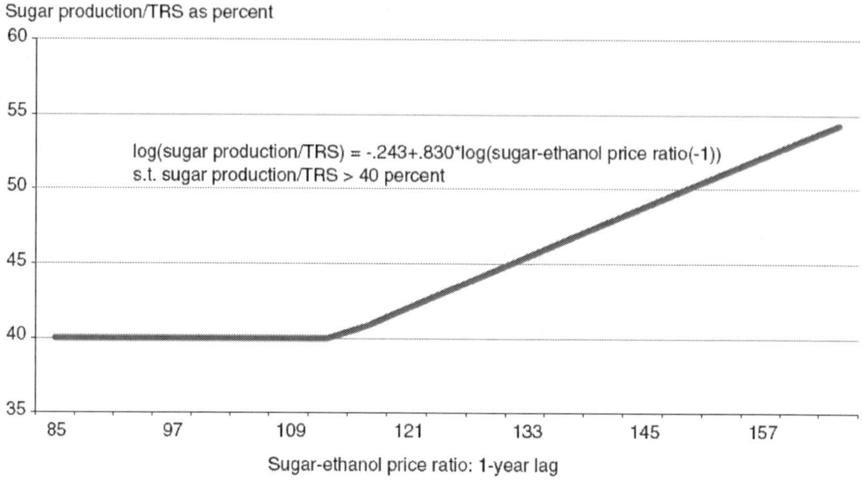

Source: USDA, Economic Research Service.

Figure 7. Brazil Center-South sugar production share of total reducing sugars (TRS).

FRAMEWORK FOR OTHER COUNTRIES AND REGIONS

Appendix 2, table 2 lists all other countries and regions in the analytical framework and provides a general specification of the sugar supply and demand in each country/region. The equations shown in the table are a starting point for estimation and are modified where necessary to provide for the best fit. Appendix 2, table 3 provides estimation results in detail.

The other-country specification is fairly simple: there is no detail regarding policies that influence production, consumption, or trade. The approach is very much one of reduced form, emphasizing quantitative responses to world sugar price changes with no regard for the intervening policy filters. Mostly, each region's equations provide a response mechanism to changes coming from Brazil. Although not ideal, the implemented specification is an approach that can be further refined in the future.[6]

Table 4. World sugar supply and use, base projection, 2013/14-2024/25

	2014/15	2015/16	2016/17	2017/18	2018/19	2019/20	2020/21	2021/22	2022/23	2023/24	2024/25
				1,000 metric tons, raw value (MTRV)							
Beginning stocks	43,379	41,030	40,389	37,376	40,870	41,622	40,823	41,161	42,734	44,252	45,637
Beet sugar production	36,676	36,787	37,867	39,570	40,090	40,898	41,716	42,242	42,743	43,290	43,784
Cane sugar production	140,287	146,117	145,431	154,964	155,531	156,502	160,542	165,467	169,167	172,749	177,128
Total sugar production	176,963	182,904	183,298	194,535	195,621	197,400	202,258	207,709	211,910	216,039	220,912
Total imports	56,189	59,031	57,860	60,383	61,102	61,842	62,953	64,659	66,480	68,514	70,535
Total supply	276,532	282,965	281,547	292,294	297,593	300,864	306,034	313,530	321,124	328,805	337,083
Total exports	56,189	59,031	57,860	60,383	61,102	61,842	62,953	64,659	66,480	68,514	70,535
Human dom. consumption	178,490	182,723	185,489	190,219	194,046	197,377	201,097	205,314	209,569	213,832	218,298
Other disappearance	822	822	822	822	822	822	822	822	822	822	822
Total use	179,312	183,545	186,311	191,041	194,869	198,200	201,919	206,137	210,392	214,655	219,120
Ending stocks	41,030	40,389	37,376	40,870	41,622	40,823	41,161	42,734	44,252	45,637	47,428
Ending stocks-to-use ratio (percent)	22.88	22.01	20.06	21.39	21.36	20.60	20.39	20.73	21.03	21.26	21.64
Production surplus	-2,349	-641	-3,013	3,494	753	-799	338	1,572	1,519	1,385	1,791
World price (cents/lb)	17.22	15.42	19.81	16.57	16.96	19.19	20.37	19.99	19.82	19.93	19.65

Production surplus = Total sugar production - Total use.

Source: USDA, Economic Research Service.

Model Projections

The model is run to generate a base solution for world sugar supply and use and for world raw sugar prices. Values of exogenous variables (such as exchange rates, per capita income, and population) are the same as those used in USDA's *Agricultural Projections to 2023.* The Brazil ethanol-gasoline mix ratio is set at 25 percent. The lower limit of sugar's TRS share is 40 percent.

Table 4 shows the evolution of world sugar supply and use through 2024/25. (Results for individual countries and regions are detailed in Appendix 3, table 1). Production, use, and stocks projections are shown in figure 8, along with earlier period results starting in 2000/01. Figure 9 shows world sugar production surpluses/deficits (that is, production minus use) and stocks-to-use ratios.[7]

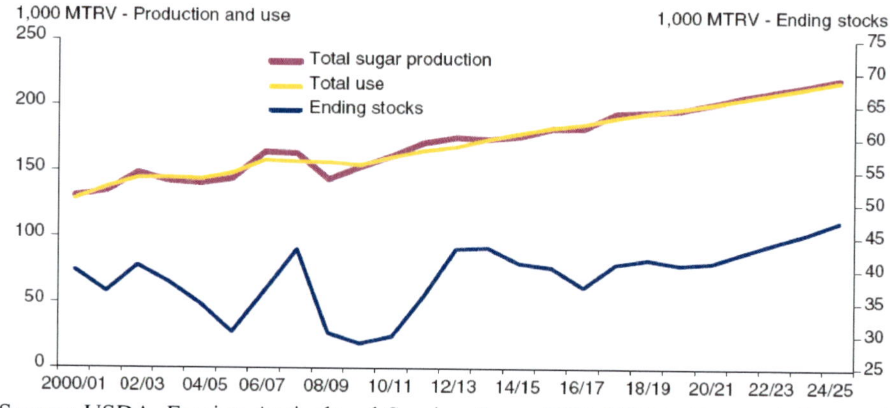

Source: USDA, Foreign Agricultural Service, Sugar PSD; USDA, Economic Research Service.

Figure 8. World sugar supply and use - estimated: 2000/01-2012/13 and projected: 2013/14-2024/25.

Total world sugar production grows from 174.8 million metric tons, raw value (MTRV) in 2013/14 to 220.9 million MTRV in 2024/25. Annual trend growth is 2.16 percent. Cane sugar and beet sugar increase at about the same rate, implying that the cane sugar share of total production is about 80 percent throughout.

Total use grows from 173.8 million MTRV in 2013/14 to 219.1 million MTRV in 2024/25. The annual trend growth is 1.98 percent. Per capita human consumption grows from 24.35 kilograms in 2012/13 to 27.49 kilograms in

2024/25, 12.9 percent higher. Production growth is more variable than consumption growth, especially in the first half of the projections period. Ending stocks show some variability in the first half, decreasing from above 25 percent in 2013/14 to the 20.7-22.1 percent range. Starting in 2020/21, stocks grow from 21.0 percent of use to 22.3 percent in 2024/25.

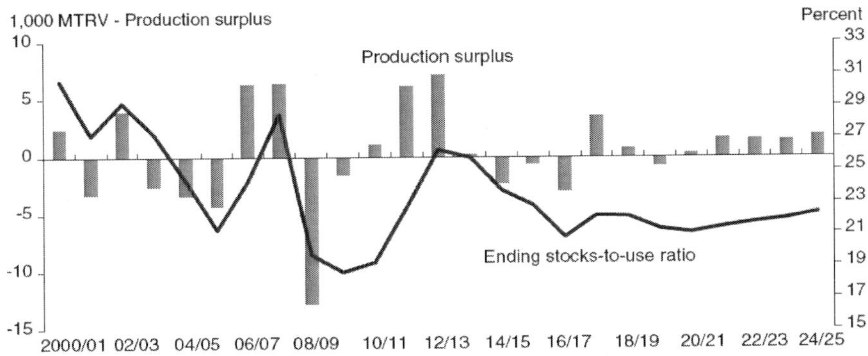

Source: USDA, Foreign Agricultural Service, Sugar PSD; USDA, Economic Research Service.

Figure 9. World sugar production surplus and stocks-to-use: estimated 2000/01-2012/13 and projected 2013/14-2024/25.

There are four instances of production deficits in the first 6 years of projections (2014/15 through 2019/20). The largest deficit—3.01 million MTRV in 2016/17—is completely offset by the next year's surplus of 3.49 million MTRV. The farther out one goes into the projections period, the more stable the production gains. As one might expect in a projections framework, there is much less production surplus/deficit and stocks-to-use variability compared with the historical period before the projections. This reflects the constancy of assumptions about policy and weather-related phenomena.

Table 5 shows projections for Brazil's sugarcane, total reducing sugars, sugar, and ethanol. Sugarcane area, production, and total reducing sugar production all increase 26.5–27.4 percent from 2014/15 to 2024/25. Ethanol production grows about 28.0 percent over the period, and sugar grows about 26.5 percent (fig. 10). Sugar's share of total reducing sugar production averages about 42.0 percent. Brazil's sugar exports in the first 6 years of the projections period average 27.850 million MTRV, compared with 32.179 million MTRV in the final 5 years. Brazil's share of total world exports varies between 45.0 and 49.5 percent.

Table 5. Base results for Brazil sugarcane sector

	2013/14	2014/15	2015/16	2016/17	2017/18	2018/19	2019/20	2020/21	2021/22	2022/23	2023/24	2024/25
Sugar blend price (reais/mt)	752.20	775.28	768.70	868.32	926.46	879.79	973.85	1,090.89	1,136.15	1,148.64	1,174.56	1,196.71
Anhydrous (sugar eq: reais/mt)	777.16	697.32	796.12	823.62	901.97	952.88	996.89	1,052.66	1,127.88	1,176.30	1,232.72	1,298.37
Hydrous (sugar eq: reais/mt)	695.90	624.41	712.88	737.51	807.67	853.26	892.66	942.60	1,009.96	1,053.31	1,103.84	1,162.62
Blend TRS price (reais/mt)	742.07	703.33	757.68	812.64	882.67	890.74	954.58	1,034.80	1,097.89	1,129.81	1,172.62	1,219.61
Cultivated area (1,000 hectares)	9,800	9,880	10,071	10,280	10,516	10,740	10,985	11,263	11,562	11,865	12,176	12,497
Sugarcane (1,000 mt)	640,000	667,208	680,568	695,158	711,614	727,196	744,280	763,612	784,457	805,498	827,134	849,489
TRS (1,000 mt)	87,322	91,436	93,273	95,279	97,540	99,682	102,030	104,687	107,551	110,443	113,416	116,489
Sugar (TRS eq: 1,000mt)	41,773	37,947	41,583	39,488	41,836	42,082	42,201	43,270	45,641	46,023	46,784	48,020
Anhyrous (TRS eq: 1,000 mt)	20,668	20,449	22,313	23,146	24,874	26,297	27,741	29,398	31,357	33,028	34,856	36,838
Hydrous (TRS eq: 1,000mt)	24,881	33,041	29,377	32,644	30,830	31,304	32,088	32,018	30,553	31,392	31,776	31,630
Ethanol (TRS eq: 1,000 mt)	45,548	53,490	51,690	55,790	55,704	57,600	59,829	61,417	61,910	64,420	66,632	68,468
Sugar (percent of TRS)	47.84	41.50	44.58	41.45	42.89	42.22	41.36	41.33	42.44	41.67	41.25	41.22
Total Exports (1,000 MTRV)	27,250	25,320	28,719	26,577	28,735	28,861	28,868	29,795	31,983	32,250	32,885	33,982
Brazil's share of world exports (percent)	46.44	45.06	48.65	45.93	47.59	47.23	46.68	47.33	49.46	48.51	48.00	48.18
World price (cents/lb)	16.92	17.22	15.42	19.81	16.57	16.96	19.19	20.37	19.99	19.82	19.93	19.65

Source: USDA, Economic Research Service.

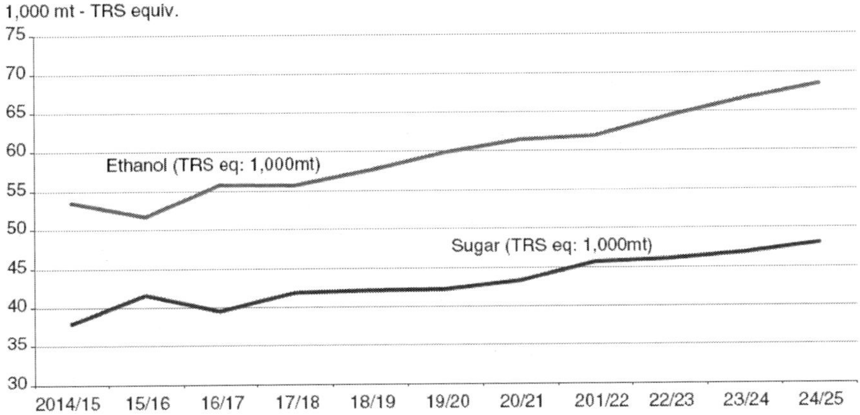

Source: USDA, Economic Research Service.

Figure 10. Brazil sugar and ethanol production projections, 2014/15-2024/25.

World prices are projected to range between 15.42 and 20.37 cents/lb. Prices are lower in the first half of the projections period: the average for the first 6 years (2014/15-2019/20) is 17.53 cents/lb, but the average for the remaining 5 years is much higher at 19.95 cents/lb. Prices in the latter half, like the supply and use measures, are less variable than in the first half.

Figure 11 pairs actual and projected world prices since 2000/01 with an index of Brazil Center/South dollar production costs. Prices in the early period averaged below 10 cents/lb. Starting in 2002/03, Center/South production costs began rising, and about a year later prices started rising as well. As noted earlier, Haley (2013) showed that world raw sugar prices and Center/South production costs are cointegrated, meaning that they are in a long-run equilibrium relationship with each other. The relationship holds because of Brazil's dominant share of the world sugar export market. During the projections period (2013-2025), production costs show only a weakly rising trend. This has a stabilizing effect on world prices, as seen in the figure, and is essentially true without the assumption of any destabilizing weather- or policy-related events taking place.

Table 6. Framework projections for Brazil and world sugar prices, 2014/15-2024/25 and 11-year averages

	2014/15	2015/16	2016/17	2017/18	2018/19	2019/20	2020/21	2021/22	2022/23	2023/24	2024/25	Average
Sugar blend price												
Base	775.3	768.7	868.3	926.5	879.8	973.8	1,090.9	1,136.2	1,148.6	1,174.6	1,196.7	994.5
20 percent mix ratio	777.8	727.4	818.6	920.6	863.5	989.8	1,094.5	1,092.0	1,164.5	1,192.6	1,206.4	986.2
Gas price 50 percent increase above inflation	774.3	786.5	885.2	943.2	895.2	946.0	1,031.9	1,106.9	1,134.0	1,123.8	1,126.5	977.6
10 percent per capita income reduction	777.1	736.2	829.6	922.1	869.4	986.9	1,099.1	1,106.5	1,160.3	1,196.1	1,213.9	990.7
10 percent exchange rate depreciation	824.5	793.3	929.6	973.9	912.9	1,078.4	1,157.8	1,169.2	1,247.8	1,260.3	1,291.9	1,058.1
20 percent exchange rate depreciation	858.7	817.8	1,013.5	1,010.5	929.9	1,192.0	1,183.9	1,187.8	1,342.5	1,282.7	1,373.2	1,108.4
Hydrous ethanol price (reais/mt, sugar equivalent)												
Base	624.4	712.9	737.5	807.7	853.3	892.7	942.6	1,010.0	1,053.3	1,103.8	1,162.6	900.1
20 percent mix ratio	573.6	674.8	671.5	743.2	800.3	810.8	883.6	941.7	966.1	1,032.5	1,069.9	833.4

	2014/15	2015/16	2016/17	2017/18	2018/19	2019/20	2020/21	2021/22	2022/23	2023/24	2024/25	Average
Gas price 50 percent increase above inflation	647.2	748.5	808.6	884.2	955.9	1,023.2	1,092.3	1,163.3	1,237.1	1,314.6	1,395.2	1,024.6
10 percent per capita income reduction	584.7	688.2	686.5	761.1	816.8	833.5	902.3	969.2	993.4	1,058.0	1,100.6	854.0
10 percent exchange rate depreciation	635.0	730.8	733.2	827.7	853.9	878.1	964.6	1,009.6	1,044.2	1,115.3	1,142.2	903.1
20 percent exchange rate depreciation	651.8	742.2	733.5	858.7	838.8	857.9	995.9	958.0	1,025.5	1,115.9	1,084.3	896.6
Total reducing sugars (TRS) blend price												
Base	703.3	757.7	812.6	882.7	890.7	954.6	1,034.8	1,097.9	1,129.8	1,172.6	1,219.6	968.8
20 percent mix ratio	669.9	714.9	747.4	838.8	848.4	905.3	1,000.0	1,035.0	1,078.1	1,133.0	1,160.2	921.0
Gas price 50 percent increase	716.8	785.6	863.1	934.3	959.5	1,023.0	1,102.1	1,177.9	1,235.7	1,280.7	1,333.0	1,037.4
10 percent per capita income reduction	678.5	728.8	763.9	852.7	863.8	921.8	1,015.3	1,061.4	1,096.8	1,153.5	1,186.9	938.5
10 percent exchange rate depreciation	732.2	780.2	835.3	918.8	905.5	988.4	1,081.9	1,113.7	1,167.1	1,218.2	1,246.3	998.9

Table 6. (Continued)

	2014/15	2015/16	2016/17	2017/18	2018/19	2019/20	2020/21	2021/22	2022/23	2023/24	2024/25	Average
20 percent exchange rate depreciation	759.9	798.5	870.0	958.1	903.8	1,022.4	1,120.6	1,090.7	1,203.3	1,234.0	1,246.5	1,018.9
Cultivated area (1,000 hectares)	0.001											
Base	9,880	10,071	10,280	10,516	10,740	10,985	11,263	11,562	11,865	12,176	12,497	11,076
20 percent mix ratio	9,856	10,018	10,182	10,387	10,579	10,789	11,038	11,291	11,553	11,828	12,102	10,875
Gas price 50 percent increase	9,889	10,100	10,343	10,616	10,887	11,181	11,509	11,869	12,250	12,643	13,054	11,304
10 per percent capita income reduction	9,862	10,034	10,209	10,424	10,627	10,848	11,109	11,380	11,656	11,947	12,241	10,940
10 percent exchange rate depreciation	9,900	10,107	10,333	10,595	10,830	11,100	11,412	11,727	12,059	12,406	12,752	11,202
20 percent exchange rate depreciation	9,919	10,140	10,390	10,680	10,918	11,213	11,554	11,861	12,221	12,584	12,939	11,311

	2014/15	2015/16	2016/17	2017/18	2018/19	2019/20	2020/21	2021/22	2022/23	2023/24	2024/25	Average
Sugarcane production (1,000 mt)												
Base	667,208	680,568	695,158	711,614	727,196	744,280	763,612	784,457	805,498	827,134	849,489	750,565
20 percent mix ratio	665,604	676,918	688,429	702,699	716,147	730,752	748,109	765,755	783,968	803,172	822,245	736,709
Gas price 50 percent increase above inflation	667,857	682,547	699,517	718,466	737,340	757,794	780,588	805,592	832,050	859,402	887,928	766,280
10 percent per capita income reduction	666,018	677,994	690,282	705,230	719,423	734,833	752,979	771,886	791,081	811,372	831,798	741,172
10 percent exchange rate depreciation	668,598	683,065	698,783	717,003	733,433	752,217	773,892	795,836	818,916	843,010	867,124	759,261
20 percent exchange rate depreciation	669,936	685,314	702,718	722,880	739,452	759,973	783,671	805,045	830,080	855,341	879,998	766,764
Sugar production (TRS basis, 1,000 mt)												
Base	37,947	41,583	39,488	41,836	42,082	42,201	43,270	45,641	46,023	46,784	48,020	43,171
20 percent mix ratio	37,857	44,145	39,112	42,359	43,921	41,446	45,200	47,047	45,943	48,306	48,034	43,943

Table 6. (Continued)

	2014/15	2015/16	2016/17	2017/18	2018/19	2019/20	2020/21	2021/22	2022/23	2023/24	2024/25	Average
Gas price 50 percent increase above inflation	37,983	40,578	39,732	40,780	41,824	42,956	44,218	45,602	47,068	48,582	50,162	43,589
10 percent per capita income reduction	37,880	43,565	39,216	42,248	43,393	41,674	44,486	46,770	45,796	47,644	47,760	43,676
10 percent exchange rate depreciation	38,912	43,227	39,691	44,546	43,458	42,644	47,059	47,885	47,979	50,515	49,958	45,080
20 percent exchange rate depreciation	40,317	43,969	39,911	47,908	44,051	43,077	52,320	48,453	51,225	55,161	51,663	47,096
Ethanol production (TRS basis, 1,000 mt)												
Base	53,490	51,690	55,790	55,704	57,600	59,829	61,417	61,910	64,420	66,632	68,468	59,723
20 percent mix ratio	53,359	48,627	55,242	53,957	54,245	58,726	57,358	57,937	61,544	61,820	64,713	57,048
Gas price 50 percent increase above inflation	53,542	52,967	56,145	57,701	59,251	60,930	62,800	64,851	67,021	69,265	71,605	61,462

	2014/15	2015/16	2016/17	2017/18	2018/19	2019/20	2020/21	2021/22	2022/23	2023/24	2024/25	Average
10 percent per capita income reduction	53,393	49,355	55,393	54,416	55,222	59,059	58,741	59,055	62,668	63,608	66,299	57,928
10 percent exchange rate depreciation	52,715	50,389	56,085	53,735	57,080	60,476	59,039	61,229	64,306	65,081	68,952	59,008
20 percent exchange rate depreciation	51,493	49,955	56,406	51,180	57,314	61,108	55,121	61,925	62,594	62,128	69,015	58,022
Sugar exports (1,000 mt)												
Base	25,320	28,719	26,577	28,735	28,861	28,868	29,795	31,983	32,250	32,885	33,982	29,816
20 percent mix ratio	25,233	31,197	26,214	29,241	30,640	28,138	31,661	33,342	32,172	34,357	33,996	30,563
Gas price 50 percent increase above inflation	25,355	27,746	26,813	27,714	28,612	29,598	30,711	31,945	33,260	34,624	36,054	30,221
10 percent per capita income reduction	25,255	30,635	26,314	29,133	30,129	28,358	30,971	33,075	32,030	33,716	33,731	30,304
10 percent exchange rate depreciation	26,253	30,309	26,773	31,355	30,192	29,296	33,460	34,153	34,142	36,494	35,857	31,662

Table 6. (Continued)

	2014/15	2015/16	2016/17	2017/18	2018/19	2019/20	2020/21	2021/22	2022/23	2023/24	2024/25	Average
20 percent exchange rate depreciation	27,613	31,027	26,986	34,607	30,766	29,715	38,547	34,702	37,280	40,987	37,506	33,612
World price (U.S. cents/lb)												
Base	17.22	15.42	19.81	16.57	16.96	19.19	20.37	19.99	19.82	19.93	19.65	18.63
20 percent mix ratio	17.32	13.74	19.45	16.76	16.29	20.41	19.42	19.49	20.88	19.59	20.33	18.52
Gas price 50 percent increase above inflation	17.18	16.13	19.80	17.14	16.95	18.22	19.28	20.06	19.33	18.84	18.58	18.32
10 percent per capita income reduction	17.30	14.11	19.54	16.71	16.52	20.08	19.87	19.53	20.68	19.86	20.27	18.59
10 percent exchange rate depreciation	16.18	14.57	19.75	15.24	16.52	19.93	18.52	19.44	20.05	19.00	20.02	18.11
20 percent exchange rate depreciation	14.80	14.32	20.00	13.48	16.23	20.76	15.59	19.86	19.32	17.40	20.79	17.50

Source: USDA, Economic Research Service.

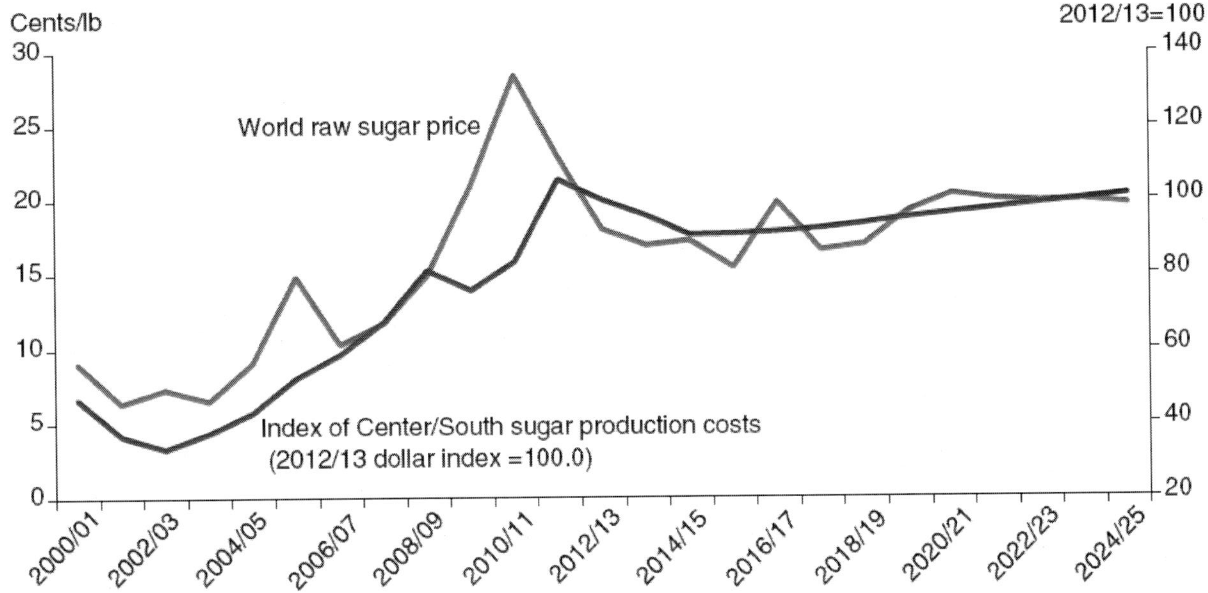

Source: Intercontinental Exchange No.11; LMC International; USDA, Economic Research Service.

Figure 11. World raw sugar price and Brazil Center/South production costs.

Table 7. Framework projections for Brazil and world raw sugar price: average percentage changes relative to the base scenario

Scenarios	Sugar blend price	Hydrous ethanol price	TRS blend price	Sugarcane production	Sugar production	Ethanol production	Sugar exports	Sugar worldprice
20 percent mix ratio	-0.84	-7.40	-4.93	-1.85	1.79	-4.48	2.50	-0.60
Gas price 50 percent increase above inflation	-1.70	13.83	7.09	2.09	0.97	2.91	1.36	-1.67
10 percent per capita income reduction	-0.38	-5.12	-3.12	-1.25	1.17	-3.01	1.64	-0.22
10 percent exchange rate depreciation	6.40	0.34	3.11	1.16	4.42	-1.20	6.19	-2.78
20 percent exchange rate depreciation	11.46	-0.39	5.18	2.16	9.09	-2.85	12.73	-6.04

Source: USDA, Economic Research Service.

Alternative Scenarios

The framework is tested by varying assumptions made in the base run. Specifically, these include: (1) lowering Brazil's ethanol/gasoline ratio to 20 percent; (2) specifying that the price of gasoline increases 50 percent above the inflation rate; (3) reducing projected income per capita by 10 percent (which implies lower demand for fuel because of fewer automobile purchases); (4) a 10-percent currency depreciation as measured by the exchange rate; and (5) a 20-percent currency depreciation. Annual projection results are shown in table 10 for the main Brazil sugarcane sector products and the world sugar price, along with averaged values covering the whole projections period for each variable. In table 7, these averages are divided by the corresponding average for the base period to facilitate comparisons.

These simulated changes cause aggregate TRS production to change. This type of expansion/ contraction change affects sugar and ethanol in the same direction. The exogenous changes also affect the relative amounts of ethanol and sugar produced—a substitution effect favoring one product over the other. Both the 20-percent mix-ratio scenario and the 10-percent per capita income reduction imply small reductions in sugarcane area and production, but the stronger reduction effect on ethanol production implies more sugar production. Sugar exports expand, and the world sugar price decreases slightly (less than 1 percent).

An increase in the gasoline price of 50 percent above inflation (a price equal to inflation is the base assumption) has the strongest effect on the TRS blend price in spite of a lower sugar-blend price. Under that same scenario, sugarcane production expands by 2.1 percent. This expansion effect is strong enough to imply an increase in sugar production of 0.9 percent, although the effect on ethanol production is much greater (2.9 percent). Although U.S. gasoline prices fell more than 30 percent between June and December 2014, mainly due to reductions in the price of petroleum in world markets, it is not clear that this phenomenon will affect Brazil. Gasoline prices have not fallen in Brazil because the national government controls the price of gasoline. If authorities were to lower gasoline prices to reflect lower petroleum prices, the producer return on ethanol sales would be lower and, all else constant, lead to more production of sugar. Over the longer term, the return to sugarcane would likely be reduced, with, consequently, less sugarcane grown.

The strongest effect on sugar production and exports comes from the depreciations of the currency as measured by the exchange rate. The value of world sugar increases in terms of reais proportionate to the exchange rate change, thereby favoring sugar over ethanol (little of which is traded or linked to world oil prices, at least as specified in the framework). Although sugarcane production increases (which could result in more ethanol), the relative price effect dominates so that sugar expands proportionately more than sugarcane production, and ethanol production contracts. The 10-percent currency depreciation results in a world sugar price reduction of 2.8 percent. The 20-percent depreciation, in turn, results in a 6.0 percent world raw sugar price decline.

The next section presents an analysis of forecast world prices from the base and alternative solutions on U.S. Federal expenditure using ERS's U.S.-Mexico baseline model.

Modeling Impacts on U.S. Sugar Policy

In addition to examining the impacts of alternative scenarios for Brazil or other countries on world sugar prices, the model can also be used to estimate the implications for U.S. sugar policy. With a sufficiently high level of U.S. sugar imports from Mexico, low world sugar prices can increase the likelihood of sugar loan rate forfeitures in the United States. As seen in 2012/13, sugar from Mexico competes with sugar imported by the United States from countries that have raw sugar tariff-rate quota (TRQ) allocations. If the TRQ sugar is not needed because of plentiful supplies from Mexico (and/or from domestic sources), the margin between U.S. and world prices contracts to discourage those TRQ imports from being supplied. If the margin (whose minimum value is probably about 3 cents/lb.) plus the world price add up to less than what a U.S. sugar processor needs to sell sugar to repay loans to the USDA, then the processor has an incentive to settle the loan by forfeiting ownership of the sugar collateral to the USDA, as set out in both the 2008 and 2014 Farm Acts. These Acts also contain provisions that require the USDA to purchase a sufficient amount of sugar in the market for resale to ethanol producers to forestall the risk of loan forfeitures. The difference between the sugar purchase price and the subsequent price at which the sugar is sold constitutes a subsidy expense for USDA. Table 8 details how domestic raw sugar prices and the unit subsidy can be determined in the model.

For illustrative purposes, table 9 shows the estimated impacts of the alternative Brazil scenarios (see table 7) on loan forfeitures and U.S. budget outlays. All of the illustrative scenarios indicate sufficiently low raw sugar prices to imply forfeitures in 2014/15, 2015/16, 2017/18, and 2018/19. The present value of the USDA budget expense in those years to purchase sugar and then resell it for ethanol is $214.4-$214.5 million, except for the final scenario. In the final scenario, a 20-percent exchange rate depreciation implies a sufficiently low world price in 2023/24 to add an additional $41.8 million (present value) to the total.

Table 8. U.S. raw sugar pricing and CCC-budget outlay estimation

Method 1 - U.S. raw sugar price when supported by world price
Margin between third-quarter U.S. and world raw sugar prices is a function of projected ending stocks-to-use ratio: U.S. raw sugar price = world raw sugar price + margin Margin = max(28.284 - 1.2673*[stocks-to-use ratio], 3 cents per pound) If the initial margin is less than 3 cents per pound, then: Minimum margin of 3 cents per pound achieved by increasing the tariff-rate quota shortfall up to 50 percent of initial allocation; and, if necessary, divert a required percentage of total Mexico exports to third-country destinations: these actions reduce U.S. sugar supply and thereby stocks so that the ending stocks-to-use ratio rises to a level that implies a 3-cent price margin
Method 2 - U.S. raw sugar price when supported by U.S. sugar loan rate program
U.S.raw sugar price in 3rd quarter is a function of projected ending stocks-to-use ratio: U.S. raw sugar price = max(43.301*[stocks-to-use ratio]^(-0.2532), minimum price-to-avoid-forfeiture) Minimum price-to-avoid forfeiture = loan rate + interest payable on loan + transportation cost less discount If U.S. raw sugar price = minimum, then private stocks-to-use ratio = (Minimum price^(-1/0.2532))/43.301 USDA purchase of sugar for ethanol = (total stocks-to-use ratio - private stocks-to-use ratio)*(total supply - use) Note: USDA purchase equal to zero if raw sugar price is above the minimum price-to-avoid forfeiture USDA sells sugar to ethanol producers at a price consistent with the value of corn used for ethanol production: $(\text{Sugar price})_{\text{cents/lb}}$-[(corn price - byproduct credit)$_{\text{dollar/bushel}}$*(100*1.378618)/56 + Premium-to-motivate purchase$_{\text{cents/lb}}$ where 1.378618= ratio of corn-to-sugar in pounds to produce the same amount of ethanol
U.S. raw sugar price = Max(Method 1, Method 2)

Source: USDA, Economic Research Service.

Table 9. Illustrative impacts of alternative Brazil-related scenarios on U.S. Federal Budget expense for Feedstock Flexibility Program (FFP)

Scenario	Present value in 2013/14[1]	2014/15	2015/16	2016/17	2017/18	2018/19	2019/20	2020/21	2021/22	2022/23	2023/24	2024/25
						1,000 dollars						
Base	214,372	60,691	62,615	0	53,354	52,589	0	0	0	0	0	0
20 percent mix ratio	214,467	60,691	62,615	0	53,376	52,672	0	0	0	0	0	0
Gas price 50 percent increase	214,375	60,691	62,615	0	53,355	52,591	0	0	0	0	0	0
10 percent per capita income reduction	214,443	60,691	62,615	0	53,370	52,651	0	0	0	0	0	0
10 percent exchange rate depreciation	214,389	60,691	62,615	0	53,358	52,604	0	0	0	0	0	0
20 percent exchange rate depreciation	256,226	60,654	64,174	0	53,435	52,624	0	0	0	0	48,779	0

[1]interest rate = 0.018.

Source: USDA, Economic Research Service.

REFERENCES

Haley, Stephen. "World Sugar Prices: The Influence of Brazilian Costs of Production and World Surplus/Deficit Measures." USDA/ERS, *Sugar and Sweeteners Outlook* SSS-M-297-01, May 2013.

McConnell, Michael J., E. Dohlman, and S. Haley. "World Sugar Price Volatility Intensified by Market and Policy Factors." *Amber Waves.* USDA/ERS, September 2010.

Organisation for Economic Co-Operation and Development (OECD) and the Food and Agriculture Organization (FAO), Agricultural Outlook 2013-2022. http://www.oecd.org/site/oecd-faoagriculturaloutlook/highlights-2013-EN.pdf.

"The Road to Forfeitures." USDA/ ERS, *Sugar and Sweeteners Outlook* SSS-M-303, November 2013.

"Long-term Projection of U.S. and Mexico Sugar Supply and Use Through 2024/25." USDA/ERS, *Sugar and Sweetener Outlook*, SSS-M-306, February 2014.

"World Sugar and High Fructose Syrup Production Costs: 2001/02-2012/13." USDA/ERS, *Sugar and Sweetener Outlook*, SSS-M-309, May 2014.

APPENDIX 1

Table 1. Brazil sugar-ethanol model component: Brazil hydrous fuel ethanol price determination

Stage 1 - project automotive vehicle growth
Stage 2 - project automotive vehicle fuel demand
Stage 3 - ethanol supply: size of current sugarcane crop plus production capacity proportions determined from price expectations formed in the previous year
Stage 4 - ethanol split into hydrous and anhydrous ethanol proportions based on policy-determined ethanol/gasoline mix ratio
Stage 5 - gasoline price is exogenous: policy-determined and assumed to grow at the inflation rate
Stage 6 - estimate: %A (hydous ethanol-gasoline price ratio) = ö*%A (hydrous ethanol use/gasoline use)
Stage 7 - project hydrous ethanol price based previous year's prices plus %A from stage 6
Stage 8 - project hydrous ethanol producer price based on consumption price
Stage 9 - anhydrous ethanol producer price set as proportion of hydrous price

Source: USDA, Economic Research Service

Table 2. Brazil sugar-ethanol model component: Net returns for sugarcane based products

Regions for each stage: Center/South and North/Northeast
Stage 1 - project costs of production from LMC International over projection period; Types of costs: average field, factory, administrative costs, plus cash/non-cash proportions as functions of sugarcane and total reducing sugar (TRS) yields and production plus inflation
Stage 2 - calculate April/March world raw sugar price denominated in reais per metric ton (mt) weighted function of October/ September world price, current and 1-year lagged, multiplied by corresponding period real/dollar exchange rate:
World raw: April/Mar, real/mt = 0.478*world raw:Oct/Sept,dollar/mt * real:dollar exch.rate + (1-0.478)*world raw (-1):Oct/ Sept,dollar/mt * real:dollar exch.rate (-1)
Stage 3 - calculate a blend sugar price of VHP (very high polarity) export (Sao Paulo:SP) and of crystal sugar in domestic market, both of which are functionally related to real-denominated world raw sugar price
VHP export (reais/mt) = 0.873*world raw (reais/mt)
Crystal sugar (reais/mt) = 3.114*world raw (reais/mt) - 2.142*VHP export (reais/mt)
Sugar blend (reais/mt:TRS basis) = (sugar proportion for export)*VHP export + (sugar proportion for consumption)*crystal sugar
Stage 4 - calculate blend ethanol producer price as weighted average of hydrous and anhydrous producer prices
Ethanol blend (reais/mt: TRS eq.) = (hydrous proportion)*hydrous producer (TRS eq.) + (anhydrous proportion)*anhydrous producer (TRS eq.)
Stage 5 - calculate blend TRS price as weighted average of TRS-equivalent sugar and ethanol prices
Blend TRS (reais/mt)= (sugar proportion of TRS)*sugar blend + (ethanol proportion of TRS)*ethanol blend
Stage 6 - calculate sugarcane products net return as difference between blend TRS price total average cost of production Sugarcane products net return (reais/mt:sugar basis) = Blend TRS/1.0495 - total cost, average

Source: USDA, Economic Research Service.

Table 3. Brazil sugarcane and products model component: production of sugarcane and products, and use

Regions for each stage: Center/South and North/Northeast

Stage 1 - set regional base area expansion
Center/South = 3 percent North/Northeast = 1 percent

Stage 2 - set projected area expansion on the linear evaluation of TRS net return:
Case 1: net return > total average cost --> projected > base
Case 2: net return = total average cost --> projected = base
Case 3: cash average cost < net return < total average cost --> 0 < projected < base
Case 4: net return = 0 --> projected = 0
Case 5: net return < 0 --> projected < 0

Stage 3 - sugarcane and total reducing sugars (TRS) yields set at predetermined values, allowing calculation of sugarcane and TRS
Stage 4 - determine split between sugar and ethanol for next year:
Max(estimated sugar/TRS ratio as function of world sugar price/producer price of hydrous ethanol, 100 - maximum ethanol share (60 percent initially))
Stage 5 - use stage 4 coefficient to calculate sugar and ethanol production
Stage 6 - sugar consumption set as fixed per capita (amount times population) and ending year stocks set at -295,000 mt, raw value (MTRV) and imports set at zero
Stage 6 - calculate sugarcane products net return as difference between blend TRS price total average cost of production Stage 7 - Sugar exports = Sugar production - sugar consumption

Source: USDA, Economic Research Service.

APPENDIX 2

Table 1. Brazil model: data sources and equation structure

Symbols:
LOG - natural log
D - difference operator
DX or DXtoY: X,Y - year or year month indicator - DX=1 or DXtoY=1 for period X or X to Y, 0 otherwise
Mix ratio - Policy-determined ratio of anhydrous ethanol blended with gasoline A to produce Gasoline C
(-1) - 1-year lag indicator
C/S - Center/South Brazil

N/NE - North/Northeast Brazil
SP - Sao Paulo
3-year average - average over 2011/12 - 2013/14

Automotive sector - hydrous ethanol price determination	
Data	**Source**
Population	USDA-ERS long term projections database: to 2024/25
Exchange rate: real/dollar	USDA-ERS long term projections database: to 2024/25
Per capita income 2000$	USDA-ERS long term projections database: to 2024/25
Crude oil price: $/barrel EIA refiner acquisition cost	USDA-ERS long term projections database: to 2024/25
Automotive fleet (no. of vehicles)	ANFAVEA
Fuel consumption per vehicle	ANP

Equations

DLOG(Population/vehicle) = -0.021914-0.502289*D2009-0.564284*DLOG(percap income) adj. R2 = 0.492
Automotive fleet projection = Population/(Population/vehicle)
Total fuel (1,000 liters): gasoline C + hydrous ethanol (gas basis) = Number of vehicles*fuel consumption per vehicle (2012/13level)
Fuel ethanol = 0.800*total ethanol from domestic production* (determined in production sector - see below)
Hydrous fuel ethanol = (Fuel ethanol - (mix ratio)*(total fuel))/(1-(mix ratio)*0.7)
Hydrous fuel ethanol: gasoline basis = hydrous fuel ethanol*0.7
Gasoline C = Total fuel - hydrous fuel ethanol: gasoline basis
Anhydrous fuel ethanol = (mix ratio)*Gasoline C
Hydrous ethanol sales ratio = 100*(Hydrous fuel ethanol: gasoline basis)/total fuel
Projected change in consumer prices = change in exchange rate
Gasoline C price = Gasoline C price (-1)*change in consumer prices - Note: gasoline price is policy determined
Fuel price ratio = 100*hydrous pump price/gasoline price
DLOG(fuel price ratio) = -0.0601*D200706to200707+0.0480*D200711to200712-0.0419*D201103to201104+0.4405*D201105
-0.2764*DLOG(hydrous ethanol sales ratio)+[ar(1)=0.4228] adj. R2 = 0.790
Hydrous ethanol pump price =.01*Gasoline C price*(projected fuel price ratio)
Hydrous ethanol producer price per liter = 0.916007*hydrous ethanol pump price-0.6553 from normalized cointegration coefficients
Hydrous ethanol producer price, sugar equivalent, per metric ton = 1000*(1.0495/1.676)*hydrous ethanol producer price per liter
Hydrous ethanol producer price, TRS basis, per metric ton = (1/1.0495)*Hydrous ethanol producer price, sugar basis, per metric ton

Anhydrous ethanol producer price, TRS basis, per metric ton = 1.11676*hydrous ethanol producer price, TRS basis, per metric ton
Pricing and Cost of Production sector - net returns determination

Data	Source
Field, Factory, Administrative Costs: total, cash, and non-cash, dollars per metric tons	LMC International.

Equations
Field costs, average, C/S (reais/mt) = 3.1805*change in consumer prices - 0.7574*TRS_yield, adj. R2 = 0.949
Factory costs, average, C/S (reais/mt) = -11.396+2.557*change in consumer prices+27.545*D2009-0.002269*TRS adj. R2 = 0.980
Administrative costs, average, C/S (reais/mt) = -8.895 + 0.683*change in consumer prices, adj. R2 = 0.951
Total costs, average, C/S (reais/mt) = Field + Factory + Administrative
Total costs, average, N/NE (reais/mt) = 267.49 + 6.163*change in consumer prices - 0.0053*sugarcane production, N/NE
Cash field cost, average, C/S (reais/mt) = ((Field labor: 3-yr average + Field inputs: 3-year average)/Total field (3-year average))*projected field costs
Cash factory cost, average, C/S (reais/mt) = ((Factory labor: 3-yr average + Factory inputs: 3-year average)/Total factory (3-year average))*projected factory costs
Cash costs, average, C/S (reais/mt) = Cash field + cash factory + administrative costs
Cash costs, average, N/NE (reais/mt) = Cash average: 3-yr average/Total costs: 3=yr average
World raw sugar price, April/March (reais/mt) = 0.478*(world sugar price, Oct/Sept (dollar/mt)*exchange rate(reais/dollar)) + (1-0.478)*(world sugar price (-1), Oct/Sept (dollar/mt)*exchange rate (-1) (reais/dollar))
VHP export price (reais/mt) = 0.873*world raw sugar price (reais/mt)
Crystal sugar price (reais/mt) = 3.114*world raw sugar price (reais/mt) - 2.142*VHP export price (reais/mt)
Sugar blend price, TRS basis (reais/mt) = (sugar proportion for export)*VHP export price/1.0495+(sugar proportion for domestic use)*crystal sugar price/1.0495
Ethanol blend price, TRS basis (reais/mt) = (hydrous proportion of total ethanol)*Hydrous ethanol producer price, TRS basis +(anhydrous proportion of total ethanol)*anhydrous ethanol producer price, TRS basis
Blend TRS price (reais/mt) = (sugar proportion of total TRS)*sugar blend price + (ethanol proportion of total TRS)*ethanol blend price
Sugarcane products net return, sugar basis, C/S, N/NE (reais/mt) = Blend TRS price/1.0495 - total cost, average, C/S, N/NE
Sugarcane production and use sector

Data	Source
Sugarcane, sugar, hydrous and anhydrous production, and share production data	UNICA.

Sugar consumption, trade, and stocks data	USDA, FAS, Production, Supply, and Distribution (PSD)

Equations

Base area expansion rate (percent): C/S = 3 percent; N/NE = 1 percent.
Projected area expansion rate, C/S, N/NE (percent) = Base area expansion rate*(100+100*(sugarcane products net return/(Total cost, average, C/S,N/NE-cash costs, average, C/S, N/NE)*.01
Sugarcane area (1,000 hectares): C/S, N/NE = sugarcane area(-1)*(1+projected area expansion: C/S, N/NE)
Sugarcane production (1,000 mt): C/S, N/NE = sugarcane area: (C/S, N/NE) * yield(C/S = 70mt/hectare, N/NE = 50mt/hectare)
TRS production (1,000 mt) = sugarcane production*average TRS/sugarcane ratio(C/S =.0001*137.50, N/NE =.0001*132.50)
Calculated sugar/TRS percent, C/S = exp(-0.243+.083*log(world raw sugar price, April/March (reais/mt)/Hydrous ethanol producer price, sugar equiv (reais/mt)))
Sugar/TRS ratio, C/S = max(calculated sugar/TRS, C/S,100-maximum ethanol percent share (initially assumed constant at 60 percent))
Sugar/TRS ratio, N/NE = 70 percent
Sugar production: C/S, N/NE (1,000 mt) = Sugar/TRS ratio: C/S, N/NE * TRS production: C/S, N/NE/1.0495
Ethanol production, TRS basis, C/S, N/NE (1,000 mt) = TRS production: C/S, N/NE - sugar production - 1.0495*sugar production: C/S, N/NE
Total ethanol production, hydrous basis (1,000 liters) = 1,000*(ethanol production, TRS basis, C/S + ethanol production, TRS basis, N/NE)/1.676
Sugar consumption (1,000 mt, raw basis) = Average per capita sugar consumption (54.14 kilogram)*population (millions)
Sugar imports (1,000 mt, raw basis) = 0
Sugar ending stocks (1,000 mt, raw basis) = -295
Sugar exports (1,000 mt, raw basis) = Sugar production(1,000 mt, raw basis) - Sugar consumption (1,000 mt, raw basis)

Source: USDA, Economic Research Service.

Table 2. World sugar model and region listing for countries/regions other than Brazil, with general equation specifications

Regions	Sub-regions or countries
North America	Canada, Mexico, United States
Caribbean	Cuba, Dominican Republic, Other Caribbean
Central America	Guatemala, Other Central America
South America	Argentina, Colombia, Other South America
Europe	European Union - 28, Other Europe
Former Soviet Union	Russia, Ukraine, Other Former Soviet Union
Middle East	Turkey, Other Middle East
North Africa	Egypt, Other North Africa
Sub-Sahara Africa	South Africa, Other Sub-Sahara Africa
South Asia	India, Pakistan, Other South Asia

East Asia	China, Japan, Other East Asia
Southeast Asia	Thailand, Philippines, Other Southeast Asia
Oceania	Australia, Other Oceania

Measure units/symbol definition:
Area = 1,000 hectares, for sugarcane (CANE) or sugarbeets (BEET)
Cost of Production (COP) = U.S. Dollars per metric ton of sugar
Yield = Metric ton per hectare, for crop (YIELD) or sugar (SUYIELD)
WPRICE = world raw sugar price
T = trend
EXRATE = exchange rate
Sugar consumption per capita (SUGAR_PERCAP) = kilograms
Stocks-to-use (STKSUSE) or Stocks-to-consumption (STKSCONS) = percent
Sugar quantities (production, TRADE:export, import, consumption, stocks, etc) = 1,000 metric tons

Supply and use components	Estimated equation structure
Area	LOG(AREA) = β0 + β1*LOG(AREA(-1)) + β2*(WPRICE(-1)/COP(-1))
Cost of production	COP = β0 + β1*EXRATE + β2*SUYIELD + β3*T + β4*WPRICE
Crop yield	YIELD = β0 + β1*T + β2*WPRICE(-1)
Sugar yield	SUYIELD = β0 + β1*YIELD + β2*T
Sugar production	SUGAR = AREA*SUYIELD
Sugar consumption per capita	SUGAR_PERCAP = β0 + β1*INCOME_PERCAP + β2*WPRICE + β3*T
Sugar consumption (CONS)	SUGAR_CONS = POPULATION*SUGAR_PERCAP
Stocks-to-use	STKSTOUSE = β0 + β1*(WPRICE or WPRICE/COP)
Stocks	STOCKS = STKSTOUSE*USE
Trade	TRADE = STOCKS(-1) + SUGAR - SUGAR_CONS - STOCKS

Source: USDA, Economic Research Service.

Table 3. Detailed equation structure for countries and regions other than Brazil

Measure units:
Area = 1,000 hectares
Cost of Production (COP) = U.S. Dollars per metric ton of sugar
Yield = Metric ton per hectare
WPRICE = world raw sugar price
T = trend
DXXXX or DXXXXtoYYYY=1 for year XXXX or 1 for years XXXX to YYYY, zero otherwise
Sugar consumption per capita (Sugar_percap) = kilograms
Stocks-to-use (Stkstouse) or Stocks-to-consumption (Stkstocons) = percent
Sugar quantities (production, export, import, consumption, stocks, etc) = 1,000 metric tons

Regions/supply and use components	Estimated equation structure	Sample period	Adj. R2
Argentina			
Cane_Area	LOG(CANE_AREA) = 2.384+0.5893*LOG(CANE_AREA (-1))+0.1281*LOG((WPRICE_11(-1)/CANE_COP(-1)))	1981-2013	0.713
Cane_COP	CANE_COP = 915.015-183.420*D2003-80.313*CANE_SUYIELD+19.138*EXRATE	1995-2013	0.772
Cane_Suyield	CANE_SUYIELD = -0.670*D1987TO1990+0.020*T+0.103 *CANE_YIELD	1995-2013	0.772

Regions/supply and use components	Estimated equation structure	Sample period	Adj. R2
Sugar_Percap	LOG(SUGAR_PERCAP) = -0.235*D1997+0.513*LOG(INCOME_PERCAP)-0.117*LOG (WPRICE_11)	1980-2013	0.939
Stkstouse	DLOG(STKSTOUSE) = 0.279-1.033*D2006TO2007-1.503*DLOG(WPRICE_11/CANE_COP)	1995-2009, 2012-2012	0.269
Australia			
Cane_Area	LOG(AUST_AREA) = 0.598-0.196*D2011+0.900*LOG(AUST_AREA (-1))+0.051*LOG(WPRICE_11(-1)/AUST_COP(-1))+0.104*D2000+0.134*D2012	1981-2013	0.966
Cane_COP	AUST_COP = 1274.615-278.877*EXRATE-50.072*AUST_SUYIELD	1995-2014	0.770
Cane_Yield	AUST_YIELD = 112.400-0.917*T-21.275*D2001TO2002	1995-2014	0.780
Cane_Suyield	AUST_SUYIELD = -1.496*D1999+0.140*AUST_YIELD	1980-2014	0.839
Sugar_Percap	SUGAR_PERCAP = 55.0		
Stkstouse	STKSTOUSE = 2.5 percent		
Other Oceania			
Sugar_Export	SUGAR_EXPORT = 175		
Sugar_Import	SUGAR_IMPORT = 295		

Appendix 2-Table 3. (Continued)

Regions/supply and use components	Estimated equation structure	Sample period	Adj. R2
Canada			
Beet_Area	BEET_AREA = 0.835*BEET_AREA(-1)+4.801*(1.07*WPRICE_11 (-1)+65)/BEET_COP(-1)	1981-2013	0.714
Beet_COP	BEET_COP = 791.60	2010-2013	
Beet_Yield	BEET_YIELD = 53.7	2009-2013	
Beet_Suyield	BEET_SUYIELD = 0.067*T+0.106*BEET_YIELD	1980-2013	0.829
Sugar_Percap	SUGAR_PERCAP = 34.367	2010-2014	
Stkstouse	STKSTOCONS = 20.494 percent	2010-2014	
China			
Cane_Area	LOG(CANE_AREA) = 0.224*D2003+0.187*D2008+1.013*LOG(CANE_AREA (-1))+0.231*LOG(WPRICE_11(-1)/CANE_COP(-1))	1995-2013	0.913
Cane_COP	CANE_COP = 375.580+27.282*T-84.267*CANE_SUYIELD	1995-2012	0.828
Cane_Yield	CANE_YIELD = 64.076	2000-2013	
Cane_Suyield	CANE_SUYIELD = 0.598*D2004+0.049*T+0.104* CANE_YIELD+[AR(1)=0.349]	1991-2013	0.944
Beet_Area	BEET_AREA = 250		
Beet_Yield	BEET_YIELD = 1.237*T+8.331*D2007TO2008	2005-2013	0.781
Beet_Suyield	BEET_SUYIELD = 0.114*BEET_YIELD	1980-2013	0.958

Regions/supply and use components	Estimated equation structure	Sample period	Adj. R2
Sugar_Percap	LOG(SWT_PERCAP) = -0.935-0.119*D2000TO2002+0.448*LOG(INCOME_PERCAP)-0.048* LOG(WPRICE_11)	1995-2012	0.966
Stkstouse	DLOG(STKSTOCONS) = 1.129*D2008-1.092*DLOG(WPRICE_11)	1996-2012	0.477
Colombia			
Cane_Area	CANE_AREA = 1.005*CANE_AREA(-1)		
Cane_COP	DLOG(CANE_COP) = -0.241*D1991+0.299*D1994-0.550*DLOG (CANE_SUYIELD)	1981-2014	0.292
Cane_Yield	CANE_YIELD = 113.145	1995-2014	
Cane_Suyield	CANE_SUYIELD = -0.959*D1985TO1988+0.094*T+0.106*CANE_YIELD	1980-2014	0.919
Sugar_Percap	SUGAR_PERCAP = 29.873+0.00170*INCOME_PERCAP-5.042*D1999	1980-2014	0.439
Stkstouse	STKSTOCONS = 20.611 percent	2010-2014	
Cuba			
Cane_Area	LOG(CANE_AREA) = 1.045+0.857*LOG(CANE_AREA(-1))+0.271*LOG(WPRICE_11(-1)/CANE_COP(-1))	1995-2013	0.901
Cane_COP	CANE_COP = 387.563-142.855*CANE_SUYIELD+25.215*T-122.937*D2002TO2005	1995-2013	0.940
Cane_Yield	CANE_YIELD = 32.311	1995-2013	
Cane_Suyield	CANE_SUYIELD = 1.181-0.028*T+0.087*CANE_YIELD	1980-2013	0.951
Sugar_Percap	SUGAR_PERCAP = 61.766-13.460*D2012	1995-2014	0.235
Stkstouse	LOG(STKSTOUSE) = 2.127-0.307*LOG(WPRICE_11/CANE_COP)	1980-2012	0.117
Dominican Republic			
Cane_Area	LOG(CANE_AREA) = -0.244*D1998TO1999+1.00472225*LOG(CANE_AREA(-1))+0.050*LOG((WPRICE_11(-1)/CANE_COP(-1)))	1981-2013	0.911

Appendix 2-Table 3. (Continued)

Regions/supply and use components	Estimated equation structure	Sample period	Adj. R2
Cane_COP	CANE_COP = 550.185+82.002*D2001-93.061*D2003TO2004-54.294*CANE_SUYIELD+5.539*EXRATE	1995-2013	0.475
Cane_Yield	CANE_YIELD = 13.526+1.223*T	1995-2013	0.584
Cane_Suyield	CANE_SUYIELD = 0.062*T+0.068*CANE_YIELD	1995-2013	0.912
Sugar_Percap	LOG(SUGAR_PERCAP) = 4.183+0.245*D1985TO1987-0.072*LOG(INCOME_PERCAP)	1980-2014	0.548
Stkstouse	LOG(STKSTOUSE) = 1.520+1.208*D1995TO1998-0.343*LOG(WPRICE_11/CANE_COP)	1995-2012	0.533
Egypt			
Cane_Area	CANE_AREA = 101.166+0.161*T	1980-2013	0.016
Cane_Yield	CANE_YIELD = 82.500+0.606*T+17.474*D2003TO2004-7.878*D2008TO2014	1980-2013	0.787
Cane_Suyield	CANE_SUYIELD = 12.229+0.045*T-0.039*CANE_YIELD	1996-2013	0.466
Beet_Area	BEET_AREA = 10.520+1.036*BEET_AREA(-1)-7.358*(WPRICE_11(-1)*1.07+65)/BEET_COP(-1)	1989-2013	0.943
Beet_Yield	BEET_YIELD = 45.662	1993-2013	
Beet_Suyield	BEET_SUYIELD = 0.058*T+0.100*BEET_YIELD	1993-2013	0.823
Sugar_Percap	LOG(SUGAR_PERCAP) = 0.534*LOG(INCOME_PERCAP)-0.068*LOG(WPRICE_11)	1995-2012	0.754
Stkstouse	LOG(STKSTOCONS) = 2.607-2.223*D2000-0.688*LOG(WPRICE_11/CANE_COP)	1995-2012	0.575

Regions/supply and use components	Estimated equation structure	Sample period	Adj. R2
Other North Africa			
Cane_Production	CANE_PRODUCTION = 350		
Beet_Production	BEET_PRODUCTION = 60		
Sugar_consumption	SUGARNA_CONS = 1078.145802 + 71.82620865*T - 637.7582697*D2011	1995-2014	
Stkstouse	STKSTOCONS = 11.41 percent	2010-2014	
European Union			
Beet_Yield	BEET_YIELD = 20.821+1.522*T	2005-2013	0.743
Beet_Suyield	BEET_SUYIELD = 0.152*BEET_YIELD	1995-2013	0.945
Sugar_Percap	SUGAR_PERCAP =.35402		
Stkstouse	STKSTOUSE = WPRICE_11^(-0.25)		
Other Europe			
Beet_Production	BEET_PRODUCTION = MOVING AVERAGE(5 year)		
Sugar_exports	SUGAR_EXPORTS = 325		
Sugar_consumption	SUGAR_CONS = 0.995*(SUGAR_CONS(-1))		
Stkstouse	STKSTOCONS = 33.0 percent		
Guatemala			
Cane_Area	LOG(CANE_AREA) = 0.342+0.942*LOG(CANE_AREA (-1))+0.060*LOG(WPRICE_11(-1)/CANE_COP(-1))	1990-2013	0.985
Cane_COP	CANE_COP = -137.470*D1999TO2003-52.684*CANE_SUYIELD+ 115.300*EXRATE	1995-2013	0.784
Cane_Yield	CANE_YIELD = 88.258	1995-2013	
Cane_Suyield	CANE_SUYIELD = 0.054*T+0.098*CANE_YIELD+0.829*D2000TO2005	1995-2013	0.889
Sugar_Percap	DLOG(SUGAR_PERCAP) = -0.044 - 0.095*D2005+0.068*D2007TO2009+3.652*DLOG(INCOME_PERCAP)	1995-2014	0.536

Appendix 2-Table 3. (Continued)

Regions/supply and use components	Estimated equation structure	Sample period	Adj. R2
Stkstouse	LOG(STKSTOUSE) = 2.158-1.095*D1998TO2004-0.986*LOG(WPRICE_11/CANE_COP)+[AR(1)=0.5200015723]	1983-2012	0.747
India			
Cane_Area	LOG(INDIA_AREA) = 0.175*LOG(WPRICE_11(-1)/INDIA_COP(-1))-0.272*LOG(INDIA_AREA(-2))-0.132*LOG(INDIA_AREA (-3)) 0.009*LOG(INDIA_AREA(-4)) + 0.149*LOG(INDIA_AREA(-5)) + 0.29*LOG(INDIA_AREA(-6))+0.43*LOG(INDIA_AREA(-7)) +0.571*LOG(INDIA_AREA(-8))	1989-2013	0.780
Cane_COP	CANE_COP = -58.562*INDIA_SUYIELD+18.0824*EXRATE	1995-2013	0.496
Cane_Yield	INDIA_YIELD = 68.102-8.716*D2004	1995-2013	0.352
Cane_Suyield	INDIA_SUYIELD = -0.531*D1996+0.110*INDIA_YIELD	1995-2013	0.807
Sugar_Percap	LOG(INDIA_CONSPERCAP) = 1.011+0.366*LOG(INDIA_PERCAPINCOME)-0.096*LOG(WPRICE_11)	1990-2012	0.897
Stkstouse	DLOG(INDIA_STKSTOUSE)=0.194-4.048833623*DLOG(INDIA_CONS)-0.696*DLOG(WPRICE_11)	1981-2012	0.228
Japan			
Cane_Area	CANE_AREA = 22		
Cane_Suyield	CANE_SUYIELD = 0.118*CANE_YIELD	1980-2013	0.836
Beet_Area	BEET_AREA = 60		
Beet_Yield	BEET_YIELD = 51.011+0.292*T	1980-2013	0.264
Beet_Suyield	BEET_SUYIELD = 0.166*BEET_YIELD	1995-2013	0.806
Sugar_Percap	SWT_PERCAP(20.75) - HFCS_PERCAP(6.00)		

Regions/supply and use components	Estimated equation structure	Sample period	Adj. R2
Stkstouse	STKSTOCONS = 26.607 percent	2009-2014	
Other East Asia			
Cane_Production	CANE_PRODUCTION = 65		
Sugar_Percap	ROASIACONS = 1645.720+29.268*T-0.595*WPRICE_11+209.739*D1997	1995-2012	0.802
Stkstouse	STKSTOCONS = 31.0 percent	Stkstouse	
Mexico			
Cane_Area	LOG(CANE_AREA) = 1.007*LOG(CANE_AREA(-1))+0.060*LOG (WPRICE_11(-1)/CANE_COP(-1))	1993-2013	0.863
Cane_COP	CANE_COP = -29.135*CANE_SUYIELD+53.012*EXRATE	1998-2013	0.771
Cane_Yield	CANE_YIELD = 70.853	2000-2014	
Cane_Suyield	CANE_SUYIELD = 0.0179*T+0.106*CANE_YIELD	1998-2014	0.868
Swt_Percap	SWT_PERCAP = 23.266+0.003*INCOME_PERCAP	1987-2014	0.825
HFCS	HFCS: as specified in USDA sugar baseline model		
Sugar_Percap	SUGAR_PERCAP = (SWT_PERCAP*POP-HFCS)/POP		
Stkstocons	STKSTOCONS = 22.0 percent		
Other Central America			
Cane_Area	LOG(CANE_AREA) = 0.966+0.836*LOG(CANE_AREA(-1))+0.069*LOG(WPRICE_11(-1)/CANE_COP(-1))	1995-2013	0.815
Cane_COP	CANE_COP = 136.166+18.951*CANE_SUYIELD+0.360*WPRICE_11+99.651*D2008TO2009+[AR(1)=-0.5187034158]	1995-2012	0.923
Cane_Yield	CANE_YIELD = 60.471+0.522*T	1980-2013	0.776
Cane_Suyield	CANE_SUYIELD = 0.102*CANE_YIELD+[AR(1)=0.6802225293]	1995-2013	0.813

Appendix 2-Table 3. (Continued)

Regions/supply and use components	Estimated equation structure	Sample period	Adj. R2
Sugar_Percap	SUGAR_PERCAP = 34.358+0.305*T+1.382*D1998-2.131*D2005TO2011	1995-2014	0.926
Stkstouse	LOG(STKSTOUSE) = 2.945-0.280*LOG(WPRICE_11/CANE_COP)+[AR(1)=0.8923098015]	1995-2012	0.453
Other South America			
Cane_Area	CANE_AREA = CANE_AREA(-1)*(1+PERCENTCHANGE (WORLDPRICE(-1))		
Cane_Yield	CANE_YIELD = 61.935+0.169*T	1995-2013	0.103
Cane_Suyield	CANE_SUYIELD = 0.043*T+0.084*CANE_YIELD	1980-2013	0.795
Beet_Area	BEET_AREA = BEET_AREA(-1)*(1+PERCENTCHANGE (WORLDPRICE(-1))		
Beet_Yield	BEET_YIELD = 40.122+1.945*T-17.560*D2009-11.144*D1996TO2002	1983-2012	0.940
Beet_Suyield	BEET_SUYIELD = 0.145*BEET_YIELD	1983-2013	0.968
Sugar_Percap	SUGAR_PERCAP=1.005*SUGAR_PERCAP(-1)		
Stkstouse	LOG(STKSTOCONS) = 3.553-0.1864388644*LOG(WPRICE_11/CANE_COP)+[AR(1)=0.8156111093]	1995-2012	0.811
Pakistan			
Cane_Area	LOG(CANE_AREA) = 0.297*D1989TO1995-0.100*LOG(CANE_AREA (-2))+0.135*LOG(CANE_AREA(-3)) +0.369*LOG(CANE_AREA (-4))+0.604*LOG(CANE_AREA(-5))	1987-2013	0.882
Cane_COP	CANE_COP = 320.415-120.091*D2002+180.630*D2009TO2010+4.221*EXRATE- 27.782*CANE_SUYIELD	1980-2013	0.878
Cane_Yield	CANE_YIELD = 35.736+0.548*T	1980-2013	0.845

Regions/supply and use components	Estimated equation structure	Sample period	Adj. R2
Cane_Suyield	CANE_SUYIELD = 0.022*T+0.086*CANE_YIELD	1980-2013	0.920
Sugar_Percap	SUGAR_PERCAP = 20.735+2.806*D1996+1.220*D1998+1.934*D2001+0.00175* INCOME_PERCAP	1995-2014	0.839
Stkstouse	LOG(STKSTOCONS) = 0.593*D2004TO2008+0.711*D2011TO2012+0.891*LOG (SUGAR_PERCAP)	1995-2014	0.667
Philippines			
Cane_Area	LOG(CANE_AREA) = 1.008*LOG(CANE_AREA(-1))+0.110*LOG (WPRICE_11(-1)/CANE_COP(-1))	1995-2013	0.723
Cane_COP	CANE_COP = 361.669+192.326*D2009TO2013	1995-2013	0.727
Cane_Yield	CANE_YIELD = 59.268-9.491*D2010	1995-2013	0.149
Cane_Suyield	CANE_SUYIELD = 3.081-0.949*D1986TO2000-0.724*D2001-0.024*T+0.053*CANE_YIELD	1980-2013	0.867
Sugar_Percap	SUGAR_PERCAP = 20.9	2014	
Stkstouse	STKSTOUSE = 35.0 percent		
Other Southeast Asia			
Cane_Production	SEASIA_PROD = 744.618+10.847*T+0.681* SEASIA_PROD(-1)	1981-2014	0.841
Sugar_Consumption	SEASIA_CONS = 552.233+256.9*T	2000-2014	0.972
Russia			
Beet_Area	PERCENTCHANGE_AREA = PERCENTCHANGE(WORLDPRICE(-1)*EXRATE(-1)/COP(-1))^.578	2013	

Appendix 2-Table 3. (Continued)

Regions/supply and use components	Estimated equation structure	Sample period	Adj. R2
Beet_COP	BEET_COP = 42.410*EXRATE-136.487*BEET_SUYIELD	2009-2013	0.633
Beet_Suyield	BEET_SUYIELD = 0.681*D2010+0.00235*T+0.1074*BEET_YIELD	2000-2013	0.952
Sugar_Percap	SUGAR_PERCAP = 40.0		
Stkstouse	LOG(STKSTOCONS) = 1.579+1.253*D2001TO2003-1.666*LOG((1.07*WPRICE_11+65)/BEET_COP)	2000-2012	0.831
South Africa			
Cane_Area	CANE_AREA = 275		
Cane_COP	CANE_COP = 424.009-111.475*D2000TO2003-28.173*CANE_SUYIELD+17.008*EXRATE	1980-2013	0.750
Cane_Yield	CANE_YIELD = 65.678	1996-2013	Cane_Yield
Cane_Suyield	CANE_SUYIELD = 0.021*T+0.115*CANE_YIELD	1980-2013	Cane_Suyield
Sugar_Percap	SUGAR_PERCAP = 1.01*SUGAR_PERCAP(-1)		
Stkstouse	DLOG(STKSTOCONS) = -0.757*D2007TO2009-0.578*DLOG (WPRICE_11)	1981-2012	0.447
Sub-Saharan Africa			
Cane_Production	LOG(SS_CANEPRODN) = 2.286+0.737*LOG(SS_CANEPRODN (-1))+0.0515*LOG(WPRICE_11(-1)/SS_COP(-1))	2001-2013	0.927
Cane_COP	DLOG(SS_COP) = -0.810*DLOG(SS_SUYIELD) + 0.00153*T	1996-2013	0.096
Sugar_Percap	SS_PERCAPCONS = 5.401+0.007*SS_PERCAPINCOME	1998-2014	0.873
Stkstouse	LOG(SS_STKSTOCONS) = 2.425-0.312*D1997TO1999+0.863*LOG(SS_PERCAPCONS)-0.198*LOG (WPRICE_11)	1995-2012	0.759

Regions/supply and use components	Estimated equation structure	Sample period	Adj. R2
Thailand			
Cane_Production	LOG(THAI_AREA) = 2.130+0.232*LOG(WPRICE_11(-1)/THAI_COP(-1))+0.696*LOG(THAI_AREA(-1))	1982-2013	0.814
Cane_COP	THAI_COP = -36.399*THAI_SUYIELD+20.552*T+[AR(1)=0.834]	1995-2013	0.842
Cane_Yield	THAI_YIELD = 32.496+1.223*T	1995-2013	0.473
Cane_Suyield	THAI_SUYIELD = 0.015*T+0.104*THAI_YIELD	1985-2013	0.965
Sugar_Percap	LOG(THAI_CONSPERCAP) = 2.176-0.035*D1990TO1997-0.016*D 2004TO2008 +0.266*LOG(THAI_PERCAPINCOME)-0.0198*LOG (WPRICE_11)	1980-2012	0.995
Ending stocks	THAI_STOCKS = 1,500.		
Turkey			
Beet_Area	LOG(BEET_AREA) = 2.657-0.328*D1996+0.528*LOG(BEET_AREA (-1))+0.0678*WPRICE_BTEQ(-1)/BEET_COP(-1)+0.0977*WPRICE_BTEQ (-2)/BEET_COP(-2)	1982-2013	0.424
Beet_COP	BEET_COP = 339.567-153.960*D2001TO2003-16.975*BEET_SUYIELD+240.843*EXRATE+[AR(1)=0.706]	1981-2013	0.892
Beet_Yield	BEET_YIELD = 18.812+0.892*T	1995-2013	0.754
Beet_Suyield	BEET_SUYIELD = 0.022*T+0.125*BEET_YIELD	1980-2013	0.937
Sugar_Percap	SUGAR_PERCAP = 1.603+0.002022*INCOME_PERCAP+3.572*D2010+[AR(1)=0.9678]	1995-2014	0.756
Stkstouse	LOG(STKSTOCONS) = 5.899-0.470*LOG(WPRICE_11)	1995-2012	0.256
Other Middle East			
Beet_Production	BEET_PRODUCTION = 800	2014	
Cane_Production	CANE_PRODUCTION = 350	2014	

Appendix 2-Table 3. (Continued)

Regions/supply and use components	Estimated equation structure	Sample period	Adj. R2
Beet_Production	BEET_PRODUCTION = 800	2014	
Sugar_Percap	LOG(ME_CONSPERCAP) = -4.153-0.145*D2011+0.891*LOG(ME_INCOMEPERCAP)+[AR(1)=0.562]	1995-2014	0.919
Stkstouse	LOG(ME_STKSTOCONS) = 4.145+0.444*D2005TO2008-0.186*LOG(WPRICE_11)	1995-2012	0.753
Ukraine			
Beet_Area	BEET_AREA = -389.184*D2009+0.9062521522*BEET_AREA (-1)+109.137*WPRICE_BTEQ(-1)/BEET_COP(-1)	1993-2013	0.966
Beet_COP	BEET_COP = 526.718+380.666*D2008+48.194*EXRATE	1992-2013	0.744
Beet_Yield	BEET_YIELD = 45.0	2014 forecast	
Beet_Suyield	BEET_SUYIELD = 0.120*BEET_YIELD	1992-2013	
Sugar_Percap	SUGAR_PERCAP = 41.0		
Stkstouse	STKSTOCONS = 20.25 percent	2010-2013	
United States			
Cane_Area	CANE_AREA = 338.533		
Cane_Yield	CANE_YIELD = 75.726	1995-2014	
Cane_Suyield	CANE_SUYIELD = 0.038*T+0.109*CANE_YIELD	1995-2014	0.871
Beet_Area	LOG(BEET_AREA) = -0.210*D2009+0.9311167084*LOG(BEET_AREA (-1))+0.072*DNAFTA*LOG(1.07*WPRICE_11(-1)+65)	2008-2013	0.099
Beet_Yield	BEET_YIELD = 31.422+0.875*T	1995-2014	0.675
Beet_Suyield	BEET_SUYIELD = 2.298+0.596*D2009+0.112*T+0.054*BEET_YIELD	1995-2014	0.967
TRQ_Shortfall	TRQ_SHORTFALL = 100 +.25*MAX(0, IMPORTS from MEXICO - 1,000)		
Sugar_Percap	SUGAR_PERCAP = 32.12	2010-2013	

Source: USDA, Economic Research Service.

Appendix 3

Table 1. World sugar supply and use, all countries/regions, base projection, 2013/14-2024/25

	2013/14	2014/15	2015/16	2016/17	2017/18	2018/19	2019/20	2020/21	2021/22	2022/23	2023/24	2024/25
					1,000 metric tons, raw value (MTRV)							
Brazil												
Beginning stocks	-535	-295	-295	-295	-295	-295	-295	-295	-295	-295	-295	-295
Beet sugar production	0	0	0	0	0	0	0	0	0	0	0	0
Cane sugar production	38,750	36,699	40,216	38,190	40,461	40,698	40,814	41,848	44,141	44,510	45,246	46,442
Total sugar production	38,750	36,699	40,216	38,190	40,461	40,698	40,814	41,848	44,141	44,510	45,246	46,442
Total imports	0	0	0	0	0	0	0	0	0	0	0	0
Total supply	38,215	36,404	39,921	37,895	40,166	40,403	40,519	41,553	43,846	44,215	44,951	46,147
Total exports	27,250	25,320	28,719	26,577	28,735	28,861	28,868	29,795	31,983	32,250	32,885	33,982
Human dom. consumption	11,260	11,380	11,497	11,613	11,726	11,837	11,946	12,053	12,158	12,261	12,361	12,459
Other disappearance	0	0	0	0	0	0	0	0	0	0	0	0
Total use	11,260	11,380	11,497	11,613	11,726	11,837	11,946	12,053	12,158	12,261	12,361	12,459
Ending stocks	-295	-295	-295	-295	-295	-295	-295	-295	-295	-295	-295	-295
Argentina												
Beginning stocks	446	186	217	252	166	199	194	163	151	157	160	160

Appendix 3-Table 1. (Continued)

	2013/14	2014/15	2015/16	2016/17	2017/18	2018/19	2019/20	2020/21	2021/22	2022/23	2023/24	2024/25
					1,000 metric tons, raw value (MTRV)							
Beet sugar production	0	0	0	0	0	0	0	0	0	0	0	0
Cane sugar production	1,800	2,505	2,557	2,554	2,636	2,626	2,629	2,673	2,721	2,744	2,755	2,763
Total sugar production	1,800	2,505	2,557	2,554	2,636	2,626	2,629	2,673	2,721	2,744	2,755	2,763
Total imports	0	0	0	0	0	0	0	0	0	0	0	0
Total supply	2,246	2,691	2,775	2,805	2,802	2,824	2,823	2,836	2,873	2,901	2,915	2,923
Total exports	220	589	563	684	554	533	539	524	494	461	419	362
Human dom. consumption	1,830	1,874	1,950	1,945	2,039	2,087	2,111	2,151	2,211	2,270	2,326	2,388
Other disappearance	10	10	10	10	10	10	10	10	10	10	10	10
Total use	1,840	1,884	1,960	1,955	2,049	2,097	2,121	2,161	2,221	2,280	2,336	2,398
Ending stocks	186	217	252	166	199	194	163	151	157	160	160	163
Colombia												
Beginning stocks	300	390	368	375	381	387	394	401	407	414	421	428
Beet sugar production	0	0	0	0	0	0	0	0	0	0	0	0
Cane sugar production	2,400	2,343	2,369	2,395	2,422	2,449	2,476	2,503	2,530	2,558	2,586	2,614
Total sugar production	2,400	2,343	2,369	2,395	2,422	2,449	2,476	2,503	2,530	2,558	2,586	2,614

	2013/14	2014/15	2015/16	2016/17	2017/18	2018/19	2019/20	2020/21	2021/22	2022/23	2023/24	2024/25
					1,000 metric tons, raw value (MTRV)							
Total imports	290	253	257	262	266	271	275	280	285	290	294	299
Total supply	2,990	2,986	2,994	3,032	3,069	3,107	3,145	3,184	3,222	3,262	3,302	3,342
Total exports	600	826	797	797	797	796	795	794	793	791	789	787
Human dom. consumption	1,995	1,787	1,818	1,849	1,880	1,912	1,944	1,977	2,010	2,044	2,079	2,114
Other disappearance	5	5	5	5	5	5	5	5	5	5	5	5
Total use	2,000	1,792	1,823	1,854	1,885	1,917	1,949	1,982	2,015	2,049	2,084	2,119
Ending stocks	390	368	375	381	387	394	401	407	414	421	428	436
Other South America												
Beginning stocks	1,590	1,569	1,554	1,579	1,605	1,631	1,657	1,683	1,709	1,735	1,761	1,787
Beet sugar production	330	355	351	361	355	356	361	363	362	362	362	362
Cane sugar production	3,073	3,084	3,114	3,106	3,219	3,191	3,223	3,291	3,336	3,355	3,377	3,404
Total sugar production	3,403	3,439	3,465	3,467	3,574	3,547	3,584	3,654	3,698	3,717	3,739	3,766
Total imports	1,724	1,741	1,838	1,912	1,902	2,003	2,050	2,070	2,111	2,174	2,233	2,288
Total supply	6,717	6,749	6,857	6,959	7,082	7,181	7,291	7,407	7,519	7,626	7,733	7,841
Total exports	555	526	531	529	549	544	549	561	569	572	576	580
Human dom. consumption	4,593	4,670	4,747	4,824	4,902	4,980	5,058	5,137	5,215	5,293	5,371	5,448
Other disappearance	0	0	0	0	0	0	0	0	0	0	0	0

Appendix 3-Table 1. (Continued)

	2013/14	2014/15	2015/16	2016/17	2017/18	2018/19	2019/20	2020/21	2021/22	2022/23	2023/24	2024/25
					1,000 metric tons, raw value (MTRV)							
Total use	4,593	4,670	4,747	4,824	4,902	4,980	5,058	5,137	5,215	5,293	5,371	5,448
Ending stocks	1,569	1,554	1,579	1,605	1,631	1,657	1,683	1,709	1,735	1,761	1,787	1,813
Cuba												
Beginning stocks	149	150	149	152	136	144	139	129	125	125	124	122
Beet sugar production	0	0	0	0	0	0	0	0	0	0	0	0
Cane sugar production	1,600	1,578	1,547	1,461	1,474	1,400	1,335	1,313	1,302	1,275	1,239	1,199
Total sugar production	1,600	1,578	1,547	1,461	1,474	1,400	1,335	1,313	1,302	1,275	1,239	1,199
Total imports	0	0	0	0	0	0	0	0	0	0	0	0
Total supply	1,749	1,728	1,696	1,614	1,610	1,544	1,474	1,442	1,427	1,401	1,363	1,321
Total exports	850	897	864	798	788	729	670	643	630	606	573	535
Human dom. consumption	749	681	680	679	678	677	675	674	672	670	668	666
Other disappearance	0	0	0	0	0	0	0	0	0	0	0	0
Total use	749	681	680	679	678	677	675	674	672	670	668	666
Ending stocks	150	149	152	136	144	139	129	125	125	124	122	119
Dominican Republic												
Beginning stocks	50	39	38	40	37	40	40	39	38	39	40	41

	2013/14	2014/15	2015/16	2016/17	2017/18	2018/19	2019/20	2020/21	2021/22	2022/23	2023/24	2024/25
					1,000 metric tons, raw value (MTRV)							
Beet sugar production	0	0	0	0	0	0	0	0	0	0	0	0
Cane sugar production	541	575	581	584	593	597	602	609	618	627	634	642
Total sugar production	541	575	581	584	593	597	602	609	618	627	634	642
Total imports	40	0	0	0	0	0	0	0	0	0	0	0
Total supply	631	614	619	623	630	637	641	648	657	666	675	683
Total exports	212	193	192	195	196	199	201	204	209	214	219	223
Human dom. consumption	380	384	388	391	395	398	402	405	409	412	415	418
Other disappearance	0	0	0	0	0	0	0	0	0	0	0	0
Total use	380	384	388	391	395	398	402	405	409	412	415	418
Ending stocks	39	38	40	37	40	40	39	38	39	40	41	42
Other Caribbean												
Beginning stocks	128	128	138	140	141	143	144	145	147	148	150	151
Beet sugar production	0	0	0	0	0	0	0	0	0	0	0	0
Cane sugar production	210	189	191	193	195	197	199	201	203	205	207	209
Total sugar production	210	189	191	193	195	197	199	201	203	205	207	209
Total imports	405	435	431	435	439	444	448	453	457	462	466	471

Appendix 3-Table 1. (Continued)

	2013/14	2014/15	2015/16	2016/17	2017/18	2018/19	2019/20	2020/21	2021/22	2022/23	2023/24	2024/25
					1,000 metric tons, raw value (MTRV)							
Total supply	743	753	760	768	775	783	791	799	807	815	823	831
Total exports	150	145	146	148	149	151	152	154	155	157	158	160
Human dom. consumption	465	470	474	479	484	489	494	499	504	509	514	519
Other disappearance	0	0	0	0	0	0	0	0	0	0	0	0
Total use	465	470	474	479	484	489	494	499	504	509	514	519
Ending stocks	128	138	140	141	143	144	145	147	148	150	151	153
Guatemala												
Beginning stocks	120	73	82	96	75	92	96	90	90	98	106	113
Beet sugar production	0	0	0	0	0	0	0	0	0	0	0	0
Cane sugar production	2,600	2,940	3,026	3,151	3,233	3,310	3,403	3,499	3,579	3,645	3,700	3,739
Total sugar production	2,600	2,940	3,026	3,151	3,233	3,310	3,403	3,499	3,579	3,645	3,700	3,739
Total imports	0	0	0	0	0	0	0	0	0	0	0	0
Total supply	2,720	3,013	3,107	3,247	3,307	3,402	3,499	3,589	3,669	3,743	3,806	3,852
Total exports	1,850	2,117	2,178	2,311	2,324	2,383	2,453	2,505	2,540	2,567	2,583	2,577
Human dom. consumption	797	814	833	861	891	923	957	993	1,030	1,070	1,110	1,153
Other disappearance	0	0	0	0	0	0	0	0	0	0	0	0

	2013/14	2014/15	2015/16	2016/17	2017/18	2018/19	2019/20	2020/21	2021/22	2022/23	2023/24	2024/25
					1,000 metric tons, raw value (MTRV)							
Total use	797	814	833	861	891	923	957	993	1,030	1,070	1,110	1,153
Ending stocks	73	82	96	75	92	96	90	90	98	106	113	122
Other Central												
America												
Beginning stocks	618	602	639	659	670	689	700	710	724	740	755	768
Beet sugar production	0	0	0	0	0	0	0	0	0	0	0	0
Cane sugar production	2,697	2,702	2,768	2,806	2,890	2,930	2,971	3,034	3,104	3,163	3,214	3,262
Total sugar production	2,697	2,702	2,768	2,806	2,890	2,930	2,971	3,034	3,104	3,163	3,214	3,262
Total imports	0	0	0	0	0	0	0	0	0	0	0	0
Total supply	3,315	3,304	3,407	3,465	3,560	3,618	3,670	3,744	3,828	3,903	3,969	4,029
Total exports	1,275	1,311	1,370	1,393	1,445	1,467	1,485	1,520	1,563	1,599	1,628	1,652
Human dom. consumption	1,418	1,334	1,358	1,382	1,407	1,431	1,455	1,480	1,504	1,529	1,553	1,578
Other disappearance	20	20	20	20	20	20	20	20	20	20	20	20
Total use	1,438	1,354	1,378	1,402	1,427	1,451	1,475	1,500	1,524	1,549	1,573	1,598
Ending stocks	602	639	659	670	689	700	710	724	740	755	768	779
Canada												
Beginning stocks	260	260	247	249	251	253	255	256	258	260	261	263
Beet sugar production	125	144	148	149	156	158	160	165	171	175	179	183

Appendix 3-Table 1. (Continued)

	2013/14	2014/15	2015/16	2016/17	2017/18	2018/19	2019/20	2020/21	2021/22	2022/23	2023/24	2024/25
					1,000 metric tons, raw value (MTRV)							
Cane sugar production	0	0	0	0	0	0	0	0	0	0	0	0
Total sugar production	125	144	148	149	156	158	160	165	171	175	179	183
Total imports	1,195	1,109	1,129	1,137	1,139	1,146	1,153	1,156	1,158	1,162	1,166	1,169
Total supply	1,580	1,514	1,524	1,535	1,546	1,556	1,567	1,577	1,587	1,597	1,606	1,615
Total exports	45	60	60	60	60	60	60	60	60	60	60	60
Human dom. consumption	1,275	1,206	1,215	1,224	1,233	1,242	1,251	1,259	1,267	1,275	1,283	1,291
Other disappearance	0	0	0	0	0	0	0	0	0	0	0	0
Total use	1,275	1,206	1,215	1,224	1,233	1,242	1,251	1,259	1,267	1,275	1,283	1,291
Ending stocks	260	247	249	251	253	255	256	258	260	261	263	265
Mexico												
Beginning stocks	1,548	1,044	1,066	1,046	1,067	1,090	1,107	1,117	1,132	1,150	1,168	1,187
Beet sugar production	0	0	0	0	0	0	0	0	0	0	0	0
Cane sugar production	6,890	6,398	6,530	6,616	6,800	6,909	7,025	7,191	7,383	7,566	7,744	7,924
Total sugar production	6,890	6,398	6,530	6,616	6,800	6,909	7,025	7,191	7,383	7,566	7,744	7,924
Total imports	231	231	231	231	231	231	231	231	231	231	231	231
Total supply	8,669	7,673	7,827	7,893	8,098	8,230	8,363	8,540	8,746	8,947	9,143	9,341

	2013/14	2014/15	2015/16	2016/17	2017/18	2018/19	2019/20	2020/21	2021/22	2022/23	2023/24	2024/25
					1,000 metric tons, raw value (MTRV)							
Total exports	2,485	1,400	1,665	1,614	1,694	1,731	1,808	1,900	2,008	2,108	2,203	2,294
Human dom. Consumption	4,743	4,846	4,756	4,852	4,954	5,032	5,078	5,148	5,228	5,311	5,394	5,481
Other disappearance	397	360	360	360	360	360	360	360	360	360	360	360
Total use	5,140	5,206	5,116	5,212	5,314	5,392	5,438	5,508	5,588	5,671	5,754	5,841
Ending stocks	1,044	1,066	1,046	1,067	1,090	1,107	1,117	1,132	1,150	1,168	1,187	1,206
United States												
Beginning stocks	1,980	2,175	2,117	2,257	2,366	2,532	2,729	2,974	3,305	3,695	4,154	4,677
Beet sugar production	4,559	4,521	4,577	4,638	4,691	4,749	4,796	4,870	4,906	4,960	5,015	5,070
Cane sugar production	3,495	3,254	3,267	3,280	3,293	3,306	3,319	3,332	3,345	3,358	3,371	3,384
Total sugar production	8,054	7,775	7,844	7,918	7,984	8,056	8,115	8,202	8,252	8,318	8,386	8,454
Total imports	3,059	2,972	3,173	3,140	3,203	3,235	3,295	3,365	3,447	3,524	3,596	3,666
Total supply	13,093	12,922	13,134	13,315	13,553	13,822	14,139	14,541	15,003	15,537	16,136	16,797
Total exports	227	181	181	181	181	181	181	181	181	181	181	181
Human dom. consumption	10,523	10,431	10,503	10,575	10,647	10,719	10,791	10,863	10,935	11,010	11,085	11,161
Other disappearance	168	192	192	192	192	192	192	192	192	192	192	192
Total use	10,691	10,624	10,696	10,768	10,840	10,912	10,984	11,055	11,127	11,202	11,277	11,353
Ending stocks	2,175	2,117	2,257	2,366	2,532	2,729	2,974	3,305	3,695	4,154	4,677	5,263

Appendix 3-Table 1. (Continued)

	2013/14	2014/15	2015/16	2016/17	2017/18	2018/19	2019/20	2020/21	2021/22	2022/23	2023/24	2024/25
					1,000 metric tons, raw value (MTRV)							
European Union - 28												
Beginning stocks	4,044	3,894	3,764	3,878	3,648	3,821	3,804	3,693	3,642	3,663	3,673	3,670
Beet sugar production	15,700	16,444	16,526	16,609	18,361	18,453	18,564	18,757	18,900	18,979	19,066	19,167
Cane sugar production	300	275	275	275	275	275	275	275	275	275	275	275
Total sugar production	16,000	16,719	16,801	16,884	18,636	18,728	18,839	19,032	19,175	19,254	19,341	19,442
Total imports	3,650	2,989	3,185	2,793	1,472	1,216	1,034	920	864	788	696	620
Total supply	23,694	23,602	23,751	23,554	23,757	23,765	23,677	23,645	23,681	23,704	23,710	23,731
Total exports	1,500	1,500	1,500	1,500	1,500	1,500	1,500	1,500	1,500	1,500	1,500	1,500
Human dom. consumption	18,300	18,337	18,373	18,406	18,435	18,461	18,484	18,503	18,519	18,531	18,541	18,547
Other disappearance	0	0	0	0	0	0	0	0	0	0	0	0
Total use	18,300	18,337	18,373	18,406	18,435	18,461	18,484	18,503	18,519	18,531	18,541	18,547
Ending stocks	3,894	3,764	3,878	3,648	3,821	3,804	3,693	3,642	3,663	3,673	3,670	3,684
Other European												
Beginning stocks	374	374	387	385	383	381	379	377	375	373	372	370
Beet sugar production	684	712	711	706	700	703	706	705	704	704	704	705

	2013/14	2014/15	2015/16	2016/17	2017/18	2018/19	2019/20	2020/21	2021/22	2022/23	2023/24	2024/25
					1,000 metric tons, raw value (MTRV)							
Cane sugar production	0	0	0	0	0	0	0	0	0	0	0	0
Total sugar production	684	712	711	706	700	703	706	705	704	704	704	705
Total imports	690	838	818	818	817	809	800	795	791	785	779	773
Total supply	1,748	1,924	1,916	1,908	1,901	1,893	1,885	1,878	1,870	1,863	1,855	1,848
Total exports	156	325	325	325	325	325	325	325	325	325	325	325
Human dom. consumption	1,178	1,172	1,166	1,160	1,155	1,149	1,143	1,137	1,132	1,126	1,120	1,115
Other disappearance	40	40	40	40	40	40	40	40	40	40	40	40
Total use	1,218	1,212	1,206	1,200	1,195	1,189	1,183	1,177	1,172	1,166	1,160	1,155
Ending stocks	374	387	385	383	381	379	377	375	373	372	370	368
Russia												
Beginning stocks	275	260	427	427	427	426	426	425	424	423	423	421
Beet sugar production	4,400	4,737	4,596	5,436	5,155	5,379	5,918	6,302	6,448	6,636	6,886	7,077
Cane sugar production	0	0	0	0	0	0	0	0	0	0	0	0
Total sugar production	4,400	4,737	4,596	5,436	5,155	5,379	5,918	6,302	6,448	6,636	6,886	7,077
Total imports	1,100	1,392	1,363	519	795	563	0	0	0	0	0	0
Total supply	5,775	6,389	6,386	6,382	6,376	6,369	6,343	6,727	6,872	7,060	7,308	7,498
Total exports	100	250	250	250	250	250	234	630	787	989	1,252	1,457

Appendix 3-Table 1. (Continued)

	2013/14	2014/15	2015/16	2016/17	2017/18	2018/19	2019/20	2020/21	2021/22	2022/23	2023/24	2024/25
					1,000 metric tons, raw value (MTRV)							
Human dom. Consumption	5,400	5,697	5,694	5,690	5,685	5,678	5,669	5,658	5,647	5,634	5,620	5,606
Other disappearance	15	15	15	15	15	15	15	15	15	15	15	15
Total use	5,415	5,712	5,709	5,705	5,700	5,693	5,684	5,673	5,662	5,649	5,635	5,621
Ending stocks	260	427	427	427	426	426	425	424	423	423	421	420
Ukraine												
Beginning stocks	629	209	365	363	361	358	356	353	351	348	346	343
Beet sugar production	1,700	2,561	2,663	2,730	2,867	2,942	3,021	3,134	3,261	3,375	3,479	3,580
Cane sugar production	0	0	0	0	0	0	0	0	0	0	0	0
Total sugar production	1,700	2,561	2,663	2,730	2,867	2,942	3,021	3,134	3,261	3,375	3,479	3,580
Total imports	5	0	0	0	0	0	0	0	0	0	0	0
Total supply	2,334	2,770	3,028	3,093	3,228	3,300	3,377	3,487	3,612	3,723	3,825	3,923
Total exports	325	600	872	952	1,101	1,188	1,278	1,404	1,543	1,669	1,786	1,900
Human dom. consumption	1,800	1,804	1,793	1,781	1,769	1,757	1,745	1,733	1,720	1,708	1,695	1,683
Other disappearance	0	0	0	0	0	0	0	0	0	0	0	0
Total use	1,800	1,804	1,793	1,781	1,769	1,757	1,745	1,733	1,720	1,708	1,695	1,683
Ending stocks	209	365	363	361	358	356	353	351	348	346	343	341

	2013/14	2014/15	2015/16	2016/17	2017/18	2018/19	2019/20	2020/21	2021/22	2022/23	2023/24	2024/25
					1,000 metric tons, raw value (MTRV)							
Other Former												
Soviet Union												
Beginning stocks	931	1,156	751	764	778	791	805	819	832	846	860	873
Beet sugar production	1,010	960	960	960	960	960	960	960	960	960	960	960
Cane sugar production	3	3	3	3	3	3	3	3	3	3	3	3
Total sugar production	1,013	963	963	963	963	963	963	963	963	963	963	963
Total imports	1,684	1,333	1,788	1,824	1,861	1,897	1,934	1,970	2,007	2,043	2,079	2,115
Total supply	3,628	3,452	3,502	3,551	3,601	3,652	3,702	3,752	3,802	3,852	3,901	3,951
Total exports	506	700	700	700	700	700	700	700	700	700	700	700
Human dom. consumption	1,966	2,002	2,038	2,074	2,110	2,147	2,183	2,220	2,256	2,292	2,328	2,364
Other disappearance	0	0	0	0	0	0	0	0	0	0	0	0
Total use	1,966	2,002	2,038	2,074	2,110	2,147	2,183	2,220	2,256	2,292	2,328	2,364
Ending stocks	1,156	751	764	778	791	805	819	832	846	860	873	887
Turkey												
Beginning stocks	157	82	234	254	233	260	265	257	257	267	275	282
Beet sugar production	2,200	2,047	2,029	2,022	2,035	2,068	2,058	2,071	2,106	2,133	2,143	2,149
Cane sugar production	0	0	0	0	0	0	0	0	0	0	0	0

Appendix 3-Table 1. (Continued)

	2013/14	2014/15	2015/16	2016/17	2017/18	2018/19	2019/20	2020/21	2021/22	2022/23	2023/24	2024/25
					1,000 metric tons, raw value (MTRV)							
Total sugar production	2,200	2,047	2,029	2,022	2,035	2,068	2,058	2,071	2,106	2,133	2,143	2,149
Total imports	5	461	425	462	570	587	659	731	784	836	906	985
Total supply	2,362	2,590	2,687	2,737	2,838	2,916	2,983	3,059	3,147	3,236	3,324	3,416
Total exports	20	20	20	20	20	20	20	20	20	20	20	20
Human dom. consumption	2,260	2,336	2,413	2,485	2,558	2,631	2,705	2,782	2,861	2,940	3,022	3,104
Other disappearance	0	0	0	0	0	0	0	0	0	0	0	0
Total use	2,260	2,336	2,413	2,485	2,558	2,631	2,705	2,782	2,861	2,940	3,022	3,104
Ending stocks	82	234	254	233	260	265	257	257	267	275	282	292
Other Middle East												
Beginning stocks	1,572	1,587	1,641	1,740	1,721	1,841	1,896	1,916	1,962	2,040	2,118	2,193
Beet sugar production	800	800	800	800	800	800	800	800	800	800	800	800
Cane sugar production	350	350	350	350	350	350	350	350	350	350	350	350
Total sugar production	1,150	1,150	1,150	1,150	1,150	1,150	1,150	1,150	1,150	1,150	1,150	1,150
Total imports	9,448	10,009	10,473	10,656	11,123	11,471	11,845	12,289	12,753	13,214	13,694	14,198
Total supply	12,170	12,746	13,264	13,545	13,994	14,463	14,891	15,355	15,865	16,404	16,963	17,541
Total exports	1,005	1,167	1,205	1,130	1,086	1,118	1,141	1,136	1,122	1,121	1,128	1,129

	2013/14	2014/15	2015/16	2016/17	2017/18	2018/19	2019/20	2020/21	2021/22	2022/23	2023/24	2024/25
					1,000 metric tons, raw value (MTRV)							
Human dom. consumption	9,578	9,938	10,319	10,695	11,068	11,448	11,835	12,257	12,702	13,165	13,642	14,134
Other disappearance	0	0	0	0	0	0	0	0	0	0	0	0
Total use	9,578	9,938	10,319	10,695	11,068	11,448	11,835	12,257	12,702	13,165	13,642	14,134
Ending stocks	1,587	1,641	1,740	1,721	1,841	1,896	1,916	1,962	2,040	2,118	2,193	2,278
Egypt												
Beginning stocks	160	160	297	311	317	333	344	352	362	373	385	396
Beet sugar production	1,100	1,069	1,096	1,124	1,153	1,183	1,213	1,244	1,276	1,308	1,341	1,375
Cane sugar production	920	1,060	1,062	1,065	1,067	1,069	1,071	1,073	1,076	1,078	1,080	1,082
Total sugar production	2,020	2,129	2,158	2,189	2,220	2,252	2,284	2,317	2,351	2,386	2,421	2,457
Total imports	1,200	1,478	1,471	1,498	1,638	1,717	1,768	1,833	1,921	2,006	2,092	2,186
Total supply	3,380	3,766	3,926	3,998	4,175	4,302	4,396	4,503	4,634	4,765	4,898	5,040
Total exports	400	400	400	400	400	400	400	400	400	400	400	400
Human dom. consumption	2,820	3,070	3,216	3,281	3,442	3,558	3,644	3,741	3,861	3,981	4,101	4,231
Other disappearance	0	0	0	0	0	0	0	0	0	0	0	0
Total use	2,820	3,070	3,216	3,281	3,442	3,558	3,644	3,741	3,861	3,981	4,101	4,231
Ending stocks	160	297	311	317	333	344	352	362	373	385	396	409
Other North Africa												

Appendix 3-Table 1. (Continued)

	2013/14	2014/15	2015/16	2016/17	2017/18	2018/19	2019/20	2020/21	2021/22	2022/23	2023/24	2024/25
					1,000 metric tons, raw value (MTRV)							
Beginning stocks	419	419	410	418	426	434	443	451	459	467	475	484
Beet sugar production	350	350	350	350	350	350	350	350	350	350	350	350
Cane sugar production	60	50	50	50	50	50	50	50	50	50	50	50
Total sugar production	410	400	400	400	400	400	400	400	400	400	400	400
Total imports	3,870	3,783	3,872	3,944	4,016	4,088	4,159	4,231	4,303	4,375	4,447	4,519
Total supply	4,699	4,602	4,682	4,762	4,842	4,922	5,002	5,082	5,162	5,242	5,322	5,402
Total exports	585	600	600	600	600	600	600	600	600	600	600	600
Human dom. consumption	3,695	3,592	3,664	3,736	3,808	3,879	3,951	4,023	4,095	4,167	4,238	4,310
Other disappearance	0	0	0	0	0	0	0	0	0	0	0	0
Total use	3,695	3,592	3,664	3,736	3,808	3,879	3,951	4,023	4,095	4,167	4,238	4,310
Ending stocks	419	410	418	426	434	443	451	459	467	475	484	492
South Africa												
Beginning stocks	172	362	190	203	172	190	189	177	172	176	179	180
Beet sugar production	0	0	0	0	0	0	0	0	0	0	0	0
Cane sugar production	2,450	2,287	2,293	2,299	2,305	2,310	2,316	2,322	2,328	2,333	2,339	2,345

	2013/14	2014/15	2015/16	2016/17	2017/18	2018/19	2019/20	2020/21	2021/22	2022/23	2023/24	2024/25
					1,000 metric tons, raw value (MTRV)							
Total sugar production	2,450	2,287	2,293	2,299	2,305	2,310	2,316	2,322	2,328	2,333	2,339	2,345
Total imports	225	227	229	232	234	237	240	242	245	247	250	253
Total supply	2,847	2,876	2,712	2,734	2,711	2,737	2,745	2,741	2,745	2,757	2,768	2,778
Total exports	600	786	587	620	557	563	561	540	518	506	493	477
Human dom. consumption	1,880	1,895	1,916	1,938	1,959	1,980	2,002	2,024	2,046	2,068	2,090	2,112
Other disappearance	5	5	5	5	5	5	5	5	5	5	5	5
Total use	1,885	1,900	1,921	1,943	1,964	1,985	2,007	2,029	2,051	2,073	2,095	2,117
Ending stocks	362	190	203	172	190	189	177	172	176	179	180	184
Other Sub-Sahara												
Africa												
Beginning stocks	2,210	2,242	2,290	2,456	2,447	2,651	2,761	2,816	2,910	3,052	3,192	3,328
Beet sugar production	0	0	0	0	0	0	0	0	0	0	0	0
Cane sugar production	6,179	6,233	6,279	6,277	6,359	6,361	6,371	6,419	6,475	6,512	6,536	6,556
Total sugar production	6,179	6,233	6,279	6,277	6,359	6,361	6,371	6,419	6,475	6,512	6,536	6,556
Total imports	5,406	5,645	6,102	6,305	6,843	7,141	7,482	7,906	8,343	8,752	9,176	9,636
Total supply	13,795	14,120	14,671	15,038	15,649	16,153	16,613	17,140	17,728	18,316	18,904	19,521
Total exports	1,935	1,969	1,983	1,983	2,009	2,009	2,013	2,028	2,046	2,057	2,065	2,071

Appendix 3-Table 1. (Continued)

	2013/14	2014/15	2015/16	2016/17	2017/18	2018/19	2019/20	2020/21	2021/22	2022/23	2023/24	2024/25
					1,000 metric tons, raw value (MTRV)							
Human dom. Consumption	9,567	9,810	10,182	10,558	10,939	11,333	11,735	12,153	12,580	13,016	13,462	13,918
Other disappearance	51	50	50	50	50	50	50	50	50	50	50	50
Total use	9,618	9,860	10,232	10,608	10,989	11,383	11,785	12,203	12,630	13,066	13,512	13,968
Ending stocks	2,242	2,290	2,456	2,447	2,651	2,761	2,816	2,910	3,052	3,192	3,328	3,482
India												
Beginning stocks	10,425	9,475	9,704	10,976	9,310	11,088	11,247	10,542	10,389	10,893	11,327	11,645
Beet sugar production	0	0	0	0	0	0	0	0	0	0	0	0
Cane sugar production	25,450	27,449	27,499	27,916	32,740	32,859	33,273	33,934	34,322	36,414	38,254	40,166
Total sugar production	25,450	27,449	27,499	27,916	32,740	32,859	33,273	33,934	34,322	36,414	38,254	40,166
Total imports	1,800	0	2,220	0	0	0	0	0	2	0	0	0
Total supply	37,675	36,924	39,422	38,892	42,050	43,946	44,520	44,476	44,714	47,308	49,581	51,812
Total exports	2,000	60	0	855	753	1,547	2,166	1,408	0	1,021	1,851	2,341
Human dom. consumption	26,200	27,160	28,446	28,727	30,210	31,152	31,812	32,679	33,820	34,960	36,084	37,309
Other disappearance	0	0	0	0	0	0	0	0	0	0	0	0
Total use	26,200	27,160	28,446	28,727	30,210	31,152	31,812	32,679	33,820	34,960	36,084	37,309
Ending stocks	9,475	9,704	10,976	9,310	11,088	11,247	10,542	10,389	10,893	11,327	11,645	12,161

	2013/14	2014/15	2015/16	2016/17	2017/18	2018/19	2019/20	2020/21	2021/22	2022/23	2023/24	2024/25
					1,000 metric tons, raw value (MTRV)							
Pakistan												
Beginning stocks	639	729	763	785	807	830	854	879	905	934	963	995
Beet sugar production	40	40	40	40	40	40	40	40	40	40	40	40
Cane sugar production	4,930	3,965	4,663	5,169	5,090	4,797	4,554	5,214	5,488	5,219	4,997	5,160
Total sugar production	4,970	4,005	4,703	5,209	5,130	4,837	4,594	5,254	5,528	5,259	5,037	5,200
Total imports	10	654	45	0	0	229	585	42	0	286	638	613
Total supply	5,619	5,388	5,511	5,993	5,936	5,896	6,033	6,175	6,433	6,478	6,639	6,807
Total exports	440	0	0	358	173	0	0	0	110	0	0	0
Human dom. consumption	4,450	4,625	4,726	4,829	4,934	5,042	5,154	5,269	5,390	5,514	5,644	5,779
Other disappearance	0	0	0	0	0	0	0	0	0	0	0	0
Total use	4,450	4,625	4,726	4,829	4,934	5,042	5,154	5,269	5,390	5,514	5,644	5,779
Ending stocks	729	763	785	807	830	854	879	905	934	963	995	1,029
Other South Asia												
Beginning stocks	702	702	723	743	763	784	806	828	851	874	898	923
Beet sugar production	0	0	0	0	0	0	0	0	0	0	0	0
Cane sugar production	290	290	290	290	290	290	290	290	290	290	290	290

Appendix 3-Table 1. (Continued)

	2013/14	2014/15	2015/16	2016/17	2017/18	2018/19	2019/20	2020/21	2021/22	2022/23	2023/24	2024/25
					1,000 metric tons, raw value (MTRV)							
Total sugar production	290	290	290	290	290	290	290	290	290	290	290	290
Total imports	2,263	2,344	2,415	2,490	2,566	2,645	2,726	2,809	2,894	2,982	3,072	3,165
Total supply	3,255	3,336	3,428	3,522	3,619	3,719	3,822	3,927	4,035	4,146	4,261	4,378
Total exports	10	0	0	0	0	0	0	0	0	0	0	0
Human dom. consumption	2,543	2,613	2,685	2,759	2,835	2,913	2,993	3,076	3,161	3,248	3,337	3,429
Other disappearance	0	0	0	0	0	0	0	0	0	0	0	0
Total use	2,543	2,613	2,685	2,759	2,835	2,913	2,993	3,076	3,161	3,248	3,337	3,429
Ending stocks	702	723	743	763	784	806	828	851	874	898	923	949
China												
Beginning stocks	6,790	8,345	6,883	4,160	2,947	3,649	3,687	3,256	3,135	3,315	3,465	3,562
Beet sugar production	1,000	1,284	1,284	1,284	1,284	1,284	1,284	1,284	1,284	1,284	1,284	1,284
Cane sugar production	13,800	14,128	14,934	15,270	16,414	16,813	17,190	17,953	18,885	19,656	20,290	20,844
Total sugar production	14,800	15,411	16,218	16,554	17,698	18,097	18,474	19,237	20,169	20,939	21,574	22,127
Total imports	2,800	1,000	0	1,514	3,260	2,955	2,746	2,993	3,176	3,197	3,336	3,741
Total supply	24,390	24,756	23,101	22,229	23,905	24,700	24,906	25,485	26,480	27,452	28,374	29,430
Total exports	45	0	177	0	0	0	0	0	0	0	0	0

	2013/14	2014/15	2015/16	2016/17	2017/18	2018/19	2019/20	2020/21	2021/22	2022/23	2023/24	2024/25
					1,000 metric tons, raw value (MTRV)							
Human dom. Consumption	16,000	17,873	18,763	19,281	20,256	21,014	21,650	22,350	23,164	23,987	24,812	25,686
Other disappearance	0	0	0	0	0	0	0	0	0	0	0	0
Total use	16,000	17,873	18,763	19,281	20,256	21,014	21,650	22,350	23,164	23,987	24,812	25,686
Ending stocks	8,345	6,883	4,160	2,947	3,649	3,687	3,256	3,135	3,315	3,465	3,562	3,744
Japan												
Beginning stocks	550	549	524	532	531	530	528	527	525	524	522	520
Beet sugar production	600	653	656	659	662	666	669	672	675	678	681	684
Cane sugar production	150	156	156	156	156	156	156	156	156	156	156	156
Total sugar production	750	809	813	816	819	822	825	828	831	834	837	841
Total imports	1,365	1,135	1,195	1,179	1,171	1,163	1,154	1,145	1,136	1,126	1,115	1,105
Total supply	2,665	2,493	2,532	2,527	2,521	2,515	2,508	2,500	2,492	2,484	2,475	2,465
Total exports	1	0	0	0	0	0	0	0	0	0	0	0
Human dom. consumption	2,115	1,969	2,000	1,996	1,991	1,986	1,981	1,975	1,969	1,962	1,955	1,947
Other disappearance	0	0	0	0	0	0	0	0	0	0	0	0
Total use	2,115	1,969	2,000	1,996	1,991	1,986	1,981	1,975	1,969	1,962	1,955	1,947
Ending stocks	549	524	532	531	530	528	527	525	524	522	520	518
Other East Asia												

Appendix 3-Table 1. (Continued)

	2013/14	2014/15	2015/16	2016/17	2017/18	2018/19	2019/20	2020/21	2021/22	2022/23	2023/24	2024/25
					1,000 metric tons, raw value (MTRV)							
Beginning stocks	706	708	758	774	765	788	795	795	799	810	820	828
Beet sugar production	0	0	0	0	0	0	0	0	0	0	0	0
Cane sugar production	65	65	65	65	65	65	65	65	65	65	65	65
Total sugar production	65	65	65	65	65	65	65	65	65	65	65	65
Total imports	2,783	2,994	3,017	2,954	3,075	3,086	3,077	3,098	3,146	3,182	3,213	3,254
Total supply	3,554	3,767	3,840	3,793	3,905	3,938	3,937	3,958	4,010	4,057	4,098	4,147
Total exports	423	440	443	434	452	454	452	455	462	468	472	478
Human dom. consumption	2,298	2,444	2,497	2,469	2,541	2,565	2,565	2,579	2,613	2,644	2,672	2,705
Other disappearance	125	125	125	125	125	125	125	125	125	125	125	125
Total use	2,423	2,569	2,622	2,594	2,666	2,690	2,690	2,704	2,738	2,769	2,797	2,830
Ending stocks	708	758	774	765	788	795	795	799	810	820	828	839
Thailand												
Beginning stocks	3,240	2,790	1,500	1,500	1,500	1,500	1,500	1,500	1,500	1,500	1,500	1,500
Beet sugar production	0	0	0	0	0	0	0	0	0	0	0	0
Cane sugar production	10,900	11,035	11,128	10,860	11,268	11,048	10,915	11,098	11,344	11,432	11,436	11,420

	2013/14	2014/15	2015/16	2016/17	2017/18	2018/19	2019/20	2020/21	2021/22	2022/23	2023/24	2024/25
					1,000 metric tons, raw value (MTRV)							
Total sugar production	10,900	11,035	11,128	10,860	11,268	11,048	10,915	11,098	11,344	11,432	11,436	11,420
Total imports	0	0	0	0	0	0	0	0	0	0	0	0
Total supply	14,140	13,825	12,628	12,360	12,768	12,548	12,415	12,598	12,844	12,932	12,936	12,920
Total exports	8,700	9,533	8,294	7,985	8,353	8,091	7,918	8,060	8,266	8,313	8,277	8,221
Human dom. consumption	2,650	2,793	2,834	2,875	2,916	2,957	2,997	3,038	3,079	3,119	3,159	3,199
Other disappearance	0	0	0	0	0	0	0	0	0	0	0	0
Total use	2,650	2,793	2,834	2,875	2,916	2,957	2,997	3,038	3,079	3,119	3,159	3,199
Ending stocks	2,790	1,500	1,500	1,500	1,500	1,500	1,500	1,500	1,500	1,500	1,500	1,500
Philippines												
Beginning stocks	887	827	802	816	830	845	859	873	887	901	915	929
Beet sugar production	0	0	0	0	0	0	0	0	0	0	0	0
Cane sugar production	2,500	2,565	2,645	2,696	2,825	2,904	2,993	3,128	3,292	3,458	3,631	3,817
Total sugar production	2,500	2,565	2,645	2,696	2,825	2,904	2,993	3,128	3,292	3,458	3,631	3,817
Total imports	40	0	0	0	0	0	0	0	0	0	0	0
Total supply	3,427	3,392	3,447	3,512	3,655	3,748	3,852	4,001	4,179	4,359	4,547	4,746
Total exports	350	299	299	309	398	436	485	579	703	830	963	1,109
Human dom. Consumption	2,250	2,291	2,332	2,372	2,413	2,454	2,494	2,534	2,575	2,615	2,655	2,694

Appendix 3-Table 1. (Continued)

	2013/14	2014/15	2015/16	2016/17	2017/18	2018/19	2019/20	2020/21	2021/22	2022/23	2023/24	2024/25
					1,000 metric tons, raw value (MTRV)							
Other disappearance	0	0	0	0	0	0	0	0	0	0	0	0
Total use	2,250	2,291	2,332	2,372	2,413	2,454	2,494	2,534	2,575	2,615	2,655	2,694
Ending stocks	827	802	816	830	845	859	873	887	901	915	929	943
Other Southeast Asia												
Beginning stocks	1,442	2,022	2,080	2,133	2,187	2,240	2,294	2,347	2,401	2,454	2,508	2,561
Beet sugar production	0	0	0	0	0	0	0	0	0	0	0	0
Cane sugar production	3,305	3,374	3,433	3,483	3,528	3,570	3,609	3,646	3,683	3,718	3,754	3,788
Total sugar production	3,305	3,374	3,433	3,483	3,528	3,570	3,609	3,646	3,683	3,718	3,754	3,788
Total imports	6,849	6,634	6,824	7,024	7,229	7,437	7,647	7,858	8,070	8,283	8,497	8,711
Total supply	11,596	12,031	12,336	12,640	12,944	13,247	13,549	13,852	14,154	14,456	14,758	15,060
Total exports	488	498	507	514	521	527	533	538	544	549	554	559
Human dom. consumption	9,086	9,453	9,696	9,939	10,183	10,426	10,669	10,913	11,156	11,399	11,643	11,886
Other disappearance	0	0	0	0	0	0	0	0	0	0	0	0
Total use	9,086	9,453	9,696	9,939	10,183	10,426	10,669	10,913	11,156	11,399	11,643	11,886
Ending stocks	2,022	2,080	2,133	2,187	2,240	2,294	2,347	2,401	2,454	2,508	2,561	2,615
Australia												

	2013/14	2014/15	2015/16	2016/17	2017/18	2018/19	2019/20	2020/21	2021/22	2022/23	2023/24	2024/25
					1,000 metric tons, raw value (MTRV)							
Beginning stocks	83	65	114	117	118	121	122	122	124	125	126	126
Beet sugar production	0	0	0	0	0	0	0	0	0	0	0	0
Cane sugar production	4,300	4,510	4,600	4,646	4,739	4,772	4,800	4,847	4,896	4,928	4,944	4,951
Total sugar production	4,300	4,510	4,600	4,646	4,739	4,772	4,800	4,847	4,896	4,928	4,944	4,951
Total imports	90	92	93	94	95	96	97	98	99	100	101	102
Total supply	4,473	4,667	4,807	4,858	4,953	4,989	5,019	5,067	5,119	5,152	5,171	5,179
Total exports	3,190	3,302	3,425	3,462	3,541	3,564	3,580	3,615	3,652	3,673	3,679	3,675
Human dom. consumption	1,218	1,251	1,265	1,278	1,291	1,304	1,317	1,329	1,342	1,354	1,366	1,378
Other disappearance	0	0	0	0	0	0	0	0	0	0	0	0
Total use	1,218	1,251	1,265	1,278	1,291	1,304	1,317	1,329	1,342	1,354	1,366	1,378
Ending stocks	65	114	117	118	121	122	122	124	125	126	126	126
Other Oceania												
Beginning stocks	101	101	105	105	105	105	105	105	105	105	105	105
Beet sugar production	0	0	0	0	0	0	0	0	0	0	0	0
Cane sugar production	220	225	225	225	225	225	225	225	225	225	225	225
Total sugar production	220	225	225	225	225	225	225	225	225	225	225	225

Appendix 3-Table 1. (Continued)

	2013/14	2014/15	2015/16	2016/17	2017/18	2018/19	2019/20	2020/21	2021/22	2022/23	2023/24	2024/25
					1,000 metric tons, raw value (MTRV)							
Total imports	313	299	295	295	295	295	295	295	295	295	295	295
Total supply	634	625	625	625	625	625	625	625	625	625	625	625
Total exports	180	175	175	175	175	175	175	175	175	175	175	175
Human dom. consumption	353	345	345	345	345	345	345	345	345	345	345	345
Other disappearance	0	0	0	0	0	0	0	0	0	0	0	0
Total use	353	345	345	345	345	345	345	345	345	345	345	345
Ending stocks	101	105	105	105	105	105	105	105	105	105	105	105
Unrecorded												
Beginning stocks	0	0	0	0	0	0	0	0	0	0	0	0
Beet sugar production	0	0	0	0	0	0	0	0	0	0	0	0
Cane sugar production	0	0	0	0	0	0	0	0	0	0	0	0
Total sugar production	0	0	0	0	0	0	0	0	0	0	0	0
Total imports	6,138	6,141	6,141	6,141	6,141	6,141	6,141	6,141	6,141	6,141	6,141	6,141
Total supply	6,138	6,141	6,141	6,141	6,141	6,141	6,141	6,141	6,141	6,141	6,141	6,141
Total exports	0	0	0	0	0	0	0	0	0	0	0	0
Human dom. consumption	6,138	6,141	6,141	6,141	6,141	6,141	6,141	6,141	6,141	6,141	6,141	6,141

	2013/14	2014/15	2015/16	2016/17	2017/18	2018/19	2019/20	2020/21	2021/22	2022/23	2023/24	2024/25
					1,000 metric tons, raw value (MTRV)							
Other disappearance	0	0	0	0	0	0	0	0	0	0	0	0
Total use	6,138	6,141	6,141	6,141	6,141	6,141	6,141	6,141	6,141	6,141	6,141	6,141
Ending stocks	0	0	0	0	0	0	0	0	0	0	0	0
World												
Beginning stocks	43,162	43,379	41,030	40,389	37,376	40,870	41,622	40,823	41,161	42,734	44,252	45,637
Beet sugar production	34,598	36,676	36,787	37,867	39,570	40,090	40,898	41,716	42,242	42,743	43,290	43,784
Cane sugar production	140,228	140,287	146,117	145,431	154,964	155,531	156,502	160,542	165,467	169,167	172,749	177,128
Total sugar production	174,826	176,963	182,904	183,298	194,535	195,621	197,400	202,258	207,709	211,910	216,039	220,912
Total imports	58,678	56,189	59,031	57,860	60,383	61,102	61,842	62,953	64,659	66,480	68,514	70,535
Total supply	276,666	276,532	282,965	281,547	292,294	297,593	300,864	306,034	313,530	321,124	328,805	337,083
Total exports	58,678	56,189	59,031	57,860	60,383	61,102	61,842	62,953	64,659	66,480	68,514	70,535
Human dom. consumption	173,773	178,490	182,723	185,489	190,219	194,046	197,377	201,097	205,314	209,569	213,832	218,298
Other disappearance	836	822	822	822	822	822	822	822	822	822	822	822
Total use	174,609	179,312	183,545	186,311	191,041	194,869	198,200	201,919	206,137	210,392	214,655	219,120
Ending stocks	43,379	41,030	40,389	37,376	40,870	41,622	40,823	41,161	42,734	44,252	45,637	47,428

Source: USDA, Economic Research Service.

End Notes

[1]See "The Road to Forfeitures" in *Sugar and Sweeteners Outlook*, SSS-M-303, Nov. 2013.

[2]Situation and Outlook Report No. SSSM-297-01, May 2013, "World Sugar Prices: The Influence of Brazilian Costs of Production and World Surplus/Deficit Measures."

[3]For a discussion of world sugar pricing volatility, see M. J. McConnell, E. Dohlman, and S. Haley, "World Sugar Price Volatility Intensified by Market and Policy Factors," in *Amber Waves,* (USDA, Economic Research Service, September 2010).

[4]See Haley (2013), referenced previously.

[5]In Portuguese, total recoverable sugar has the abbreviation ATR.

[6]As discussed, an important goal of this report is to describe a framework that generates world price forecasts for use in analysis of U.S. and Mexico sugar and sweetener sectors. The model equations for the United States and Mexico are not currently specified in order to allow endogenous policy-specific reactions to world price changes. The next step in model development would be to incorporate equations similar to those in ERS's U.S.-Mexico sugar baseline model into the world model framework. See the *Sugar and Sweetener Outlook*, February 2014, pp. 3-17, for a discussion of the baseline modeling framework and results for 2014/15-2023/24.

[7]The drop in ending stocks and the associated increase in world prices in 2016/17 seen in the model projections in table 4, figures 8 and 9, and later tables and charts are the result of the approach used to model India's sugarcane production cycles. The specification chosen (see Appendix II, table 3) provides favorable statistical characteristics but incorporates a long lag structure that carries the effects of a sharp, largely policy-induced, cyclical downturn in production in 2009 to 2017. This result is likely to disappear as the projection period for the model is moved forward.

INDEX

D

E

F

G

H

I

J

L

R

S

T

U

V

W

Y